AN
IMPERIAL HISTORY OF INDIA

Owing to the antiquity and rarity of this book, certain pages are regrettably absent, and readability is compromised due to the blurring of the original text. If you possess any insights regarding the availability of these missing sections, kindly inform us. Your assistance is crucial in ensuring the completion of this significant work for the benefit of future generations.

AN
IMPERIAL HISTORY OF INDIA

IN A SANSKRIT TEXT

[C. 700 B.C. - C. 770 A.D.]

WITH A SPECIAL COMMENTARY ON LATER GUPTA PERIOD

BY

K. P. JAYASWAL

RAHULA SANKRITYAYANA

GYAN

Published by

Gyan Publishing House
5, Ansari Road
Daryaganj, New Delhi-110002
Phone: 011-47034999, 9811692060
E-mail: books@gyanbooks.com

Distribution Network
gyanbooks.com
India, USA, Canada, UK, Australia

ISBN: 978-93-6280-128-9 (HB)
First Published, 1934

2nd Impression 2024

Printed at: Gyan Press, Delhi.

AN IMPERIAL HISTORY OF INDIA
Author: K. P. JAYASWAL, RAHULA SANKRITYAYANA

AN IMPERIAL HISTORY OF INDIA

AN IMPERIAL HISTORY OF INDIA

IN A SANSKRIT TEXT

[C. 700 B.C. — C. 770 A.D.]

WITH A SPECIAL COMMENTARY ON LATER GUPTA PERIOD

By

K. P. JAYASWAL

With the Sanskrit Text
Revised by

VEN. RAHULA SAṄKṚITYAYANA

PUBLISHED BY

MOTILAL BANARSI DASS
THE PUNJAB SANSKRIT BOOK DEPOT
SAIDMITHA, LAHORE
1934

To

PROFESSOR SYLVAIN LÉVI

साहित्ये सुकुमारवस्तुनि, दृढन्यायग्रहग्रन्थिले,

शास्त्रे वा त्वयि संविधातरि समं लीलायते भारती ।

MATERIAL

1. The Sanskrit Text as printed in the *Trivandrum Sanskrit Series*, No. LXXXIV, 1925, pp. 579—656, ed. T. Gaṇapati Sāstrī.

2. The Tibetan Text in the *Snar-thang* edition of the SKAḤ-ḤGYUR, Vol. De, leaves 425*b*—485*b*.

3. A part of the Tibetan Text, for Ślokas 549—558, *viz.*, the text kindly supplied by Prof. Sylvain Lévi from the Peking red edition, Vol. XIII, p. 275*b* (Bibliotheque Nationale, Paris, Tibetan 13).

ARRANGEMENT

(*a*) The pagination of Gaṇapati Sāstrī's edition is denoted on each page by the letter G. and that of the Tibetan version by the letter T.

(*b*) The Tibetan variants are given in footnotes.

(*c*) Ordinary corrections in the Sanskrit Text have been made from the Tibetan version in footnotes. The passages requiring correction have been underlined in the G. Text.

(*d*) Passages which are not in the Tibetan Text have been put in *smaller Sanskrit type*.

(*e*) Texts found in Tibetan and omitted in the G. Text have been added in round brackets in the body of the G. Text.

(*f*) The divisions, in English, into sections have been made to correspond with my commentary above.

(g) Proper names have been put in *Italics* (Sanskrit Type).

K. P. J.

CONTENTS

PAGES

§ 3. *Kings of the time of the Buddha* (*Sixth Century* B.C.)

§ 4. *"100 years after the Buddha"*

Revival of Buddhism

Emperor Aśoka; His Stūpas and Pillars

§ 5. *Early Emperors before the Buddha*

§ 6. *Imperial Dynasty of Benares, before 600 B.C.*

§ 7. *Magadha Kings and their Ministers*

Subsequent to Udāyin (C. 450 B.C.—338 B.C.)

§ 8. *Maurya Dynasty*

PAGES

PAGES

Comments on the MMK History of Nepal

PAGES

Comments

[Caste of the Maitrakas]

Madhyadesa: Imperial History

§ 17. Śāka Dynasty—Śaka Emperors (the Kushans, 78 A.D.—350 A.D.). Northern Madhyadeśa

§ 18. The Dynasty of Nāga-Senas [150 A.D.—348 A.D.]

Comments on §§ 17—18

§ 19-19(c). [Post-Guptan Imperial Rulers of Madhyadeśa] [530 A.D.—647 A.D.]

§ 19. Vishṇu, (520—533 A.D.). *Hara* (533—550 ?)

§ 19c. The Maukharis (550 A.D.—600 A.D.)

Comments

§ 19 (C.). The Vaiśya Dynasty and Śrīkaṇṭha-Sthāṇvīśvara (560 A.D.—647 A.D.)

Comments

Southern India

[Mainly kings contemporary of Harshavardhana]

§ 20. The Sātavāhana [223 A.D.—231 A.D.]

PAGES

§ 21. *Contemporaries of King Mahendra* (600—640 A.D.)

Comments

§ 22. *The Dvīpas in the Southern Sea, (Indian Archipelago) and Further India*

Comments

EAST

IMPERIAL [MAGADHA]-GAUḌA DYNASTIES

[(*a*) Before 320 A.D.; and (*b*) 320—750 A.D.]

§ 23. *Loka* [*Gauḍa Dynasty*] (*before* 320 A.D.)

§ 24. *Imperial Guptas* (348 A.D.—500 A.D.)

§ 25. *Break-up and Division of the Empire*

Comments on §§ 23-24

(Gupta Imperial History)

PAGES

§ 56. *Śūdras and Śakas*

§ 57. *Brahmins again*

Vishṇugupta

S. (Subandhu)

Southern Brahmins

V., an artist abroad

Bh.

Madhyadeśa Brahmins

Comments

INTRODUCTORY

1. History of India from the pre-Mahābhārata War down to 320—348 A.D. (the beginning of the Gupta Period) is chronicled in the *Purāṇas*. For the subsequent period we have been dependent on inscriptions; and it had been believed that there was no text or written history for it. The inscriptions left certain 'blanks', and gave us a fragmentary view. It is therefore a matter of no small satisfaction to recover a text which turns out to give a connected history where we needed it most. From 78 A.D. we have in our new text a connected history down to the close of the eighth century. And what is still more gratifying is the imperial feature of that history. Some of the matters of great importance that this written record discloses are:—

(1) a full and complete history of the Imperial Gupta epoch (348 A.D. to 500 A.D.), describing its break-up (500 A.D.),

(2) imperial history from (*a*) Vishṇuvardhana (520—535 A.D.), then following the (*b*) imperial family of the Maukharis (555—600 A.D.) down to (*c*) his descendants' re-rise in the person of Prabhākaravardhana and Harshavardhana (606—647 A.D.),[with a full history of Śaśāṅka, who was a Brahmin by caste and a popular leader rising from Bengal],

(3) history of a Revived Gupta Empire, following the death of Harshavardhana, with its decline and fall,

(4) then a vivid description of two popular elections of kings in Bengal and the rise of Gopāla.

Numerous important details, e.g., that Mahāpadma Nanda had been the Prime Minister of Magadha before his kingship, that there was a short-lived republic in Bengal after Śaśāṅka—come in as additions to our knowledge. Further, Indian Imperial history for the first time receives personal touches when the author gives his estimate of character of individual emperors. All this welcome information is stored in a long section—which is a book by itself, being in 1000 ślokas—in the Mahāyāna work entitled *Ārya-Mañjuśrī-Mūlakalpa*, published [Part III] in the year 1925 by the late MM. Gaṇapati Śāstrī of the State of Travancore in the Trivandrum Sanskrit Series (No. 84).

Possibly some of the Indian scholars, trained to suspect every written book in Sanskrit, would have darkly hinted (as a big historian did to my knowledge when the *Arthaśāstra* was discovered) that 'the book was a 'Southern forgery'.' But fortunately the book was translated in Tibetan in the eleventh century A.D. and the present text agrees word for word with that translation.

My friend *Bhadanta* Rāhula Sāṅkṛityāyana has collected a unique library from Tibet, including an original Sanskrit manuscript which had been taken from India and translated there. He was fortunate enough to obtain a complete set of Buston's works from the Dalai Lama, which is not available even in the rich Russian collection. Thanks to the help and co-operation of Rev. Sāṅkṛityāyana, and his Tibetan Library (deposited at the Patna Museum), I have been able to get all important passages of the *Mañjuśrī-Mūlakalpa* compared with the Tibetan text, and to derive benefit from Buston (b. 1289 A.D.—d.1363 A.D.) for the purpose of following some passages and obtaining additional light on the history of S k a n d a G u p t a.

2. According to the *Mañjuśrī-Mūlakalpa*, **Indian history** is a **succession of empires** from the time preceding the Buddha to c. 750 A.D. where it stops. To take the period from 78 A.D., it consists of the following successions:

(*a*) *Śaka dynasty* (*Śakavaṃśa*, i.e., Kushāns),
(*b*) *Nāga-Senas*, or, *Nāgas* and *Prabha-Vishṇu*, i.e., Vishṇuvṛiddha Pravara-sena (Vākāṭaka),
(*c*) Guptas (up to Budha Gupta),
(*d*) Vishṇu (vardhana) and one descendant,
(*e*) Maukharis,
(*f*) *Śrīkaṇṭha* dynasty, [Āditya (vardhana), Rājya (vardhana). etc.],
(*g*) Imperial Valabhī dynasty (two generations),
(*h*) Imperial '*Gauḍa dynasty*' i.e., Later Guptas: Ādityasena to Vishṇu-Gupta.

It will be at once noticed that (*d*), (*e*) and (*g*) go to fill up blanks in Indian History.

The Mūlakalpa, 'edited' in the Sanskrit original by the late MM. Gaṇapati Śāstrī, is a poor production as an edition. The editor took no pain to correct even ordinary orthographical mistakes. He was unfamiliar with the Buddhist technical terms, and in preparing his letter-press he misread numerous words or preserved the misreadings, e.g. the well-known तायि° ('saviour') as तापि° ('ascetic'). Dr. Gaṇapati Śāstrī was under the disadvantage of possessing a single manuscript from which he edited the text. We are, however, thankful to get the text even in its present form. Practically the whole of the historical section, Chapter 53 in Part III, has been compared by Rev. Rāhula Sāṅkṛityāyana, with the result that we are better situated than we would have been if we had only the Sanskrit or only the Tibetan text before us. I am combining the results of the two versions, indicating their difference wherever important and necessary.

3. The (A)MMK (I adopt this abbreviation for the text; the Sanskrit version will be indicated by S., and Tibetan by T.) was written in Bengal. Geographically it is to Gauḍa and Magadha that the author pays his greatest attention. In fact his history from the Nāga (C. 140 A.D.) and Gupta times (350 A.D.) to the beginning of the Pāla period (750 A.D.) is a survey from Gauḍa—written from the point of view of Gauḍa, showing an intimate concern with Gauḍa and the provinces in the proximity of Gauḍa. To him Gauḍa means the whole of Bengal and includes generally Magadha.

4. The author brings his history down from two different points to the beginning of the Pāla Period. Once he starts with Śakas, pauses with the Guptas and comes down right to Gopālaka after finishing the Gupta line. Then, again, he starts with the Nāga dynasty (Bhāraśiva), deals with Samudra [Gupta] and his brother in Gauḍa, and with Śaśāṅka whose name for some reason he conceals but whose history he makes unmistakable, and then comes down to the Gopālas, 'the *dāsajīvins* (śūdras). He does not know the later and the great Pāla kings (whom he would not have left unnamed had he known them) and their patronage of Mahāyāna. I would therefore regard the work as one of *circa* 770 A.D. (the death of Gopāla), or roughly 800 A.D.

5. It was translated into Tibetan about 1060 A.D. by the Hindu Paṇḍita Kumārakalaśa in co-operation with the Tibetan interpreter Śākya-blo-gros. The translation forms part of the *Skangyur* (rgyud D). The date of Śākya-blo-gros is fixed by that of Subhuti-Śrī-Śānti, a companion of Dīpaṅkara Śrījñāna (Atiśa). Subhuti Śrī-Śānti, and Śākya-blo-gros together translated the *Pramāṇa-*

vārttika which is in the Stanḥgyur. Dīpaṅkara reached Tibet in 1042 and died in 1054 A.D.[1]

6. The history is put in the prophetic style in the mouth of the Buddha, who undertakes to narrate the future vicissitudes of his Doctrine and Church, and in that connexion royal history is dealt with. It is not strictly speaking, history proper as in the *Purāṇas,* but a secondary reference, the primary note being the history of Buddhism. This prophetic form of history was adopted in several Mahāyāna sūtras which have been cited by B u s t o n. A commentary on one of them (Abhisamayālaṅkāra) says that a particular historical prophecy came to be true, that is, the author of that sūtra came to know of the event as a past event. In many places the writer of the *MMK* forgot to use the future tense and used the legitimate past tense in the narration. All such passages I have put in the past tense. The language and style has a striking resemblance with the *Yugapurāṇa* in the *Garga-Saṃhitā.*

7. The historical narration is a lengthy one, the chapter covering 1005 verses in the printed S. MMK (pp. 579—656; Paṭala-visara 53) and about 25 less in T. *MMK* (rgyud D, Ch. XXXVI, pp. 425*b*—483*b*). The learned editor of the S. *AMMK* has left the verses unnumbered. For convenience of reference I have numbered them. I shall refer in my summary to the verses so marked. The Tibetan text ends at verse 989 with its. first line (*ataḥ avichi-paryantaṃ na rājā tatra vidyate*). T. *MMK* is a word-for-word and termination-for-termination translation, hence the task of comparison becomes easy. T. *MMK* has 3 verses extra after verse 829.

8. Except for the opening 9 lines of prose [which is not to be found in T.] the whole text of the historical section is in *anushṭubh* verses. Their language is Gāthā Sanskrit which makes their understanding at places a matter more of guessing than of Sanskrit construction.

8*a*. In some cases it is evident from the context that the MS from which the Tibetan translation was made, was defective.

9. The length of life of many kings is exaggerated. I have left them out in my summary except where it seems to be reasonable or otherwise important. I also omit the history of future births of the virtuous and sinful kings and their careers in paradise or hell, which is

[1] Rāhula Sāṅkṛityāyana, Journal Asiatique, 1934; and तिब्बत में बौद्धधर्म.

an important concern of the Buddhist religious historian but none of the present-day historian.

10. The name of the chapter, rather the section (*parivarta*), is *Rājavyākaraṇa-parivarta,* literally '*the Section on the Kingly Exposition*' but technically '*the Section on the Prophecy about Kings*'. Dynastic names as a rule are omitted. I have supplied them [in square brackets]. In many places the names of kings—at times very important ones—are denoted by their initials only—e.g., *H.* for *Harshavardhaṇa,* R. for *Rājya-vardhana,* S. for *Skanda Gupta.* This makes the task of identification at times impossible.

11. Our Buddhist historian often gives castes of the rulers. For instance, he notes that the king who defeated Śaśāṅka ("Soma") was a Vaiśya by caste, 'Soma' was a Brahmin, the Gopālas (Pālas) were of servile caste, *etc.* Our authority is very full on Śaśāṅka and supplies certain details which were badly wanted. A most important fact which we gather from the author is that after Harshavardhana and Śaśāṅka and before the rise of the Pālas there was an Imperial Dynasty in the East with its seat at Benares and in Magadha. This seems quite natural, as without it we would have found the Chālukyas come up to the North. Our new datum helps us to correct the erroneous view of V. Smith that after Harsha there was no imperial power in the North. Another fact of importance is that the Buddhist historian specially notes the imperial position of rulers.

12. The author, after the Śuṅga and Kadphises period, divides his history geographically:

(1) of Northern India (*Uttara-Dik,* verses 549—585), (S., pp. 621—624; T., 452B—454B);

(2) of Western India (*Paśchāt Deśa,* verses 586—609), (S., pp. 624—626; T., pp. 454B—455B);

(3) of Mid-India, (*Madhyadeśa;* 'Madhyama Kings', verses 610—621), (S., p. 626; T. 455B—456A);

(4) of Southern India (*Dakshiṇa Dik,* verses 621—636), (S., pp. 626—628; T., pp. 456A—457A);

(4*a*) of the Archipelago (636—640), ('*Dvīpeshu*', S., p. 628; T., 457A);

(5) of Eastern India (*Pūrva Dik,* verses 640—683), (S., pp. 628—647; T., pp. 457A—469A);

(6) Minor references of Hindu Central India (*Madhyadeśa*, verses 903—912), (S., p. 648; T., 470A), and of Miscellaneous Provinces (913—924), (S., p. 649; T., 470B).

At verse 924 royal history ends; then there is a summing up of the scheme (925—932); and from 933 up to the end of 955 a history of Buddhist clergy and their condition is detailed, and then from 956 to 980 political Brahmaṇas and a few Śūdras are described, and finally from 981 to 988 the four heavenly Mahārājas and Gods. The passage from 989 to the 1005 is not in the T. *MMK*. It deals with semi-divine beings *etc*. and is clearly a later addition.[2] Our interest ends with verse 980 where the history of leading monks, Brahmins and Śūdras closes.

In the beginning verses 1 to 344 detail the biography of the Buddha (supposed to be given by himself) up to his Nirvāṇa. From verse 335 royal history begins with an enumeration of the ruling contemporaries of the Buddha who had come in personal contact with the Prophet. Thus from verse 345 (S., p. 605; T., p. 442) to verse 932 (S., p. 650; T., p. 471B) about 600 verses (taking into account some extra verses to be found in T. *MMK*) are devoted to history. But that history is an enlargement of history proper by the explanatory verses as to the Mahāyāna Mantra and magical processes which particular kings are alleged to have practised to attain greatness, and by invisible history of those princes in paradise or hell. Although the real matter in the 600 verses is cut down by about fifty per centum, we are immensely lucky in getting about 300 ślokas as new data on Indian History. The account of the punishment of bad kings in after life will not interest the present-day materialist reader. Our Buddhist writer does not forgive, like the modern historian, the wickedness and arbitrariness in kings. He would have thrown into the waste-paper basket all modern histories as so many veiled and covert panegyrics on force and fraud and virtueless greatness. His outlook is different. He emphasizes the relentless law of morality, the avenging principle of KARMA and he follows the rascally kings to their tortures in hell. This, to follow the current of the time, I have omitted in my analysis. Yet the material so curtailed is unexpectedly large.

I have divided our data into parts and sections, giving descriptive

[2] T. *AMMK* has not got also the first seven lines of the next chapter of the printed *AMMK* at p. 657 (up to *Mañjuśrī Kumāraḥ veditavyaḥ*).

captions to each. The importance of the sections has been pointed out in the comments attached to each section.

The *MMK* history seems to have been from one pen. It is not a book which has grown from generation to generation. Restricting ourselves to the historical section, it has drawn upon two classes of earlier literature. One of them was purely historical, drawing from which is evident in the section dealing with the Imperial History of Madhyadeśa from the Śaka-vaṃśa down to the break-up of the Imperial Guptas. Here, religious interest is wholly lacking (except for the reign of Bālāditya). The author has utilized at least three such temporal histories, one of which had been composed about 700 A.D. and which was very full on a century for the whole of India—North (Himālayan States), South, East, West, Central (Mid) India, and the Colonies. His other source-books, of temporal nature, were two independent books on the Gupta dynasty, from the beginning down to the end of the Later Guptas, which must have been available in the early Pāla period when the *MMK* was written and which was probably the record kept up from generation to generation in the royal archives of the Guptas. We should recall here that Yuan Chwang actually saw political records being maintained yearly, when he visited India in the middle of the 7th century. Two long extracts in the *MMK* from two different sources are given, one for the Magadha branch and the other for a Bengal (Gauḍa) branch of the Guptas. Then, the author is largely indebted to the sacerdotal history maintained by his own Church. This literature has been availed of not only by the *MMK*, but by various Mahāyāna texts which have been cited by Buston in his critical historical survey *Chos-ḥbyung*, e.g., *Chandragarbha-paripṛichchhā* (which cites full details of the great war of Skanda Gupta[8]), *Laṅkāvatāra-sūtra*, *Kālachakra*, etc.—and by Tārānātha amongst others.

Our author has two rest-points for his history—one is the end of Harshavardhana's reign, the disruption of the empire of Mid-India (Madhyadeśa) and the dissolution of the Nepal Kingdom under Aṃśuvarman's successor; and the other is the elections in Bengal, first of a popular leader as king, and then, of Gopāla the Śūdra. The author has utilized good and reliable material for the successive empires from 78 A.D. to 770 A.D.

[8] See below the comments on the section of the Gupta Imperial History.

The basis of such dynastic Manuals was the system noted by Yuan Chwang mentioned above, which goes back at least to the time of Khāravela (2nd century B.C.) as is evident from his inscription noting each year's important events.

PART I

MAGADHA AND MADHYA-DEŚA; IMPERIAL PERIOD

§ 1. *Śaiśunāka Dynasty*

The Buddha begins his prophecy about his own Nirvāṇa (verses 13 ff). [*Read* in verse 10 *sa eva* instead of *sa epa;*—in verse 14 *Mallānām upavartane* instead of *upaparvate;* correct similarly *Mallānām upadartate* (verse 18) into *upavartane*]. He relates his biography from verse 24 (p. 581).

[*Correct* in verse 36 *Burubilvām* into *Urubilvāṃ* (T.).]

Verse 118 gives the name *Kuśāgrapurī* of the Magadhas. The mountain Vārāha had the Paipala Cave.

Capital of Magadha.

In verse 137 the Tibetan text (p. 432) reads *Brāhmaṇaḥ* instead of *Śramaṇaḥ* before K ā ś y a p a.

Ajātaśatru.

In verse 140 the visit of A j ā t a ś a t r u, king of the Magadhas, who had been overtaken by grief for his father's death, is mentioned. The king describes his own miserable condition and appeals:

"I am abandoned by relatives as untrustworthy and so I stand before the nation. I am fallen, (destined to the terrible hell). Whose shelter shall I seek (read *kaṃ śaraṇaṃ* instead of *kaḥ śa°*, 145)? Save me, you Great Hero....."

Division of ashes of the Buddha is detailed, in verses 207 ff. The Magadha capital is called *Rāja* (elsewhere *Rājagṛiha*) and *Kuśāgrapura* in verse 232.

Revival of orthodox Hinduism.

"After my passing away, in the end of the period (yugānte) kings will fight each other (*mahīpālā bhavishyanti paraspara-vadhe* (incorrect *vidhe*) *ratā*), and bhikshus will become industrialists (*bahukarmāntā*), and the people overtaken by greed; Buddhist laity will lose faith; will kill each other, will examine each other." There will be a general decline and demoralisation in Buddhism (236—246; read *pariśeshaiva chaturvidhaḥ* for *pariśeshveva chaturvidhe*, 246).

"The country will be invaded by Devas and Tīrthikas [*Tīrthika-krāntā-bhūyishṭhā Devā-* (incorrect *sarvā*) *krāntā cha medinī*]. The people will be having faith in Brahmin caste (*bhavishyanti tadā kāle dvija-varṇa-ratā janā*). At that time men will indulge in the killing of living creatures; they will have false conduct." This is the prophecy (or description—*vyākṛita*) of Kali age (248).

From verse 250 comes the description of relic-worship, of the corporal remains of the Buddha, and, once more, that of their partition by Mahā-Kāśyapa (minor corrections which are many here are omitted). Ajāta, 'of great army', applied for a portion of the relics (257). [In verse 266 a (common) mistake *tāpin°* for *tāyin°* occurs in the printed text.] The king is called the son of Bimbisāra (307) (misspelt in S. as *Bimbāsāra* throughout, but correct in T.).

Extent of Ajātaśatru's Kingdom.

In verse 321 he is styled as *Mahārāja* Ajāta (Ajāta-śatru in T.) 'the Magadhan king.' He will be king (rājā) of Aṅga (T.) (S., 'up to Aṅga'), Magadha, up to Vārāṇasī, in the N. up to Vaiśālī (322).

Udāyin, his son, got Buddha's teaching written.

His son will be king by name U. ('*Ukārākhya*') (*i.e.*, Udāyin) (324). He will be prone to the **Buddha's teaching**, and will have it **reduced to writing.** His reign will be for 20 years. He will be for 30 years with his father (326). He will die at midnight.

Comments

The kings are:

Bimbisāra
|
Ajātaśatru
|
Udāyin (20 years)

Udāyin is stated to be the king in whose reign the words of the Buddha were committed to writing (*tadetat pravachanaṃ Śāstu lekhāpayishyati vistaram*). This is the first mention about the Teacher's words being reduced to writing.

After the Buddha's death there was a decline in Buddhism. It may be noted that the age of decline is dated in Kali Age. Of the earlier age (the *Ādi Yuga*) the kings mentioned (See § 2) are the well-known kings of Purāṇic history.

§ 2. *Ancient Kings, before the Buddha*

In the First Yuga the kings were:
Nahusha and others (332),
Pārthiva and others (332),
Budha, Śukra, Udaya (not in T., 333 up to 336),

Śāntanu, Chitra, Suchitra, the Pāṇḍavas, the Vāravatya Yātavas who came to an end (*astamitā*) cursed by the Ṛishi; Kārtika, Kārttavīrya, Daśaratha, Dāśarathi, Arjuna, the minister Aśvatthāman son of Dvi (ja) Droṇa (335). They were worshippers of the Buddha (!) (337).

§ 3. *Kings of the time of the Buddha* [*Sixth century* B.C.]

The kings between Dvāpara and Kali will be bad kings (343).
"In the present age the kings are" (344),
"(1) Prasenajit of Kosala,
(2-3) King Bimbisāra and another,
(4) Udayana, the best of the Kshatriyas, son of Śatānīka.
(5) (*a*) Subāhu,
(*b*) Sudhanu (T.) Sudhana (S.),
(*c*) Mahendra,
(*d*) Chamasa (T.), Chandrasama (S.),
(*e*) Siṃha, of the Lichchhavis at Vaiśālī ('from the Śākya family', T.)
(6) Udāvi (Udāyi), (Varshadhara, T.)
(7) Vidyota Pradyota (T.) 'Vidyota Mudyota' (S.), 'the *Mahāsena*', at Ujjayanī, also '*Chaṇḍa*'.
(8) Rājā Śuddhodana at the capital Kapila, entitled 'the *Virāṭ*' (president of a *vairājya* republic), 'very powerful' (348).

These were contemporaries of Śākyasiṃha Buddha, all Kshatriyas, all who had come in personal contact with the Buddha and respected his teachings" (349—352).

(9) Ajāta [is again mentioned after the group in verse 353 as if by a footnote.]

Comments

The group of No. 5 seems to consist of Lichchhavi rulers. They were not descendants of Ajātaśatru, as wrongly supposed by Tārānātha (J. B. O. R. S., I, 79). The description of No. 8 is noteworthy. Although he is the father of the Buddha he comes last. Probably they are given in order of political and constitutional importance.

Udayana, son of Śatānīka (of Kauśāmbī) is described as being of the best Kshatriya family amongst his contemporaries (*kshatriya-śreshṭhaḥ*), which confirms Bhāsa. The Lichchhavis are also stated as Kshatriyas, and connected with the Śākyas.

§ 4. *"100 years after the Buddha"*

Revival of Buddhism

Emperor Aśoka: His Stūpas and Stone Pillars

[Like Yuan Chwang, the author of our AMMK has fallen into a confusion between the Aśoka of the time of the Second Council who flourished a century after the Buddha and the Aśoka the Great (Maurya). He is called variously in Northern Buddhism: *'Nanda'* (Rockhill, p. 186; Schiefner, p. 61), *'Kāla-Aśoka'* (as distinguished from *'Dharma-Aśoka'*, i.e., the Maurya) and Kāma-Aśoka (Tārānātha). This Aśoka of 100 A.B. was N a n d a I or N a n d a v a r d h a n a (J. B. O. R. S., I. 81, 84). The AMMK has transformed Aśoka the Maurya into the Aśoka of A. B. 100. The other Aśoka is mentioned again as V i ś o k a. Except the date the whole datum is to be taken as on Aśoka Maurya placed out of his place.]

100 years after the Buddha in a dark age there will arise at *Kusuma-nagara* an emperor ['Protector of the (whole) earth] famous as A ś o k a (353, 355; S., p. 606; T., p. 442 B). At first he will be sharp in action, with anger, unkind; having come across a selfless Bhikshu he will become considerate as to what is right and what is wrong, very rich, scrupulous and kind (356—58). He had in his boyhood by mistake and in play done homage to Ś ā k y a s i ṃ h a B u d d h a, hence—

'Ye, king, rule over Jambudvīpa along with its Forests' (361). At the instance of his guide, he out of the old stūpa over the Buddha's relics at Veṇuvana in the *'Rāja' capital city* [*Rājagṛiha*], took out the jar of relics and divided in hundreds, he beautified the whole of this Jambudvīpa with *stūpas* at one moment through Yakshas. Thousands of **Stone Pillars (Sila-yashti)** were set up at C h a i t y a s and as h u m a n [*dehināṃ*] m e m o r i a l s (369-70). These monuments were erected in one night by Yakshas in the service of A ś o k a. Then the king D h a r m ā ś o k a on his chariot undertook a j o u r n e y o f i n s p e c t i o n, and decorated and honoured those m o n u m e n t s with gold, silver, and copper (372—377). On his death he attains divinity. For 87 years he worshipped relics and lived altogether for 100 years. He died of disease (379).

Comments

The technical name for Aśoka pillars and their two classes should be noted, viz., one set to mark old Chaityas and the other as human memorials (stūpas). Inscriptional monuments are not noted. They were mostly governmental. His tour is also noted.

§ 5. *Early Emperors before the Buddha*

He [Aśoka] knew the Mantra to be an Emperor (*Chakravartin*) which had been known to Nahusha, Sitātapatra, Sagara, Dilīpa, Mandhātā, (385—388). By virtue of mantras of Mahāyāna the following kings in the past age had attained success:

Dundhumāra,
Kandarpa, his son
Prajāpati, his son
Nābhi, his son
Ūrṇa (T.),

Ṛishabha, son of Lābhin,
Ṛishabhaputra Bharata (388—395).

Comments

The Buddha employs past tense in respect of these kings. They are implied to be ancient kings of the pre-Buddhan age by the next verse 396 where the kings of Benares who 'lived' in the Middle Time are described. This Middle Time is to be distinguished from the Future Middle Time mentioned later wherein the Gupta emperors (§ 17) are placed. The kings of the Past Middle Age were past kings in the Buddha's time.

§ 6. *Imperial Dynasty of Benares* [*before 600* B.C.]

These lived in the Middle Age (396). King Brahmadatta was at the great capital *Vārāṇasī* (398). He was a successful king, known all over, very vigorous, very kind. His son was of pious deeds, wise, and of firm undertakings. The son of the latter was Harya (Hayagrīva, T.), his was Śveta. These were successful and famous, [and their success was due, of course, to Mahāyāna mantras] (401—3).

Comments

The Dynasty of Vārāṇasī is the centre of imperial history before the rise of Magadha and Kosala. Śiśunāka, the founder of the Magadha dynasty on the fall of the very ancient dynasty of the Bṛihadrathas, was a cadet of this dynasty of Vārāṇasī or Kāśī. The dynasty of Kāśī annexed Magadha *c.* 727 B.C. (J.B.O.R.S., I, 114). Brahmadatta was the greatest king of the line; he conquered Kosala and made it a part of his empire according to the Vinaya (II). This must have taken place at least three generations before Prasenajit's father Mahā-Kosala, who owned Benares; and attacks by three earlier Kosala kings on Benares are known to the Buddhist Jātakas. The date 727 B.C. fits in with the great rise of Benares. It had an empire from Benares (from the frontiers of the kingdom of Kauśāmbī) to Kosala in the N., and to the frontiers of Aṅga in the E. A king of the line was Dhṛitarāshṭra who was defeated by Śatānīka of Kauśāmbī[4] (Śatapatha, 13, 8, 4, 19). The rivalry for imperial position was carried on by the Magadha branch of the Benares House in the period of the Buddha and finally it suppressed Kosala. The bone of contention was made Benares which was rightfully claimed by the Śaiśunākas, it being their ancestral possession. According to our history the house of Benares was imperial only for 3 generations.

[4] This must have happened just before the Buddha, as Udayana son of Śatānīka was a contemporary of the Buddha.

§ 7. *Magadha Kings and their Ministers, subsequent to Udāyin* [*c. 450* B.C.—*338* B.C.]

After various advices put in the mouth of the Buddha on magical practices for kings of the future, history is again taken up in verse 413 (S., p. 612; T., p. 445 B). After this A ś o k a - M u k h y a there will be V i ś o k a who will worship (Buddha) relics for 76 years (416). He was a good king. He died of fever. After him was Ś ū r a s e n a [*Vīrasena* of Tārānātha]. He caused stūpas to be put up to the confines of the Sea. He reigned for 17 years. After him there will be king N a n d a at P u s h p a-C i t y. He will have a large army and he will be a great power (422). He was called 'the leading vile man' (*Nīchamukhya*) (424). He had been a Prime Minister; by magical process he became king (424). 'In the capital of the Magadha-residents there will be Brahmin controversialists, lost in false (T.; S.—'success') pride; without doubt they will have false pride and claims; and the king will be surrounded by them' (425-26). The king, though a pious soul and just, will give them riches (427). Owing to his association with a good guide he built 24 monasteries (428). His m i n i s t e r was a Buddhist Brahmin V a r a r u c h i who was of high soul, kind and good. The king, though true, caused alienation of feeling of the C o u n c i l of M i n i s t e r s at P ā ṭ a l a C i t y. (434-35). The king became very ill, died at 67. His great friend was a Brahmin, P ā ṇ i n i by name. He will become a believer in me (Buddha); and had mantra of success from Lokeśa (T.) (439).

Viśoka (=Nanda-vardhana).

Sūrasena.

Nanda.

Prime Minister Vararuchi.

Brahmin Pāṇini.

Comments

[New light on the History of Mahāpadma Nanda and Pāṇini]

This is one of the most important sections of the AMMK. The history of the dynasty called the Śaiśunakas in the Pūrāṇas is found in the best form here as far as Northern Buddhist records go. (*a*) 'V i ś o k a' is undoubtedly the '*Kālāśoka*' of Burmese Buddhism and the '*Nandin*' of Vaiśālī of Tārānātha, in whose reign the S e c o n d C o u n c i l was held (JBORS., I, 73) and whom I have proposed to identify with N a n d a v a r d h a n a of the Purāṇas (*Ibid.*, 80 ff). His successor, (*b*) Ś ū r a s e n a, the good king ('*dharmāchārī*') of the AMMK, is the '*Vīrasena*' of Tārānātha, '*Bhadrasena*' of the Burmese tradition, *Nanda* of Rockhill and *Mahānanda* of the Purāṇas (JBORS., I, 73, 92). Then comes the infamous (*c*) N a n d a, the usurper, who is Mahā Nanda's successor '*Mahā Padma Nanda*' of the Purāṇas.

The account which we get of this king in the AMMK, is most important. He was the P r i m e M i n i s t e r (Mantrīn) of Śūrasena, who ruled in Magadha up to the Sea, that is, was an emperor. Nanda, the usurper, was called the '*Nīchamukhya,* the lowest man of his age.[5] This popular estimate was heard by Alexander's companions who reached India in the time of his son. He was not an incapable man and totally devoid of virtue according to the AMMK, whose greatest complaint is that though a man of judgment Nanda patronised the Brahmin opponents of Buddhism. The AMMK notes a great intellectual activity of the orthodox type under Nanda. Vararuchi was his minister who had a high reputation, and Pāṇini was his favourite. The greatness of these Brahmins the Buddhist chroniclers before the time of the AMMK, could not deny and consoled themselves by claiming them as Buddhists, for without being Buddhists how could men be great? A clever usurper has to pose as a great patron of intellect and letters. Mahāpadma Nanda was here perfect. Yet the AMMK notes an undercurrent. The king became unpopular with the Council of Ministers (*virāgayāmāsa mantrīṇāṃ Nagare Pāṭalāhvaye, virakta-mantrivargis tu satyasandho mahābalaḥ*), though the king was Satyasandha (constitutionally correct to the Hindu Ministry) (in spite of his) great power'. About causing alienation of the ministers the text is further explicit by its '*virāgayāmāsa mantrīṇāṃ Nagare Pāṭalāhvaye*' (434). The king fortunately died of illness and old age, and nothing untoward happened on account of this alienation of feeling.

After this king, Chandragupta is dealt with (§ 8). The supplanting of Nanda Mahāpadma's successor is not mentioned, hence nor his immediate successor.

It seems that here we have a true history which in the main is supported by Greek notices. We are thankful to gain some details of the constitutional situation of the reign in an Indian account.

The chronology of the AMMK is free from that confusion which we find in other Buddhist accounts for the period. The AMMK data are independent, and they support the Purāṇas. We have here a positive record about Pāṇini's date. He flourished a generation before Alexander. His mention of *Yavanānī* must refer to the Yavanas living in Afghanistan before Alexander or the Yavanas in the Persian territories. That Pāṇini knew the Persians well is proved by his '*Parśus*';

[5] The Buddhist historian found an explanation of his power in the king's having brought under his control the piśācha Pīlu.

and Pāṇini's home was near enough, if not at the time within, the Persian empire. His time on our this datum will be *c.* 366—338 B.C. (Nanda Mahāpadma; JBORS., I. 116). The *Kathāsaritsāgara* story is to be modified in view of our AMMK material. The latter is historical, while the former after all is a story. The confusion of Tārānātha that Nanda, the friend of Pāṇini, was the father of Mahāpadma is removed by the AMMK.

§ 8. *Maurya Dynasty*

Later than him (Nanda), Chandragupta will become king (439). He will rule without a rival. He (will be) very prosperous (*Mahābhogī*, T.; not *Mahāyogī* as in S.), true to his coronation oath (*satyasandha*), and of moral soul (*dharmātmā*) (440). On bad advice he killed many, on account of which he fainted with boils at his death.

K. Chandragupta.

He placed on his throne his son Bindusāra (T.; S.—Binduvāra), a minor, at midnight, with tears. Bindusāra's prime minister was wicked. As Bimbisāra (T., Bindusāra) had made a chaitya[6] he was rewarded by being born in the dynasty of Chandragupta. 'While a minor the king obtained great comfort; when of full manhood he turned out to be bold, eloquent and sweet-tongued. He ruled himself up to (the age of) 70 (448-49).

K. Bindusāra.

His prime minister was Chāṇakya, successful in wrath, who was Death (Yamāntaka) when angry. That bad brahmin lived a long time, he covered three reigns (455-6). He went to hell (458). [Then follows a homily (up to 478)].

Prime Minister Chāṇakya.

Comments

Chandragupta and Chāṇakya

Character of Bindusāra

Only these two names are given under the dynasty of Chandragupta. Aśoka the Great is already misplaced above. The succession of Bindusāra as a minor is noteworthy, and also his character sketch which was wanting up to this time. He was not a Buddhist. An explanation was therefore due. How could a king be successful without having been a Buddhist? He had as a child raised a toy stūpa of dust. This every Indian child does even to-day. The common form of their play is to raise a mound of dust.

[6] S. and T. disagree here. The S. text reads that Bimbisāra made a chaitya through *Siṃhadatta,* hence was born in the dynasty or 'royal family' of Chandragupta; while T. reads that Bindusāra in his playfulness had raised a (toy) chaitya, hence he was so born,—it has in place of *Siṃhadatta,* 'in playful sports'.

Chandragupta was not a Buddhist. His military career was punished by his illness and poisonous boils [or carbuncle, (*vishaspho-ṭaiḥ*)].

Chāṇakya has come in for a lot of abuse and deliverance into hell. In his *Arthaśāstra* he has penalised embracing monkish life without providing for one's family and without state permission. He was hard on Buddhists otherwise. The Buddhist history must have its revenge by assigning such a statesman at least to a long career in hell on paper. The historical detail about him, which is important, is that he lived in three reigns, *triṇi rājyāṇi.* Chandragupta seems to have died comparatively young. He had a reign of 24 years, both according to the Purāṇas and the Buddhist records (JBORS., I, 93). He was a young man when he ascended the throne. Probably he died about 45, leaving a minor son. Bindusāra reigned for 25 years according to the Purāṇas, for 28 according to the Mahāvaṃsa and for 27 according to the Burmese books. The difference is probably to be explained by his minority rule, which would be adjusted in the next reign where there is a difference of about 4 years in the different data, the Purāṇas giving less than the Mahāvaṃsa. Chāṇakya must have come down to the opening years of Aśoka, to be the mantrin in three reigns. He would have thus maintained the unity of the Maurya policy for over 50 years in his person. Tārānātha attributes large conquests between the Eastern and Western Seas, etc., (of the Deccan) in the reign of Bindusāra to this great Minister's régime (JBORS., II, 79). Similarly Rādhagupta's ministry lasted beyond Aśoka. Rādhagupta might have been a descendant of Vishṇugupta Chāṇakya.

It should be marked that the system of noting historically in Buddhist records the Prime Ministers' names begins from the Nanda period, or even earlier from Bimbisāra. In the period from the Śaiśunākas to the Mauryas, there is thus strong evidence of some real ruling power having been vested in the Prime Minister with his council. The council from the time of the master of Mahāpadma Nanda up to the last days of Aśoka is prominent in the Buddhist records.

Vishṇugupta Chāṇakya is taken up again in the list of political Brahmins at the end (966—70) [See § 57] where his administration is praised as being strong and just, but his anger is denounced.

§ 9. *Buddhist Saints and Teachers*

From verse 479 to verse 530, there follows a Church history.

"In that time my Bhikshus will be very learned" (479). Mātṛichīna (T.—Mātṛicheṭa) will flourish in *Nṛipa-nagara,* in Khaṇḍa forest. A *stotra* (hymn of praise) will be composed by him (480—490). Nāgā[rjuna], after 400 years of 'my Nirvāṇa' (490-91) will be born, who will live for 106 years. He will possess *Māyūrī-vidyā,* he will know the essence and truth of the Śāstras and of *niḥsvabhāva.* He will attain Buddhahood. There will be Asaṅga (T.; S., *Saṅga*), a learned bhikshu. He will divide and arrange the *sūtra*-meaning. He will be known in the world as self-possessed, and will be *a*(?)—*tuchchha-śīla,* magnanimous. His Vidyā (T.) will be called *Śāladūti.* His intellect will be great in making collections and the explanation of the Commandment (doctrine). He will live for 100 years (494—97). Not much later will be *Nanda* (T.—Arhan), a well-known Tāntrika (499-500) whose *mantra* is given in this book (*AMMK*) (up to 528). Nandaka will be in Chandanamāla (529).

Mātṛicheṭa or Mātṛichīna.

Nāgārjuna C. 144 B.C.—50 B.C.

Bhikshu Asaṅga.

Nanda.

Nandaka.

Comments

Date of Nāgārjuna

For the saint *Nāga,* that is, *Nāgārjuna* a definite date is given—beginning of the 5th century A.B. This will place his rise in the first century B.C. This seems to be the most reliable date for him. Prof. Lévi's date for him is not acceptable. He does not figure in the activities of Kanishka. He was the father of Mahāyāna. He must have therefore flourished before Kanishka. In the section last but one, Nāgārjuna is placed before Aśvaghosha, and Aśvaghosha is placed in the reign of Buddha [y]aksha, the first king of the Yaksha Dynasty. The Yaksha dynasty represents the two Kadphises (§ 11). Hence Aśvaghosha's time is the beginning of the first century A.D.

§ 10. *Low Period*

[Kings after the Mauryas]

K. Gomin [Pushyamitra, 188 B.C.—152 B.C.]

Destruction of Buddhism

In the Low Age (*yugādhame*) there will be king, the chief Gomin (*Gomimukhya,* S.; 'Gomin by name', T.) 'destroyer of my religion' (530). Having seized the East and the gate of Kashmir, he the fool, the wicked, will destroy monasteries with relics, and kill monks of good conduct. He will die in the North (532-33), being killed

along with his officers (? *sa-rāshṭrā*) and his animal relations by the fall of a mountain rock (534). He was destined to a dreadful suffering in hell (535—537).

Comments

In verse 535 the king is abused by the expression *Gomi-shaṇḍa*, 'Gomi the bull'. The name is concealed; and the real import of *Gomi* or *Gomin* is not clear. But the description shows that the hellish, the animalish king is no other than the Brahmin emperor Pushyamitra. It is definitely stated that Northern India from the Prāchī up to the Kashmir valley was under this king.

'The gate of Kashmir' which is mentioned again and again in the AMMK is probably *Dvārābhisāra*. In our text a point at or near Jammu seems to be meant.

§ *11. The Yaksha Dynasty.* [*End of 1st Cent.* B.C. *to 1st Cent.* A.D.]

Restoration of Buddhism

K. Buddha Yaksha.

After (Gomi-shaṇḍa the Wicked) the king according to the pious tradition (*śruta*) will be Buddha-paksha (read *Yaksha*). He, a *Mahā-Yaksha*, very charitable, will be undoubtedly fond of Buddhism (*Buddhānāṃ śāsane rataḥ*), in that low age (538-539). The king, extremely fond of Buddha's teaching will build in many places monasteries, gardens, chaityas, Buddha's images, stepped wells, wells, etc. He will die full of age (*gatāyusha*, 541). T. 542 a.

Gambhīra Yaksha.

His son will be king, possessed of a big army and great power—the famous Gambhīra Yaksha—over the whole land (544). He will be self-possessed. That king, the *Mahādyuti*, (*bhupatiḥ sa mahādyutiḥ*), will build in many places monasteries, rest-houses, chaityas, stepped wells (545-546). He practised mantra of Mañjughosha of 16 syllables and became very prosperous (546).

Comments

Who were the Yaksha dynasty of *Buddhapaksha* and *Gambhīra yaksha*, father and son, who restored Buddhism in India after the Śuṅga period? The answer is given by the known chronology and history. After the Śuṅga age it was under the Early Kushans—the Kadphises—that Buddhism was re-established. The AMMK itself gives us data for this identification. It describes Gambhīra as an emperor (*prithivīmakhiloditām*, 544, p. 621). It describes him by a significant term *mahādyuti* (*bhupatiḥ sa mahādyutiḥ*). 'He the Mahādyuti king' and his father are called *Yaksha* and *Mahāyaksha*, by which the Mongolian type is intended. See AMMK, XXII (p. 233)—'*Yakshāṇāṃtu tathā vāchā uttarāṃdiśi ye narā.* Tārānātha says that the first of these kings had enlisted the sympathy of the emperor of China on his side. This was true of Kadphises I. The name Gambhīra is either a translation of some title of Kadphises II or an attempt to Sanskritize an early edition of the Indian rendering of his name, for instance, *Gabhī* from *Kaphī*. *Buddha-pakha* (if the reading is not *Buddha yakha*) would mean 'the king who took up the cause of the Buddha.'

These two kings are supposed to be kings or rather emperors of Madhyadeśa, as they have been given in that imperial list as the last dynasty. Their time is again indicated by (§ 54) where Buddha-paksha is the patron of Aśvaghosha. It is significant that Kanishka is denoted in the AMMK as *Turushka* (§ 14) and a ruler of the North, rather Central Asia and Kashmir. Aśvaghosha is given as arising a generation or so before him.

The Madhyadeśa Imperial history is left here and Provincial Himalayan history is taken up; the Madhyadeśa Imperial history is resumed at § 17.

North

PROVINCIAL HISTORY

Provincial History of the Himalayas

§ 12. *Nepal—The Lichchhavi Dynasty,* [*and*] *the Western Nepal* [*Ṭhākurī*] *Dynasty* [*7th Century* A.D.]

"In the North, in that time (*tadā kāle*), in the valley of the Himâdri in the famous Province of Nepal (*Nepāla-Maṇḍale*) there will be king (1) Mānavendra [Mānavadeva, T.], in the dynasty of the Lichchhavis (549-50)". He "died" having kept the kingdom thiefless for 80 years (551-52). These several kings of the Himalayas (T.; S.—'of the Mlechchhas') will be worshippers of the Buddha:

(2) Vṛisha (T.; *Vavisha,* in S., a wrong reading) also (called) su-Vṛisha,

(3) Bhāvasu also (called) Śubhasu (Bhūmā-subhūmā in T.)

(4) Bhākrama (Parākrama, T.) also called (*kīrtyate*) Padākrama and Kamala (555-56).

§ 12(*a*). *Dynasty of the West*

'(There will be the kings) of the West'.

(1) Bhāgupta Vatsaka 'like the sun' (T., text lost in S.);

(2-3) Udaya and Jishṇu (T.; S.—Jinhuna) will be in the end (556-557).

§ 12(*b*). *Fall of Nepal Kingdom* [*c. 675* A.D.—*700* A.D.]

Then there will be various kings amongst the Mlechchhas (557). They will be with fallen dignity (*bhrashṭa-maryāda*), serving aliens and eaters of the subjects (*pra-*

jōpabbhojinaḥ, T.; S. corrupt). The *adhipati* kingship of Nepal will be destroyed by weapons; the vidyās will be lost; kings will be lost, they will become servants of the Mlechchha (foreign) usurper (*mlechchha-taskara-sēvinaḥ*) (558).

Comments on the (A) MMK History of Nepal

We have to take *'in that time,' bhavishyati tadā kāle* (549) as meaning *'then in time'* ('or in that time') *i.e.,* in the *yugādhame,* the lowest age of this chronicle. For the Nepal Lichchhavi dynasty has to be dated from the time of Samudra Gupta (*c.* 350 A.D.). (1) Mānavendra is unidentified. It is not *Mānadeva* for he flourished in 705 A.D. while the kings related here next are much earlier in the dynasty. (2) Vṛisha (T.; S., *vavisha,* a misreading) is the inscriptional Vṛisha deva of the Lichchhavi dynasty who lived about 630 A.D. (Fleet, GI., 189). In the Nepal inscriptions giving the genealogy, names before Vṛisha deva have been omitted. Mānavendra was probably one of them. (3) Bhāvasu Śubhasu corresponds with Śaṅkaradeva (about 655 A.D.) of the inscription, who was son of Vṛishadeva. (4) Bhākrama (or Parākrama, T.)—Padakrama should be the next king Dharmadeva of the inscription on account of the next kings being identified with the kings of the Ṭhākurī dynasty.

The Lichchhavi dynasty and the Ṭhākurī dynasty ruled together from the same place. The Ṭhākurīs ruled over the Western Province (GI., p. 180). The Western kings (*Paśchima*) as named in the AMMK are: (1) Bhāgupta, i.e., Aṃśuvarman the Vatsaka, who was the founder of the family. The next two, (2) Udaya and (3) Jishṇu, who are called 'the last' ones coming after Aṃśuvarman, are the inscriptional Udayadeva coming last (about 675 A.D.), while Jishṇugupta flourished just before him in 653 A.D. Hence we may construct a contemporary table thus:

Lichchhavi Dynasty		*Western Ṭhākurī Dynasty*	
AMMK	*Inscriptions*	*AMMK*	*Inscriptions*
Mānavendra	12. (missing).	Bhāgupta	Aṃśuvarman (635—650 A.D.)
Vṛisha	13. Vṛishadeva (C. 630 A.D.)	Jishṇu	Jishṇugupta, 653 A.D.
Bhāvasu	14. Śaṅkaradeva (C. 650)	Udaya	Udayadeva, (C. 675 A.D.)
Bhākrama	15. Dharmadeva, son of 14.		

The Buddhist faith of the Nepal Lichchhavis is attested by Yuan Chwang, and of the family of Aṃśuvarman by the conversion of the great Tibetan emperor Strong-tsan-Gampo through his chief queen who was Amśuvarman's daughter.

Fall of Nepal Kingdom

Our text affords new and correct information, which we do not get from the Nepal annals, when it says that Udaya and Jishṇu were the last kings of the Nepal kingdom and that after them rulers in Nepal became dependent on Mlechchha usurpers, and kingship was lost. This refers to the absorption of Nepal into Tibet. Strong-tsan-Gampo married Aṃśuvarman's daughter before he compelled the Chinese emperor to give his daughter to him as the second consort in or about 641 A.D. Under this Tibetan emperor before his death (698 A.D.) Nepal evidently totally passed under Tibet's domination, until 703 A.D. when Nepal rose to shake off the foreign domination and killed the Tibetan king in war (Parkar). The AMMK is thus recording the political condition of Nepal before 703 A.D. and after 675 A.D.

§ *13. Tibet ["Chīna"]*

[629 A.D.—698 A.D.]

The next Himālayan state dealt with is 'Chīna', i.e., Tibet as distinguished from *Mahā-Chīna* (=China). The text itself makes this distinction, e.g., in Chapter X (p. 88) it enumerates the kshetras of the *uttarāpatha* mountains in this order:

Daśabalaiḥ kathitaḥ kshetrāḥ uttarāpathaparvatāḥ.

Kaśmīre, Chīnadeśe cha Nepāle, Kāviśe tathā.

Kāviśa here is *Kapiśā.*

Mahā-Chīna it takes next (*Mahā-Chīne tu vai siddhi* (*ḥ*) *siddhikshetrāṇy aśeshataḥ*).

"There are related several kings and several of those who will be fond of Brahmins in Chīna and around (559). King Hiraṇyagarbha, however, will be one possessed of a large army and great power, an extensive political system, and a number of (political) relatives. The Mlechchhas will bow before him; he (will be) the conqueror; and a follower of the word of the Buddha" (560-61).

He as a boy had mastered the Mahāvīra formula. He, the great king, died at the age of 100 (566). He obtained Buddhahood. In that country Mañjughosha is a boy (568).

Comments

The only king to whom this description applies is the king Strong-tsan-Gampo of Tibet. (See the last comments above). He came to the throne as a boy (629 A.D.) and became the most powerful monarch in Central Asia in the latter half of the seventh century. He introduced Buddhism into Tibet, and had the Tibetan script devised by Hindus. He was deified by the Buddhist Church. He had a long reign (d. 698 A.D.), a remarkable victorious career, and extended dominions.

§ 14. *Balkh-to-Kashmir*

Turushka king =[Kanishka]

Turushka king in N. India.

"Then will rise in the North [uttarâpatha] the Turushka king, of great army and great vigour. Up to the gate of Kashmir, Bashkala, Udyāna (T.; S.—Udaya) with Kāviśa (570), for 700 yojanas he rules. 77,000 and 2,00,000 (revenue ?) will be his (571). 86,000 stupas he will make. 'He established the country the *Prajñāpāramitā*—the mother of the Buddhas and the foremost doctrine of Mahāyāna (Buddhism)' (574-75).

Mahā-Turushka.

After him Mahā-Turushka, the '*Maheśāksha*', the *mahāyaksha*, having a large army will be king, having been recognized by his relatives (*sammato bandhuvargāṇām rājā so pi bhavishyati*). He will make 8,000 monasteries (576—579).

Comments

The description of the Turushka king is undoubtedly the description of Kanishka. The centre of his kingdom according to our text was Bashkala which was connected with Udyāna-cum-Kapiśā and Kashmir. The tract thus indicated by the word *Bashkala* is *Balkh* with a transposition in the second syllable *lkh*. According to the text, Turushka (Kanishka) was primarily a king of Afghanistan (Kāviśa), Suwāt, and Kashmir on this side of the Himādri (in its wider significance), and up to Balkh which was considered as one of the northern provinces of Bhāratavarsha (I.A., 1933, p. 130).

Turushka is credited with having established in the North the Prajñāpāramitā. It should be noted that he is not credited with the holding of any Buddhist Council. Nor is Kanishka described under any other name in our history.

All Indian authorities—our text, Alberūnī's sources, Kalhaṇa, etc. —unanimously call Kanishka a Turushka, probably on account of his original country being Central Asia. The Text calls the next king a mahāyaksha (see below). His immediate successor is named Mahā-Turushka, whose succession was approved by his relatives. Does this denote a friction between Vāseshka and Huvishka? The extensive Buddhist foundations would identify the 'Mahā-Turushka' with Huvishka.

The unity of the family with the Yaksha family (§ 11) seems to be indicated by the Mahā-Turushka being called a *mahāyaksha.*

Western India

PROVINCIAL HISTORY

Lāḍa—Sea-coast—(Kachh-Sindh)

§ 15. *The Valabhī Dynasty* [595 A.D.—650 A.D.]

Beginning at Ujjayinī, up to the West country up to the sea-coast, in the country of the Lāḍas, there will be king Śīla a Buddhist. At Sila (āditya). Valabhī, he will be a *dharma-rājā.* He will make attractive (artistic, '*citrān*') monasteries with relics for public good, and beautiful Buddha images, and various worships (586—589). He will be in the dynasty of Dhara, and king of the Lāḍas. He rules for 30 years (597-98). He was followed by Chapala. Chapala (601) who ruled for half a year and one fortnight and was killed by soldiers. His successor (*anuja*) was Dhruva, who becomes king of the Lāḍas. He was subordinate, miserable and foolish (603-604).

Comments

This Śīla the Dharmarāja, of the family of Dhara is **Siladitya Dharmaditya I**, the seventh in succession from Dharasena I, founder of the Maitraka dynasty of Valabhī. His inscriptions with dates equivalent to 605 A.D.—609 A.D. have been found. His successor Chapala will correspond with Kharagraha (his nephew) of the inscriptions. His nephew Dhruvasena II[7] was the next king. Records of his, dated 629—639 A.D., have been found. Dhruva is described in the AMMK as *anuja* of Chapala, which is to be taken in its original sense '*born after*', '*a younger cadet*', and not '*younger brother*'. Yuan-Chwang saw the artistic Buddhist temple built by Śīlāditya when he visited Valabhī in the reign of Dhruva, who was a vassal and son-in-law to Harsha.

[7] Kielhorn's Table, EI, VIII. 11.

The dynastic description and the extent of the territories of Śīlāditya given here settles the controversy started by Hoernle (*JRAS.*, 1909, 122). He was king of the territory from Ujjain in Eastern Malwā up to the West Country on the sea, i.e., Kachchha, which was the limit of the West Country according to the Purāṇic geography (I. A., 1933, 126); and he was king of the L ā ḍ a s, i.e., what we call Gujarat, and of Valabhī i.e., Southern Kathiawār.

D h r u v a, according to our Text, becomes subordinate, which was a fact in Harshavardhana's time.

The history of Valabhī is here accurately given by the AMMK.

§ 16. *The Yādava Republics*

[Before 500 A.D., i.e., before Śīlāditya's family and after him.]

The other kings of the West or Lāḍa will be servants of the subjects [T.; S. 'will be crown-less' ("head-less", *mūrdhānta*)]. Their own earlier families will be rulers after Śīla. They will be mariners, sailing beyond the sea to Ś ū r a (T., Sūra=Assyria; S.—'going to Persia,' *Parshagāḥ*) (605). At V ā r a v a t ī there will be I n d r a, S u c h a n d r a, D h a n u, (and) K e t u, with the style *Pushpa*. Having occupied Valabhī, there will be the first king and his numerous successors with the names *Prabha* and *Vishṇu*: the numerous kings will be Yadavas (606—8). The last (T.) amongst them will have the name V i s h ṇ u whose 'capital with its citizens and the king himself was washed away by the sea owing to the curse of the Ṛishi. The V ā r a v a t y a s (T.; S.—D v ā r a v a t y a s) then disappeared and sunk in the sea (609).

Comments

[CASTE OF THE MAITRAKAS]

The V ā r a v a t y a s were Y ā d a v a s as mentioned at p. 604 (verse 324) *Yātavā Vārayatyāś* (*cha*). The V ā r a v a t y a s seem to be noted in the Paikuli Sassanian inscription in Asuristán in the form of *Boráspāčin* whose chief was Mitra al-Sen in 294 A.D. (*JBORS.*, XIX). It is noted in the AMMK that from the sea the Valabhī (Kathiāwār) people used to cross over to Ś ū r a, which refers to their trade ventures to and regular commerce with A s s y r i a. The port Ś ū r a p ā r a k a (S o p ā r ā) acquired that name for being the port of embarkation for Assyria.

The rulers noted by name are post-Śīlāditya, though their families had existed from before. The washing away of Vāravatī seems to have taken place towards the end of the seventh century. They according to the AMMK occupied Valabhī, probably in the 7th century. The Vāravatyas are expressly described as belonging to the family from which Śīlāditya descended; the Vāravatyas represented the earlier stock —*teshāṃ cha pūrvajā-Vaṃśāḥ Śīlahvōparate tadā.* The Maitrakas thus were a branch of the Yādavas.

The Pushpa-nāma of our text probably means the Pushpamitras.

Madhyadesa: Imperial History

§ 17. *Śaka Dynasty—Śaka Emperors [the Kushans, 78* A.D.—*350* A.D.]. *Northern Madhyadeśa*

Now the Buddhist historian leaves the West and takes up the Middle Country. These kings he calls *Madhyamas* i.e., the kings of the Madhya country. He begins with North Mid-Land:

"In the Northern Quarter on the mountains (T.; S.—*'rambha'* ?) and tableland, everywhere, many kings of different births (castes or nationalities—*jāti*) have been declared.

The Śaka dynasty (*Śaka-vaṃśa*) known to be of 30 rulers (T. with a wrong reading for 'Śakavaṃśa', '21+30'). 18 kings are known to be Emperors (*Sārvabhūmika,* T.; S.—wrongly, *'sārvabhūtika'*) of Madhyadeśa (Madhyamā) (610—612).

§ 18. *The dynasty of Nāga-Senas.* [*150* A.D.—*348* A.D.]

At the close there (will be) the Nāga-Śenas, and then they ceased (*viluptā*) (612).

Comments on §§ 17-18

The important thing to note is that the Śaka dynasty is placed in North Madhyadeśa, and that they were Imperial, that is, the reference is not to the Western Satraps, but to the Kushāns.

The Nāgasenas are the Nāga dynasty of the Bhāraśivas wherein Vīrasena Nāga was the first king (of the Nava Nāgas of the Purāṇas) who defeated them and dislodged them from Mathurā, and earlier still some king who founded *Kāntipurī* below the Vindhyas (Mirzapur) dispossessed them from Eastern Aryāvarta.[8] It seems very probable that the compound "Nāga-Ṣenas" is made up of the "Nāgas"

[8] JBORS., XIX, I.

and Pravara-"Sena" (the Vākāṭaka emperor) and other kings of the 'Sena' line. The histories of the two families are knit together. The member of the Imperial Śakas—18 kings—would bring them down to the time of Samudra Gupta (78 A.D.+18×15=348 A.D.) and the closing period of the Nāga-Vākāṭakas.

It is not possible to say how the other figure (30) is made up. Evidently the number was made up with some class of subordinate rulers, as distinguished from 'the emperors' (*shāhānushāhis*), probably it included the Śaka Satraps.

The Nāga dynasty, like all other Hindu dynasties of the Imperial Madhyadeśa, is repeated in the history of Bengal, (§ 30).

§§ *19-19(c). [Post-Guptan Imperial Rulers of Madhyadeśa]*

[530 A.D.—647 A.D.]

§ *19. Vishṇu, [520—533* A.D.]. *Hara, [533—550 ?]*

§ *19(c). The Maukharis* [*550* A.D.—*600* A.D.]

The Guptas are omitted here, as they are taken up separately under the section of the Imperial Eastern History (§ 24) and then also in the Provincial Eastern History (Pt. II).

Then (there will be) (1) Vishṇu, and (2) Hara. Another (3) Ājita [Hara (T.)] called *Kunta* (Kuntanāmā Haraḥ); (4) Īśāna, (5) Sarva and (6) Paṅkti, (7) Graha and after him Suvrata (T.) (613). Then they lose their kings and become fallen in prestige (*bhrashṭa-maryāda*) (614).

Comments

In this group whom I have numbered above, it is easy to recognise Maukhari kings in Nos. 4 to 7. *'Paṅkti'* is an easy misreading for *'vanti'* and is to be restored as Avanti (reading *Sarv=Āvanti,* instead of *Sarvapaṅkti* of the text). The list will thus agree with the Maukhari list known to us from inscriptions and Bāṇa:

AMMK	*Inscriptions etc.*
Ājita	Āditya-varman
Īśāna	Īśānavarman
Sarva	Śarvavarman
(*Paṅkti,* i.e., Avanti)	Avantivarman
Graha	Grahavarman d. 606 A.D.

Ājita is the Prakrit form of *Āditya.* Adityavarman was the first

Maukhari ruler to come into importance. He married a Gupta princess Harshaguptā. The AMMK begins with only important names. It seems that in continuing the imperial history of Madhyadeśa, it should have begun the Maukhari line with Īśānavarman who is the first Maukhari to assume the imperial title *Mahārājādhirāja* and whose rise is dated about 554 A.D. But the Maukhari and the Thanesar lines include some earlier names.

Vishṇu is the emperor Vishṇuvardhana of the Mandasor inscription (*GI.*, p. 50) of 589 ME (533 A.D.). The other name *Hara* appears to be of his descendant. The grouping in the text would indicate that. Further there is no other imperial line under which it can come. Situated as he is before the Maukharis (550 A.D.) [Īśāna (varman 554 A.D.)] and after Vishṇu (vardhana, 533 A.D.)—he very likely belonged to the line of Vishṇuvardhana.

The AMMK instead of mentioning the name Yaśodharman gives Vishṇu [dharman], and seems to support Hoernle's view that both names mean one personality (*sa eva,* as in the inscription).

The AMMK implies that the Maukharis occupied the imperial position in Northern India, i.e., from 550 A.D. to the rise of Prabhākara vardhana, 600 A.D., who is noted next. Our text also supplies the much needed confirmation that Vishṇuvardhana-Yaśodharman became the real emperor in his time. The Maukharis seem to come into prominence under his house.

§ *19(b). The Vaiśya Dynasty of Śrīkaṇṭha-Sthāṇvīśvara*

[*560* A.D.—*647* A.D.]

The origin and history of the family of Harshavardhana is given next. It is detailed that they were born of (king) Vishṇu (vardhana), they were of Vaiśya caste; they became first ministers and then they became kings. The style *vardhana* seems to have been borrowed from their imperial ancestors. They were ministers evidently to the Maukharis.

There were at the time two very prosperous rich men from Madhyadeśa, descended from (king) Vishṇu, *Bh.* by name and another. Both became chief ministers. The two noted rich men possessed of majesty, were devoted to this Religion. They practised Mahāyāna mantra of Kumāra after which they became rulers of men and (one) became king. (614—616).

Then, there (were) for 78 (T.; S., 115(?)) years three kings, residents of Srikaṇṭha—(1) Āditya by name, the Vaiśya, inhabitant of Sthāna(v)

Iśvara; (2) there will be king everywhere at the end—H (arshavardhana) an imperial sovereign (*sarvabhūminarādhipaḥ*) (617-618) [mantra prescribed for that Low Age].

Comments

The form Sthāṇvīśvara is incorrectly given as *Sthanamīśvara.* God Sthāṇu, the presiding deity of Thāneśvara, was the only god to whom their ancestor Vishṇuvardhana-Yaśodharman bent his head (*GI*, 146). The family was thus connected with Thānesvara from the time of the first founder. Vishṇuvardhana-Yaśodharman had a governor in Mālava, he himself did not live there. The history of H(arsha) is again taken up in § 34 in connection with Soma (Śaśāṅka) where he is called king of Madhyadeśa.

The dynasty here is taken to begin from *Ādityavardhana.* Their caste is definitely stated to be *Vaiśya* which is confirmed by Yuan-Chwang. This was therefore the caste of Emperor Vishṇuvardhana also.

Ādityavardhana
|
Prabhākaravardhana
|
Rājyavardhana — Harshavardhana (606—647)

are noted to have covered 115 (S.) or 78 (T.) years. In the former case Āditya's initial time will be 532 A.D. and in the latter 569 A.D. The former alone can be right, for there were two generations of rulers before Ādityavardhana. Harsha alone is called *Emperor.*

The Vaiśya dynasty and the Maukharis both arise under Emperor Vishṇuvardhana.

Southern India

[Mainly Kings contemporary of Harshavardhana]

'In the South with the sea' there will be (S. 621; p. 627):

§ 20. *The Sātavāhana* [223 A.D.—231 A.D.]

(1) "King Śvetasuchandra, called *Sātavāhana*" (613) (*Śālavāhana,* T. 456A).

§ 21. *Contemporaries of King Mahendra* (600—640 A.D.)

'The celebrated kings of the South:

(2) "Mahendra, (3) Śaṅkara, and (4) Vallabha [T. has *Chittabha* for *Vallabha*] (622-623). "Now, king Vallabha (623) (is) called *'Sukeśi* and *'Keśi'*. (5) Maṅgala is (also) called *Vṛishaketu* (T.) (*Bṛindakhetu,*—S.). (2) Mhendra is called *'Supota'* (T.; incorrect *Mutpata* in S.), *'Pota'* and *'Chandra'* (624), (7) Gopendra, *Indra* (*Chandra*—T.) *sena,* (8) Mādhava, *Pradyumna* (*Kāmadeva*—T.), (3) Gaṇa-Śaṅkara (called) *Vyāghra;* (9) Budha called *Siṃha;* (10) the Śūdra king (T.) [Budha Śuddha',—S.] Kumbha called Nikumbha; and (11) Mathita Sumati." (625-26).

[S. adds (not in T.): Bala-Pulina-sukeśi—(=Pulakeśi), and Kesins, 626.]

They died different deaths; some died from weapons, some of starvation (or famine) 628.

"They are up to 'the *Pota*' king Mahendra, and are his contemporaries" (629).

[Necessary worship for the South in the age of Kali that had arrived detailed. 630-33].

On the peaks of the Vindhyas and in the Lavaṇa Ocean (Indian Ocean) god Kārtikeya will be the giver of boons (633). And so in the country of Śrī-Parvata; in the valley of the Vindhya and its high lands (636).

Comments

(1) Śveta-su Chandra is the Sātavāhana king who was practically the last emperor in that line—Chandra sāta. The name is found in our text as *śveta* (corruption from *svāti*) *su Chandra.*

The kings (2) to (10) make a group of contemporary kings amongst whom (2), (3) and (4) were the most 'celebrated'. To take up their identification:

Pallava Mahendravarman.

(2) Mahendra who is particularised as the *Pota* king is the *Mahendrapota* of the inscriptions. Kielhorn (EI., VIII, Sup., p. 20) rightly anticipated and said that 'probably' this and also 'Mahendra' were names of Mahendravarman I. He is the great Pallava king of Kāñchī, 600—625 A.D., the builder of rock-cut temples, and the rival of Pulakeśin II.

Sañkaragaṇa.

(3) Śaṅkara and Gaṇa Śaṅkara of our text is the Śaṅkagaṇa mentioned in the Nerūr copperplates of Maṅgaleśa, uncle of Pulakeśin II (IA, VII, 161; Kielhorn's List No. 6). Maṅgaleśa defeated Buddharāja, son of Śaṅkaragaṇa (*c.* 601 A.D.). According to our AMMK, 'Gaṇa Śaṅkara' was one of the famous Southern kings of the time. He was an ancestor of the Southern Kalachuris (Kielhorn, No. 5). The name was repeated amongst the Tripurī Kalachuris.

(4) Vallabha Sukeśi is a Chālukya Pulakeśin of Bādāmī. As he is one of 'the celebrated' kings of the South; he is to be taken as Pulakeśin II (608—642 A.D.). In some inscriptions he is called only Vallabha (Kielhorn, No. 14), while in some *Polekeśi Vallabha* (Kielhorn, No. 12).

(5) Maṅgala Vallabha is the famous Maṅgaleśa or Maṅgalarāja, the predecessor and uncle of Pulakeśin II. The order (Maṅgala coming after Pulakeśin II) is due to the fact that the three 'celebrated kings' are picked out and mentioned first as a group of celebrities. The statement about him that Maṅgala is also called '*Vallabha*' is by way of a footnote.

(6) Govinda is the king defeated by Pulakeśin II (Aihole insc.; Kielhorn, No. 10).

(7) Gopendra Indrasena, who was, according to our text, a contemporary of Mahendra and Pulakeśin II, is yet unknown (as far as I know) from other sources. He would have been one of the rulers of the Southern states of the Aihole inscription.

(8) Mādhava is evidently the Kadamba king Madhuvarman who became the ruler of Vanavāsī in the time of Pulakeśin and Mahendravarman (Moraes, *Kadamba Kula*, pp. 64, 66).

(9) Budha, who comes with Gaṇa Śaṅkara, is the ruler who came in conflict with Maṅgaleśa and was the son of Śaṅkara-gaṇa. The name in the Chālukya inscriptions is spelt as Buddha.

(10) Nikumbha, a śūdra king according to T., is traceable from inscriptions of his descendants or their servants found in Khāndeś. These are dated in the 11th and 12th centuries of the Śaka era (Kielhorn, Nos. 333, 337). Kielhorn regarded the name Nikumbha of the Nikumbha Dynasty as mythical. Now this new evidence takes us four centuries back when we find Nikumbha actually a ruler, a contemporary of Mahendra. Later princes of the Nikumbha Dynasty patronized the science of astronomy, for the teaching of which a college founded by the grandson of the great Bhāskarâchārya was endowed by them.

(11) Mathita sumati is not yet known from any other source.

It seems that the author had some good history to draw upon for the time of Harsha, Śaśāṅka, Pulakeśin II and Mahendra I. His information of the period is detailed and accurate for the whole of India—North, South, West and East.

The religious information that Kārtikeya was worshipped in the South at the time is borne out by inscriptions. At Śrī Parvata, Mahāsena's worship is found after the Sātavāhanas. It is attested by the Kadamba inscriptions for the succeeding centuries.

§ 22. *The Dvīpas in the Southern Sea, (Indian Archipelago) and Further India*

The Indian Archipelago with Further India has been included as a part of Southern India in the survey of the AMMK.

The text on the Dvīpas (verses 636—640) says:

Everywhere the Dvīpas too, in the Kaliṅga seas [? Kaliṅgodreshu], (Kārtikeya will be worshipped). The Traiguṇyas [will be] in the Mlechchha countries all around. In the bays of the sea, on their coasts, there will be numerous kings; the *Kāma-rūpa-kalā* [Kāma-rūpa-kulā? Kings of the family of Kāma-rūpa?] in the valleys of snowy mountains ('in Himādri'). Many kings are stated to have been between the meetings of the Seas (*udra-sandhishu*). Many gaṇa chiefs of the Mlechchhas, worshippers of the Buddha:—Indra and Suchandra-Mahendra, inhabitants amongst the Mlechchhas will be kings. [These two kings will be Buddhists.]

Comments

The name of the seas 'Kaliṅga Seas' (*Kalingodreshu*, cf. *udrasandhishu*) is important. The Archipelago was intimately connected with Kaliṅga. In the seventh century (637—649) just about the period when the AMMK is full of contemporary details a Kaliṅga dynasty was ruling in Java. King Kaliṅga sent an embassy to China from Central Java. There was a Khmar king Mahendra(varman) whose ambassador Siṃhadeva was at the court of Śambhuvarman, king of Champā about 625 A.D. The Mahendra of the AMMK was a Mlechchha, that is, he did not belong to one of the Hindu dynasties of Further India who were all non-Buddhists at the time. Indra too of our text was a Mlechchha and Buddhist.

The Kāmarūpa branch was probably ruling in Upper Burma, where a Hindu king Samuda established his kingdom very early (Gait, *History of Assam*, p. 8).

It is significant that the Dvīpas or the Indian Archipelago and Further India (the countries on the bays of the Sea—*ambhodheḥ kukshitīrāntāḥ*) are treated here as part of the South and as being in the Lavaṇa Ocean (633). They were included in the Greater India of Samudra Gupta (JBORS. XIX. 154).

We seem to recover the Hindu name for the narrow seas of Java and Sumatra in the expression "Kaliṅga Waters".

East

Imperial [Magadha]—Gauḍa Dynasties

((*a*) Before 320 A.D.; and (*b*) 320—750 A.D.)

§ 23. *Loka* (*Gauḍa Dynasty*) [*before* 320 A.D.]

In the East, many great (good) kings (nṛipavarāḥ)—past, future and present are related (641). First I shall state the kings of the dynasty of the Gauḍas (642) (1) Loka, born at Vardhamāna, to Yaśasvin, becomes the cause of the prosperity of Gauḍa (*Gauḍa-vardhanaḥ*). He will be religious. Several kings passed (643).

§ 24. *Imperial Guptas* [348 A.D.—500 A.D.]

"Listen about the Mediæval and Madhyadeśa kings (*madhyakāle, madhyamā*) who will be in a long period emperors (*nṛipendrā*) and who will be confident and will be followers of *via media*," (in religious policy, madhyadharmiṇaḥ), (645):—

(1) Samudra, the king,
(2) Vikrama, of good fame (*kīrttitāḥ*), 'who is sung'.
(3) Mahendra, an excellent king and a leader (*nṛipavaro Mukhya*).
(4) S-initialled (Skanda) after Ma. (i.e., Mahendra).

His name (will be) *Devarāja;* he will have several names (*vividhākhya*, T., against *nirdhhākhya* of S.); he will be the best, wise and religious king in that low age (646-647).

His younger successor (5) Bāla (*Bālākhya*, T.; S.—*Balādhyaksha*) will be Buddhist; he will make the East up to the sea decorated with chaityas. He will build over the whole land monasteries, orchards, reservoirs, gardens and pavilions. His Majesty will then make passages (roads) and bridges, and will worship Buddha images. After reigning without any rival and peacefully he becomes a wanderer (Buddhist monk) and finally at the age of 36 years 1 month commits suicide by *dhyāna*, swooning away. He had become a monk owing to grief for his dead son (648-52).

(Verses 653 to 670 deal with his rebirths). In verse 671 he is called *Bāla the Easterner* (pūrvadeśakaḥ).

(6) "Following him (next to him, *tasyāparena*) the king declared is Kumāra by name, the great lord of the Gauḍas. He too (will be) exceedingly virtuous." (674).

(7) "Following him (or next to him) (is) the well-known, the prosperous (śrīmān) U." (675).

§ 25. *Break-up and division of the Empire*

(8) "After that there will be a mutual severance (*viślesha*)" (675).

Comments on §§ 23—24

(Gupta Imperial History)

The Imperial Period after the Nāgas and before Vishṇuvardhana which had been omitted from the Madhyadeśa Imperial history is taken up here under Eastern India, for the Guptas are treated as Eastern Emperors, evidently on account of their having ceremonial and official capital at Pāṭaliputra.

The Gauḍa Dynasty

The Eastern history is, however, introduced with king L o k a of the Gauḍa dynasty (*Gauḍānāṃ vaṃśajaḥ*). He was born at *Vardhamāna* (our modern Burdwān). He must have been a king before the Gupta epoch. In the summing-up, verse 876 (p. 646) we read

evaṃ prakārāḥ kathitā bhūpālāḥ Loka-vardhanā |
viditā sarvalokes' smiṃ Prāchyā cha sthitadehinī (°naḥ) ||

Does *lokavardhanā* here refer to Loka the Gauḍavardhana of our present section? There was probably a *vardhana* family of kings in Bengal in or about the third century A.D.

But after this introduction, and leaving the other kings unnamed (644), the Imperial Guptas are taken up, meaning thereby that Bengal passed under the Guptas. It should be noted here that in the succeeding part dealing with the provincial history of Gauḍa and Magadha, the dynasty with which the history commences is of the Nāga-rāja, i.e., the Bhāraśivas or Navanāgas (§§ 30; 37).

The Gupta Emperors

The author or the authorities of the MMK had a true history of the Gupta times. The account, where verifiable, is very correct. It is sober and fuller. Along with this the personal history of S a m u d r a G u p t a in § 31 should be read where his northern conquests and correct reign-period are given. There are some most valuable details which illuminate the confused portions of the Gupta history and help us in coming to a decision on debated and doubtful points.

It is not a matter of small satisfaction to recover an actual Indian record in the form of a written history on the Great Gupta epoch. The character-estimate of the Gupta emperors by the Buddhist historian is very valuable and it is fortunately very sound even when the kings were not Buddhists. The account really constitutes true history. The names under which each king is described should be assumed to be the most common names amongst their perplexing series of *virudas*, which causes no small trouble to the modern historian. Even our Buddhist historian complains, after recording two names of S k a n d a G u p t a that he had too many names (vividhākhyā, T.). It should be marked that

Chandra Gupta I is not in the list of emperors which begins with Samudra. The Gupta kings who are described as Emperors (*nṛipendrāḥ*) are from Samudra to Kumāra Gupta II's son, '*His Majesty U.* (675) whom I take to be identical with Budha Gupta (see below). After his reign the Empire is definitely stated to have been subject to 'disruption' (*viśleshа*). This datum is one of the greatest contributions of the MMK, as we shall presently see.

The Kings and their character

The kings in the Imperial list of the MMK are Samudra, 'the king', that is, *Samudra Gupta.* His character is reviewed in the Provincial History of Bengal (§ 31),—a lord, superman, severe, ever vigilant, mindful about himself, unmindful about the hereafter—sacrificing animals (horse-sacrifices). His reign in the Provincial History is most epigrammatically rendered:

(under his rule) men and manes had the various kinds of luxuries, and the king, various prosperity.

vividhākārabhogāṃś cha
mānushā pitarās tathā
vividhāṃ sampadāṃ so'pi
prāptavān nṛipatiḥ tathā.

The rise of Brāhmaṇas under Samudra is duly noted (§ 31).

Vikrama, i.e., *Vikramāditya* Chandra Gupta II, is '*of good fame*'. Here as in the Ayodhayā chronicles (noticed by Cunningham) 'Chandra Gupta' is not known, but *Vikrama.* This was the only popular name of this king.

(3) Mahendra is Mahendrāditya Kumāra Gupta I. He was an 'excellent' and 'leading' (*mukhya*) king. Here we should note that the estimate of the Indian historian regarding this king's character is different from that we read in V. Smith. By no means he seems to have been a weak king.

(4) 'After Ma.' (i.e., Mahendra) the succession of S. (i.e., Skanda) is specifically noted, and V. Smith is confirmed here. He bore the name of his grandfather (*Devarāja*) and had a variety of names (*virudas*).

The most important thing about this king is the highest praise reserved for him:

'the best (*śreshṭha*),
a wise (*buddhimān*)

and justice-loving (*dharma-vatsala*)
king in that low age (*yugādhame*)'.

This estimate of his character is noteworthy. He was in the opinion of the Indian historian, the greatest of the great Gupta sovereigns. I may be permitted to add here that this has been my own humble opinion. He was the greatest of the Gupta kings. He was the only hero in Asia and Europe who could defeat the Huns at their rise. This he did at an early age which is evident from the Bhītarī pillar inscription. His wise administration is attested to by Chakrapālita's Junagarh inscription.

[Wars of Skanda Gupta, from the *Chandragarbha* Sūtra.]

How grateful we are to our Buddhist historians, not only for this valuable information about the personality of Skanda Gupta, but for a description of his successful war. In the *Chandragarbha paripṛichchhā*,* cited by Buston in his history of Buddhist Doctrine, the war is thus described:

> King *Mahendrasena* who was born in the country of Kauśāmbī, had a son with arms of irresistible might. After he had passed the age of 12, Mahendra's kingdom was invaded upon by three foreign powers in concert—Yavanas, Palhikas and Sakunas—who first fought amongst themselves. They took possession of Gāndhāra and countries to the north of the Ganges. The young son[10] of M a h e n d r a s e n a, of weighty hands and other congenital military marks distinguishing his person, asked for permission to lead his father's army. The enemy army numbered three hundred thousand men under the commands of the foreign kings, the chief of whom was the Yavana [or Yauna]. The son of Mahendra put his army of two hundred thousand men divided under five hundred commanders, sons of ministers and other orthodox Hindus. With extraordinary quickness and a terrible drive he charged the enemy. In fury his veins on the forehead appeared like a visible mark (*tilaka*) and his body became steeled. The Prince broke the enemy army and won the battle. On his return his father crowned him king saying: 'henceforth rule the kingdom', and himself retired to religious life. For twelve years after this, the new king fought these foreign enemies and ultimately captured and executed the three kings. After that he ruled peacefully as the Emperor of Jambudvīpa.

The three foreign powers who fought amongst themselves first are to be recognized as the *Pahlavik* (the official name of the Sansanians), the Śakas (that is, the Kushāns) and the Yavanas, who stand here for the Hūṇas (Yaunas, Hyūnas). The Hūṇas, we know, actually fought the other two powers before attacking India.

*I understand, the text itself is preserved in the Kangyur.

[10] Compare Akbar taking the field at 14, and Harsha at 16.

It seems that this account is based on fact. The foreign army composed of three elements had penetrated up to the Ganges. It was the indomitable will and skill of Skanda Gupta which won the battle.

He led the flower of Orthodox Hindu India, *i.e.*, excluding Buddhists, younger sons of ministers and noblemen, and played like his grandfather Chandra Gupta II under Rāma Gupta, a game of sheer courage, in making an impetuous charge against the enemy, numerically stronger.

The battle was won, its fame spread in Hunnic Asia—'in the Mlechchha countries' as Chakrapālita puts it. But, according to the Buddhist authority, although the battle was won, the war was not over. A twelve years' war had to be waged before the foreign king were captured and punished.

Skanda Gupta ruled certainly from 455 A.D. to 467 A.D. (coins), for at least 12 years.

The view of V. Smith that Skanda Gupta fought more than one battle against the Huns proves to be correct, but his view that the empire of Skanda Gupta succumbed to repeated Hun attacks and perished after his death, is not only without any evidence, but is contradicted by the Chandragarbha sūtra, and the *MMK* which says that the next king (5) Bāla *i.e.*, Bālāditya had his reign (rājyaṃ) *niḥsapatnamakaṅṭakam*—without any rival or obstacle. In other words, the wars had been finished by Skanda Gupta, and the foreigners had been beaten back. Dr. V. Smith did not realize the distinction between Bālāditya I and Bālāditya II; in fact, in his book (p. 329), he gives Bālāditya without any distinguishing "I" or "II" who are known to the Sārnath inscription of Prakaṭāditya, and to the *MMK* (§ 39ff). He makes the two Bālādityas—the successor of Skanda Gupta, and the victor of Mihirakula who comes in 60 years later—one personality, and naturally transfers the second Hun invasion to the period of Skanda Gupta. The *MMK* (§ 25) reveals that the second Hun invasion is to be dated fifty years later, and that the break-up of the Gupta empire came about, not under Skanda Gupta, but in the reign of the king following Budha Gupta (496 A.D., coins) after 500 A.D. The second defeat of the Huns was inflicted by Bālāditya II before 533 A.D. the date of the Mandasor inscription, before which date Mihirakula had been already driven to Kashmir. We may date it about 520 A.D. for we must give a decade for the rise and *digvijaya* of Vishṇuvardhana or Yaśodharman. We have a positive proof of the existence of two Bālādityas in the same dynasty in the Sārnath inscription (GI., 281).

The omission of Pura Gupta is probably due either to a very short reign or to a loss of a portion of the text after *anuja* ('younger', 'younger brother'). But *anuja* is applied in this book elsewhere as meaning a successor, not necessarily a younger brother. It is not stated that Bāla followed S. immediately. Skanda died evidently at an age of about 30.

Bālā(ditya) is stated to be the first Buddhist king of the Gupta dynasty, which is true and correct and now proved by an inscription found at Nālandā.

Bāla died young, at the age of 36. This explains the short reign of Bālāditya gathered from the inscriptions.

In verse 668, in the glorification of religious merit, he is to be a *chakravartin* for several births. It is thus implied that he was a full and real emperor, with no diminution of territories inherited from his ancestors.

Immediately after him (Bāla, *tasyāpareṇa*) comes (6) Kumāra i.e., Kumāra Gupta II. He was exceedingly virtuous (*dharmavān*). Under him Gauḍa prospered (*Gauḍānāṃ prabhavishṇavaḥ*). His reign was short (473—476 A.D.).

(7) Kumāra's immediate successor was *U*. The kings after Skanda—Pura, Bāla (473 A.D.) and Kumāra II—had all short reigns, from or after 467 A.D. to 476, Kumāra II having three years or less (473 A.D.—*c.* 476 A.D.). Kumāra II must have died young. Budha Gupta succeeded in or before 476 A.D. There is hardly any room for another king to be the Śrīmān *U.* of the *MMK*. He was an emperor, and the empire broke up according to the *MMK* just after his death. He ruled at least up to 496 A.D., and the empire was intact from Bengal up to Malwā according to his inscriptions. The view of Mr. Allan and Dr. Smith that he was a provincial ruler of Malwa is now contradicted by the copperplates found in Dinajpur and his inscription at Sārnath. Budha Gupta's *āditya*-title was *Prakāśāditya*. On Budha Gupta's Malwa coins (silver) we have his name Budha Gupta (Allan, *G.C.*, p. 153), while we have the unidentified imperial gold coins with the name *Prakāśāditya* (Allan, p. 135). Now as we are

certain about the imperial dominions of Budha Gupta which was not known when Mr. Allan wrote, as also about his long reign, we must have his imperial coins. Thanks to the *MMK*, we can now identify *Prakāśāditya* with Budha Gupta. The *MMK* gives him the popular and well-known (*viśruta*) name *U. Prakāśāditya's* coins bear the initial *U.* below the king's picture (Allan, plate XXII). Thus the MMK's king '*His Majesty* (*Śrīmān*) *U.*' is the *Prakāśāditya* of the coin. The succession fixed by inscriptional dates and the succession noted in the *MMK*, fix his identity with Budha Gupta.

§ 25. *Disruption of the Empire*

Budha Gupta's reign closes about 500 A.D. The disruption of the Gupta Empire follows his death. After 510 A.D. (see below) we find the Huns for the second time in India, and this time established as far as Gwalior. The Hun invasion, however, is not the cause but the effect of the disruption. The MMK describes a family feud, a severance and separation (*viślesha*). The Hun king Toramāṇa, therefore, took advantage of it. He must have been before that on the frontier, in Afghanistan or thereabout. The Huns had been so thoroughly beaten by Skanda Gupta that they dared not think of invading India as long as the Gupta empire lasted. A breach in the Gupta family which seems to have arisen on the death of Budha Gupta and the breaking-up of the empire into Gauḍa and Magadha, brought in Toramāṇa at once.

The kings at the time of the breach were—Bhānu Gupta in Malwa (according to Eran inscription) and Tathāgata Gupta in Magadha, predecessor of Bālāditya (that is, Bālāditya II, victor of Mihirakula) according to Yuan Chwang. They are both given as contemporaries by the *MMK* in the Provincial History. The empire was thus broken up. It led to three great results—one was the Hun occupation for about or over 16 years, and the rise of a new All-India Emperor in the person of Yaśodharman Vishṇuvardhana as the successor of the Gupta Emperor.[11] Between these two facts—the Hun occupation and the rise of Vishṇuvardhana—there was the display, once more, of that military genius and daring which was innate in the

[11]It is wrong to suppose that this emperor was a Malwa ruler. In Malwa a viceroy is expressly mentioned with wide dominions in 533 A.D.

Guptas, in the defeat inflicted on Mihirakula by Bālāditya II, successor of Tathāgata Gupta. The ruse played by Bālāditya II before the invading army of Mihirakula, succeeded so well that the tyrant who had levied exactions all over the north, according to Cosmas Indicopleustes and Yuan Chwang, became a prisoner and India was liberated by that daring feat and strategy of the Gupta sovereign.

This event can be almost definitely dated. It is somewhat surprising that the dates about the Hun invasion and the defeat of Mihirakula should not have been more narrowly limited down in the text-books. The Eran pillar memorial to Goparāja and his *satī* wife shows the undisputable fact that up to 510 A.D. (191 *GE*) Toramāṇa had not conquered Malwa. In that year Goparāja under Bhānu Gupta fell on the battle-field and the memorial dated in the Gupta Era was raised; while in the very first year of Toramāṇa at Eran itself the Gupta Era was given up and regnal years of the Hun king was used. Toramāṇa, therefore, at Eran got established after 510 A.D., the date of Goparāja's death and memorial.

Now, the event of Mihirakula's invasion of Magadha must come after [510 A.D.+1 yr. (Toramāṇa)+15th year of Mihirakula (Toramāṇa's son) at Gwalior=] 526 A.D., and before 533 A.D., the date at Mandasor for the Emperor (*samrāṭ*) Yaśodharman who had found Mihirakula in Kashmir, confirming Yuan Chwang's account of Mihirakula's expulsion to Kashmir by Bālāditya. Within these fateful 7 years (526 A.D.—533 A.D.) the final act of the Gupta Imperial drama had been played out on the stage of time. The dynasty which had liberated India from the Kushan-Sassanian shadow, the dynasty which broke the Hun—unbreakable throughout Asia and Europe—the dynasty which made the name *Vikramāditya* a tradition immortal in their country, had to quit its monopoly of political history between those fateful years: 526 A.D.—533 A.D.

Need was once more felt, as it had been felt in the time of the Mauryas, as it had been felt in the time of the Vakāṭakas, that an All-India Empire be reconstituted and revived. Yaśodharman, '*the leader of the people,*' rose up during those seven years. He united the land under him. The parts which his "Gupta Masters" [Gupta-Nāthāḥ; not 'lords of the Guptas' (*GI.*, p. 148) which will be meaningless], the parts which his Gupta lords could not reach (that is, the South), the parts which the Huns could not succeed in reaching, that is, the East (Magadha, Bengal and Assam) recently attempted by Mihirakula, he acquired. And the Gupta empire disappeared.

Before 533 A.D. Malwa and West had come under the governorship of Dharmadosha, brother of Daksha the author of the dated stone inscription at Mandasor (*GI.*, 150), dated in the Mālava Era. Dharmadosha himself was the organizer of that state of Central India (lines 17-18). The new empire was thus a recent one; it has to be dated about 530 A.D. The forefathers of the governor must have served under the Guptas, for the present master Vishṇuvardhana was *ātmavaṃśa*, his own lineage, the very first ruler in his family.

It is evident that the very same events are recorded both in the inscription of Yaśodharman, at Mandasor, and in the inscription of 533 A.D. under the name of Vishṇuvardhana, bearing the title *Rājādhirāja*, *Parameśvara*—'*the 'supreme king of kings'*, supreme lord'. This paramount sovereign, the *Parameśvara,* acquired sovereignty over the *Prāchī* (the East) and North (*i.e.*, Kashmir etc.) (line 6). How could two persons within the very few years acquire sovereignty over the very areas and both be emperors?—both mentioned not only in records of the same place, but also in one and the same place, and in one and the same record. The conclusion is irresistible, that both these pedigree-less names, 'both' these emperors were one and the same, which is definitely stated in the inscription of Daksha itself (*sa eva*). One was not a subordinate of the other; the Parameśvara, and the supreme king of kings (of India) Vishṇuvardhana was identical with the *Samrāṭ* Yaśodharman. *Rājādhirāja* and *Samrāṭ* mean one and the same thing.

The *MMK* shows that he became known to chronicles under the name *Vishṇuvardhana*, a style carried on by his decendants *Naravardhana* to *Harshavardhana.*

The Gupta king who lost to Yaśodharman Vishṇuvardhana was either *Bālāditya II* himself or his son called *Vajra* by Yuan Chwang. Bālāditya II hardly recovered the imperial position. We have no imperial issues of his; in fact his coins have not been distinguished and seem to be concealed amongst the rougher, eastern variety which bear no obverse legend and are distinguishable from those bearing both Nara and Bālāditya legends of Bālāditya I.

From Bālāditya II down to Adityasena, who had all subordinate position from the Hun time to the last days of Harshavardhana, are omitted from the list by the *MMK* (see comments on the next section).

§ 26. *Later Imperial Guptas of Gauḍa* [*c.* 685 A.D.—730 A.D.] *and Magadha.*

"The Separatist Gauḍas (will be) terrible" (676).

(9) Thereafter, (there will be) D e v a known as king of Magadha. He, surrounded on all sides by enemies, was suppressed and killed.

(10) "Immediately next C h a n d r a will perform kingship (677).
He too will be severed by weapon on account of former (birth's) deeds."

(11) His son D v ā d a ś a (will) live for a few ('numbered') months. He too will be severed by weapon while a minor (678).

§§ 27-29. *Bengal Election, Anarchy, and Election of Gopālaka*

"While these violent kings will be engaged in injury, wishing harm to each other, there will arise at that time *Bh.* a leading king, a popular leader of the Gauḍas, but an invalid." He had a great malady and died of it (679-681).

§ 28. *Anarchy*

Immediately following, *D.* for a few ten days (will be king) (681).

In this Gauḍa country on the Ganges there be the next following *Bh.* ruling for three days. (682).

§ 29. *Pāla Dynasty begins* [*c.* 730 A.D.]

"Then, there will be king, from everyone, G o p ā l a k a".

(*Gopāla and his character*) [*c.* 730 A.D.—757 A.D.]

"That king (will be) sweet in speech (*priyavādin*), considerate (*ghṛiṇī*) and a power (mahābalaḥ)" (683).

Formerly he will, in youth, be in the hands of women, miserable, foolish, having been subdued by enemies; but coming in contact with a good (religious) friend he will become very charitable. He (will) become the maker of vihāras, chaityas, gardens, reservoirs, beautiful free hotels, bridges, Deva temples, and caves (guhā, T.). He will be ready in matters praiseworthy. (684-86). The land will become surrounded by many heretics—orthodox Hindus up to the sea. The king will be kind, a materialist (*bhogin*) but lover of justice or religion, (dharma). (688). He having ruled for 27 years died on the Ganges at the age of 80. (690).

Comments on §§ 26-29

See Introduction to Part II. After the period of H a r s h a, there was a revival of the Empire under the L a t e r G u p t a s. That history is touched upon by the MMK in the provincial history taken up next. Here the kings after Harshavardhana are taken up as introductory to the rise of G o p ā l a, the new dynast.

The *MMK* is here again helpful in fixing the order of certain Later Guptas appearing on coins.

(9) *Deva* is *Deva Gupta,* who should be called D e v a G u p t a II,

the first Deva being Chandra Gupta II. This Deva Gupta II was attacked on all sides by enemies and killed in war. His identity is fixed by Deo-Barnārk inscription where he is the son of Ādityasena and father of Vishṇu Gupta. Vishṇu Gupta according to his coins had the *viruda, Chandrāditya* (Allan, p. 145) who is given as (10) *Chandra* by the *MMK*, as the immediate successor of Deva, just as in Deo-Barnārk inscription.

(11) *Dvādaśa* of our text is the *Dvādaśāditya* (with another name) of the coins (Allan, p. 144) who, in the absence of all other evidence about him, was treated as coming before Chandrāditya (Allan, p. 144; pp. liii, lxi). Vishṇu Gupta had another son Jīvita Gupta II according to the Deo-Barnārk inscription (*GI.*, p. 213). Jīvita Gupta II has left no coins, while Dvādaśāditya, though short-lived, has left coins. According to the MMK, Dvādaśa was the last king of the Magadha Guptas who had sway over Bengal. Jīvita Gupta II seems to have been either identical with or successor to Dvādaśāditya, and to have been the last king of the dynasty which was swept away by Gopāla who succeeded to the kingship of Bengal and Bihar within a year or so of Dvādaśāditya. Jīvita Gupta like Dvādaśa seems to have had a very short reign. The MMK notes that the election by Gauḍa of its own king was required by the civil strife amongst the Guptas after the death of the boy king Dvādaśa. If Jīvita Gupta II was younger, he also must have been a minor, both being sons of the same father. It is, however, likely that Dvādaśa, the minor was the last king of the dynasty, and Jīvita Gupta (if not identical) an elder brother, had preceded him.

These Later Guptas mentioned here were important kings. Deva Gupta II's father was Ādityasena who performed three *Aśvamedha*-sacrifices (*GI.*, 213, *n.*) and had succeeded in reaching the Chola capital. Deva Gupta II bore once more the imperial title of *Paramabhaṭṭāraka, Mahārājādhirāja, Parameśvara* and so did his son Vishṇu Gupta (*GI.*, 213). The *MMK* thus has taken up here the Imperial line of the Later Guptas.

[The Cause of the fall of the Later Imperial Guptas]

Deva (Gupta) is expressly stated to have been attacked by enemies and killed. Who were these enemies? We find in the inscriptions of the contemporary Chālukya kings, the most powerful monarchy in India at the time, that "the Lord of All Northern India" (*sakala-*

Uttarāpatha-nātha; IA., VIII. 2)[12] was defeated by the Chālukya king Vinayāditya (679 A.D.—696 A.D.). Ādityasena had successfully invaded up to Chola country, evidently, in the reign of Vināyaditya's predecessor or Vinayāditya himself. He seems to have achieved that wherein Harsha had failed in the time of Pulakeśin. But the result was disastrous.

Gupta power, now revived once more after Bālāditya II, courted trouble which led to its final weakening and extinction. In 679-696 A.D. there was no power in Northern India other than that of Magadha under Ādityasena and his son which can be described as '*the emperor of ALL Uttarāpatha*'. It seems from the date that Deva Gupta must have been reigning at the time. He was, according to the dates, the Gauḍa king killed by Yaśovarman of Kanauj, *c.* 700 A.D. Thus he was attacked on all sides by enemies (MMK).

The immediate cause of Chandrāditya Vishṇu Gupta's death was family feud. It was probably Jīvita Gupta II, who was the Gauḍa king who was defeated twice and taken to Kashmir and killed by Lalitāditya (730 A.D.). It was fortunate for Gopāla that Kanauj broke down about *c.* 740 A.D. and that the Chālukya power broke down *c.* 757 A.D. The Gupta dynasty was really destroyed by the Karkoṭas of Kashmir, who at 740 A.D. succeeded to the imperial throne of Northern India.

We may assign approximate dates to these Later Guptas as following:
Mādhava Gupta [contemporary of Harsha]
Ādityasena [650 A.D.—680 A.D.]
Deva Gupta [680—710 A.D.]
Vishṇu Gupta Chandrāditya [710 A.D.?]
Dvādaśāditya Chandra Gupta III [710 A.D. (few months)].
Jīvita Gupta II [710—730 A.D.].

[BENGAL ELECTIONS]

About the period 735—740 A.D. Bengal elected her own king—*Bh.*, who was 'a leader of the people'. But unfortunately the choice fell upon a permanent invalid. He made a fairly good king *nṛipa-puṅgava.* After his death there was what is described in the Khalimpur copper-plate *mātsya-nyāya,* anarchy: *D.* and *Bh.* ruling for 10 days and 3 days. This

[12] Kielhorn, *EI.*, VIII, App. 2, 2.

was put an end to by the election of Gopālaka (*c.* 740—757 A.D.). This election was universal and unanimous, 'from all' (*sarvatāḥ* correct *sarvadaḥ*). We are glad to get a character-sketch of the dear king, who not only brought peace to Eastern India but succeeded in establishing a dynasty which lasted longest. Although Gopāla was a Śūdra as stated in the next section of the MMK, he patronised both Buddhists and Brāhmins, the latter more, as the complaint of the MMK indicates. His descendants became Buddhists, while he himself had a national outlook. His reign period (27 years) found in the MMK is a good datum. He died at the age of 80; he had been therefore elected at the age of 53, which speaks well of the choice of a mature and known man. The Gauḍas were correct in their judgment. But something greater is conveyed by this election. It shows that the Bengalees had freed their mind, emancipated themselves from the Vedic theory of caste superiority, in that early time, the 8th century A.D. By that big political act they repealed, so to say, the Institutes of Manu. The election of a Śūdra to kingship was as big a thing as the doctrine of *egâlité* in 1789 A.D. To say, make a Śūdra king, and to do it, was to break the slavery of mind perpetuated for ages. Even the great spiritual liberator, Lord Buddha, maintained the superiority of the Kshatriya. Even he probably would have said to the proposal moved in 740 A.D.—Render unto the Caesar what is due to the Caesar! Here the Gauḍas went beyond their country, law and old civilization. They were innovators, and emancipated; and Śūdra added a chapter of glory to the history of India.

PART II

GAUḌA AND MAGADHA; PROVINCIAL HISTORY

We have seen in § 25 that kings after Budha Gupta up to the end of the time of Harshavardhana have been omitted. In this section the MMK gives some of those omitted details as part of the local history of Gauḍa and Magadha. They assume the character of appendices to the Imperial History of Madhyadeśa and the East just surveyed. They seem to have been taken at least from two books, as one period (Nāga to Imperial Gupta) has been repeated and inserted as two independent pieces. The latter portion from *c.* 500 A.D. is full of interest, but its interpretation is a job like deciphering an unknown code.

It is possible that the whole of this part (IX ff.) (verses 691—824) is by a subsequent hand, who to conceal the recent character of his composition preferred to give mystic initials instead of names, so that people may realize the greatness of the ancient prophecy and its true fulfilment.

This provincial or additional notices are brought down from 140 A.D. to the dynasty of Gopāla, like the previous section. In a way it is a repetition but not inferior in worth. Owing to their furnishing matters to fill up gaps they are most useful. They show that the Gupta family was divided into two branches—Gaũḍa and Magadha —and that there was no Mālava branch, which has been supposed and formulated by historians.

"Gauḍa" Lines Again

From verse 691, p. 632 (T. 459*b*) to 882, p. 646 (T. 469*b*)—the largest section of the book—is devoted to the political history of Bengal proper, closing it with the line:

tataḥ pareṇa bhūpālāḥ Gopālā dāsajīvinaḥ

'after him, there will be the Gopālas (that is, the Pālas) of the servile caste kings'. This line really closes the historical sketch of the MMK. Two short subsequent passages—on Madhyadésa, Aṅga, Kāmarūpa, Vaiśālī and Kapilavastu—are perfunctory and negligible.

In the former section the Imperial Gupta line is brought down through the Later Guptas to their end and the rise of Gopālaka. Here again the Local Gauḍa history of royal families is brought down to the Gopālas. We have therefore to give to the word *tataḥ* in the opening line (V. 691) the meaning as beginning a new section, and not 'after that' that is, after Gopālaka, for, the dynasty of Gopāla as is well-known, has not been touched upon herein. Royal history (1) begins with Nāgarāja, then it describes Prabha Vishṇu, then Samudra, then the subsequent kings, oppression on the Gauḍa people and the rise of Soma (that is, Śaśāṅka), fight between Harshavardhana and Śaśāṇka, Śaśāṇka's son and his end; (2) then once more (V. 741) it begins with the Nāgarāja, describes Prabha Vishṇu and Śiśu (the Vākāṭaka), and at once takes 'the (formerly *Vaiśya*) *Kshatriya*' (Gupta) dynasty with Bh(ānu Gupta), Pra(kaṭāditya) and later, ending with the latter's 'subject' descendants, finally ushering the advent of the Gopālas. Hence it is evident that the history of Bengal and Bihar in its local aspect is being dealt with here from the Nāgas *i.e.*, the pre-Gupta Bhāraśivas.

§ 30. *The Nāgas* [*under the Bhāraśivas*]

[*c.* 140 A.D.—320 A.D.]

Revival of Orthodox Hinduism in Bengal

"The Nāga king, of majesty, a lover of religion (will) then rise, who caused to be made a beautiful Buddha image to a chaitya (691; p. 632, T. 459 B.). He made monasteries for the Saṅgha in the land" (692). "From that time onwards the capital of the Gauḍas became full of (covered up by) heretical Brahmins" (693).

Comments

Compare this and the subsequent section with section 37 below.

On the Nāga history see my *History of India,* 150 A.D. to 350 A.D. The Purāṇas say that the Eastern capital of the Nāgas (their Governors) was at Champāvatī (Bhagalpur).

In the beginning, according to the MMK, the Nāgas patronised Buddhism. But it is noted that orthodox revival dates from this reign in Bengal (that is, after the *Śakavaṃśa* noted above, who are said to have been superseded by the Nāga-senas (§§ 17-18).

§ 30-A. *Emperor Prabhavishṇu and Gauḍa king*

Then in this Eastern country in the capital, troubled by the Tīrthikas, *Bhagavat,* lord of the Gauḍas, was crowned king by the sacrificer (*vratin,* T.) Prabhavishṇu staying in the Southern country (694). He having ruled there came to the

West; having entered the elegant capital Sāketā he had to return (696). The East up to sea was invested by robbers; the king was killed by weapon after a rule of 3 years (698).

Comments

In this *vratin*, the sacrificer, Prabhavishṇu, it seems, Pravarasena Vishṇuvṛiddha—the Vākāṭaka emperor—is to be recognised. He installed the Gauḍa king, who invaded Sāketa. Sāketa was at that time the capital of the pre-imperial Guptas, and the invasion probably refers to the Gupta attempt, *i.e.*, of Chandra Gupta I, to declare his own independence and his defeat at Pāṭaliputra. [Compare this section with § 37.]

Prabhavishṇu being called *dakshiṇātya* may simply mean that he belonged to the country south of Madhyadeśa (Doab), the Vindhyan country. The Tibetan version has 'staying in Dakshiṇa'.

§ 31. *Emperor Samudra Gupta, the Prosperous; and his character*

Latter than him Samudra, of good fame, will be *nṛipatiḥ* (sovereign) (700). His younger brother, Bhasmama [*Bhasma*, T.] by name, that man of low intelligence and wicked mind, will have the government (of Gauḍa ?) for 3 days. He (Samudra) was lordly, shedder of excessive blood, of great powers and dominion, heartless, ever vigilant, (mindful) about his own person, unmindful about the hereafter, sacrificing animals; with bad councillor he greatly committed sin (694).

His government [or kingdom] was inundated with carping logicians, (*tārkikaiḥ*), vile Brahmins.

Men and manes had every luxury. The sovereign (*nṛipati*-Samudra) acquired prosperity of various sorts.

He marched systemetically and reached the West and in the North reached the gate of Kashmir. He was victorious on the battle-field even in the North.

He ruled after that (conquest) for 22 years and 5 months. On this earth on account of a fell disease he fainted several times (at his death), and in great pain he died, and went down (704—718).

Comments

Minus the theological venom, the character is well summed up—'Of great powers and dominion'—*Mahāsāvadyakāriṇaḥ*—probably implies a 'super man'. *Nirghṛinin*, according to Buddhist ideal, is heartless, i.e., severe.

This text furnishes a positive record that Samudra Gupta marched up to Kangra or Jammu, the very door of the Kushāns.

His reign-period as Emperor is exactly given here—dvādaśābdāni *sarvatra* māsā[n]pañcha daśas tathā—12+10 years and 5 months. This will bring his reign to end *c.* 372-73 A.D. He marched also to Western India. Here we have accurate history.

Did Bhasmama dispute the succession, or was he a governor of Gauḍa?

§ 32. *Condition of Bengal*

Later Gupta Period [*c.* 570 A.D.—590 A.D.] before the rise of Śaśāṅka

There was a civil war amongst them, greedy for the kingdom (708—709). It ended by the installation of S., the youngster who became a mere symbol. The Brahmin leaders who had done this became disunited amongst themselves. Reaching the province of Magadha in the city called *Udumbara* the leading Brahmin crowned two boys. Then he retired to the East, and arriving in the province of Gauḍa they (? one of them ?) become (s) rivalless (710—712). The two boy chiefs were killed by the wicked one in Kaliṅga, and owing to his bad guide he committed many murders : he killed all those Gauḍas who had been honoured by the kings who had fostered the civil war (713-714).

Comments

This fills up the period of the '*Separatist Gauḍas*' of § 25 above.

The account is somewhat confused. It is not clear whether the chief Brahmin Minister went to Gauḍa and punished the Gauḍas who had taken part in the family feud, or whether one of the two boys—called *bālamukhyān* (?)—evidently only one is meant from several adjectives—did this. This feud and oppression of Bengal led to the rise of Śaśāṅka (see next section).

The civil strife seems to have arisen between S. (Mahā-Sena Gupta?) and some other claimant. Mahā Sena Gupta's time is a generation before Harshavardhana (606 A.D.) and Śaśāṇka (*c.* 590 A.D.).

Udumbara, must have been a town in South Bihar, probably it is *Dumraon* in the Shahabad district.

§ 33. *Soma = Śaśāṅka*

Then, Soma, an unparalleled hero will become king up to the banks of the Ganges, up to Benares and beyond. He, of wicked intellect, will destroy the beautiful image of the Buddha. He, of wicked intellect, enamoured of the words of the Tīrthikas, will burn that great bridge of religion (Dharma), (as) prophesied by the former Jinas (Buddhas). Then that angry and greedy evil-doer of false notions and bad opinion will fell down all the monasteries, gardens, and chaityas; and rest-houses of the Jainas [Nirgranthas] (715—718).

Comments

Later on, his caste—Brahmin—is given. He was a popular product of Bengal, brought to the front on account of oppression from the Gupta feud.

His identity is established by the next section.

§ 34. *Rājyavardhana and Harshavardhana; and War with Soma* (*Śaśāṅka*)

At that time will arise in Madhyadeśa the excellent king R. (Rājyavardhana), brilliant, self-possessed, of the Vaiśya caste, and steady. He (will be) of this religion, and (will be) as powerful as Soma (Śaśāṅka). He also ends at the hand of a king of the Nagna caste (710-711).

His younger brother H. (Harshavardhana) will be an unrivalled hero.

Battle of Puṇḍravardhana.

He will be with a great army; that brave man of overpowering prowess, decides against the famous Soma. The powerful Vaiśya king with a large army marched against the Eastern country, against the excellent capital called Puṇḍra of that characterless man. Adopting the duty of Kshatra, with the sense of personal injury and indignation he, though kind, prone to religion, and learned, kills many and becomes an oppressor of living creatures, for the reason of being engaged in the duty of chastisement (712—715).

He defeated Soma, the pursuer of wicked deeds; and Soma was forbidden

Condition imposed on Soma.

to move out of his country (being ordered) to remain therein (thenceforth) (716).

H. returned, having been honoured in that kingdom of the barbarian (Mlechchha). He, an excellent king amongst followers of Artha(Śāstra) and Dharma(Śāstra), was successful in his undertaking (717). Having marched from his country with a desired course, they the entourage of Rājya and Harshin had achieved the business. Now he attained the pleasures of royalty (718-719).

[Soma had done in his former life some Buddhist pious acts which are detailed,

End of Soma.

hence] Soma the Brahmin (king) obtained high prosperity. He gave largess to Brahmins and ruled for 17 years, 1 month, 7 or 8 days. He died of a disease in his mouth, having been eaten by worms and went down (to hell). His capital was then destroyed by divine agency (724). His life was destroyed by magic (mantra) done by men; high fever brought about senselessness, and he died (735).

(Description of his life in hell follows : 726—729 ; and the prudence of being a Buddhist is emphasised, 730—736).

§§ 35-36. *Condition of Bengal*

Śaśāṅka's death. Revolutions

After the death of Soma, the Gauḍa political system (*Gauḍa-tantra*) was reduced to mutual distrust, raised weapons and mutual jealousy—one (king) for a week; another for a month; then a republican constitution—such will be the daily (condition) of the country on this bank of the Ganges where houses were built of the ruins of monasteries (745—48).

Thereafter Soma's son M ā n a v a will last for 8 months 5 (½ ?) days.

Comments on §§ 34—36

We have had no detail and no result of the expedition of Harsha from Bāṇa, and we are glad to have them now.

A battle which should be named the *Battle of Puṇḍravardhana,* was fought; Ś a ś ā ṅ k a was reduced to an abject submission, and he was confined within his own kingdom.

He died subsequently, in spite of Buddhist wishes, a natural death.

Śaśāṅka was an orthodox revivalist as against the weakening cult of Mahāyāna Buddhism, patronized and fostered by the Later Guptas. Now the caste of Śaśāṅka becomes known—he was a Brahmin.

Ś a ś ā ṅ k a ' s death brought about the end of the national monarchy of Bengal. *Gaṇajyaṃ* is a misselection for *Gaṇarājyaṃ* (T.), a republic. The same condition prevailed later before the election of G o p ā l a.

The first section of the Provincial Gauḍa history ends here.

Repetition of Nāga-Vākāṭaka History

The first section of the Provincial History ends with Soma's son. Now to introduce the Guptas in *c.* 500 A.D.—that is, the Later (non-imperial) Guptas, history is again taken up from the Nāgas and Vākāṭakas. The history of the Guptas from 500 A.D. up to the Maukhari empire, which has been omitted before, is filled up now. It is evidently extracted from another source. It is curious that the Nāgas are noted here to have been Vaiśyas.

The section is highly important. It supplies details which were most needed.

§ 37. *The Nāga kings and Prabhavishṇu*

[Then, (about) the Minor, (Ś i ś u) of the Vaiśya Caste] (not in T.). A king called N ā g a-r ā j a[1] will become king of Gauḍa. Near him will be Brahmins and other Vaiśyas by caste (T.), the Nāgas will be surrounded by Vaiśyas and will themselves be Vaiśyas. Their government becoming unfit (read *asāmprata* for *asamprāpta*)

[1] The Tibetan text in place of the first line seems to read that the Nāgas were of the lowest Brahmin class, originally; and later on their status was that of the Vaiśyas:

बृह्-पो-ल-मथि-रिग्स्-(बृमथि) गम्-से-कुन्-नस्-जेडु-रिग्स्-पूस्कोर्-मथि ।

there will be distress from famine and invasion, and from great robbers. The government will have no bounds. The rule full of danger to life and loss of life will last for 6 years. The Vaiśyas owing to their former sins will become distrustful of one another (750). Then their king will be Prabha Vishṇu who will be one who has adopted *Kshatra* status (755).

[See for 'the Minor' the next section].

Comments

Compare this with §§ 30-30-A, where the very dynasties are discussed. Here we have the further detail that Prabha Vishṇu (Vishṇu-vṛiddha Vākāṭaka) took possession of Bengal after 6 years of weak rule in the final days of the (Bhāraśiva) Nāgas. The name *Jaya* (750) is quite in line with the Bhāraśiva Nāga names we read on the coins e.g., *Haya, Traya,* etc. (*JBORS,* XIX. 1; *History of India,* (Nāga-Vākāṭaka Period) p. 35).

The Vishṇuvṛiddha Vākāṭakas accepted Kshatriya status although they had been Brahmins. But it is difficult to imagine why the Nāgas are called here Vaiśyas.

§ 38. *Confusion in the East, reign of Śiśu [Rudrasena] and the rise of the Gupta Dynasty*

The section proceeds to give the condition in 'the Gauḍa system' that is, Magadha and Gauḍa, under the Emperor Prabhavishṇu. From section 30-A it is evident that he installed a king in the East whose name was Bhagavat. Probably it was Bhagavat Varman, a possible ancestor of Sundara-varman at Pāṭaliputra mentioned in the Kaumudī-mahotsava, or some other king in Bengal. The confusion described below refers to the revolutions connected with the Kota family and Chandra Gupta I, and the victory of Samudra Gupta over Śiśu, who stands in the Purāṇas for Rudrasena I the Vākāṭaka Emperor, defeated by Samudra Gupta. The word *Gupta* seems to have been translated by *vaṇik* (*Vaiśya*).

Without doubt, in the system of Gauḍa (then) there (will) be kings, some of whom will be killed (in war) by weapon and some will die of diseases (i.e., natural death) (755-56). They were all orthodox Hindus, [they were consigned to *naraka*].

Then, again, Śiśu will be king in whose court women will hold chief influence. He will rule for a fortnight. He was killed by weapon (757).

A great famine and invasion made the Eastern Provinces distracted, terrorised and demoralised.

In that country, undoubtedly, (then) there will be a king—a great king—of

Mathurā Jāta (Jāṭ) family, born of a Vaiśālī lady (T.), originally Vaiśya. He became the king of the Magadhas (758—60).

Comments

Owing to the name *Gupta* the dynasty has been considered by the author as Vaiśya originally. But the author is careful to note the fact in the next verse that they were described before him (*prokta*) as leading Kshatriyas (*kshatriyaḥ agraṇī*) (761).

The invasion mentioned above refers to the Kota vs. Gupta fights for two generations.

It is to be marked that although the king is not named, he is described as the son of the Vaiśālī Lady in the Tibetan text. He is said to have been a Mathurā-Jāta (Sanskrit-*Jāta-vaṃśa*). *Jāta-vaṃśa,* that is, Jāta Dynasty stands for *Jarta,* that is, *Jāṭ.* That the Guptas were Jāṭ, we already have good reasons to hold (JBORS, XIX. p. 115). His Vaiśālī mother is the Lichchhavī lady. Evidently the ancestors of Samudra Gupta, according to this datum, once belonged to Mathurā.

Bhānu Gupta and Prakaṭâditya

[The course of history after 510 A.D.]

In this section the chief personality is *P.* or *Pra.* (as in Tibetan). He is the son of *Bh.* and is a contemporary of king Gopa who does not belong to the dynasty. The only king of the dynasty who had the name *Bh.* was Bhānu-Gupta, and his subordinate ruler was Gopa-rāja who fought for Bhānu-Gupta and died on the battle-field of Eran. *Pra.* was a bad boy of the family and had been imprisoned up to the age of 17. He was brought out of prison by an Invader who was very powerful and had reached the East, having come from the West. He enjoyed kingdoms acquired by others. He crowned the young Pra. as king of Magadha at Benares, and then died on his march. His name is given as *H.,* i.e., *Hūṇa. H.* was succeeded by his son who was very wicked, a patron of Brahmins; he was so pressed by his enemies that he lost his kingdom. He was marked with the appellation of Planet [Mihira = sun].

I feel certain that this *H.* was Toramāṇa and the Planet is Mihirakula. They are called Śūdras. A writer writing about 700 A.D. when describing a small community as the Hūṇas who had been settled for two centuries as Hindus, would naturally call them Śūdras.

The MMK adds to our existing knowledge of the Hun invasion, and removes the mist from the personality of Bālāditya of Yuan Chwang.

The Huns under Toramāṇa had reached Magadha and gone to some town called Bhagavatpura, where Pr. was caught hold of and set up as the king of Magadha at Benares, and Toramāṇa who was retiring westwards, died at Benares. When Mihirakula became king, Magadha was subject to him. This is confirmed by Yuan Chwang who says that Bālāditya rebelled and refused to pay tribute, and when Mihirakula was brought as a prisoner before Bālāditya, Mihirakula refused to show his face as the position between the master and the subject had been reversed.

Then, who was *Bālāditya* and who was this *Pra.*, and what became of *Bh.* (Bhānu-Gupta)?

Although *Pra.* was installed at Benares, it is stated that he actually became king *after the death of the Planet.* It is also implied that the imprisonment and release of *Pra.* took place during the life-time of *Bh.* The king intervening between the death of *H.* (Hūṇa Toramāṇa) and the death of the Planet, his son, we may take it, was Bhānu Gupta who in 510 A.D. at Eran is described as ruling and as the bravest man on the earth. Evidently Bhānu Gupta's *āditya*-name was *Bālāditya.* The name of the son of a second Bālāditya whose one ancestor at least was another Bālāditya, was Prakaṭāditya (*GI.*, p. 285). *Pra.'s* successor, according to the MMK, were two short-lived brothers who were followed by Rājyavardhana. Yuan Chwang saw pious buildings at Nālandā raised by successive kings in the following order (Beal, ii, 168, 170; Watters, ii. 164-65).

[Kumāra Gupta II] *Śakrāditya* evidently a mistake for *Śrī-kramāditya* as in several other names—e.g., *Mahirakula* for *Mihirakula.*
|
Budha Gupta [mis-spelt as *Buddha Gupta.*]
|
Tathāgata Gupta
|
Bālāditya [Bālāditya II]
|
Vajra

Then a king from Mid-India

Śīlāditya (Harsha ?)

Against this we have in the MMK;	and in Inscriptions or Coins.
Kumāra Gupta [*II*]	*Kumāra Gupta* [*II*]
|	|
U. [*Budha Gupta*]	*U. Budha Gupta*
|	|
Bh[*ānu Gupta*]	*Bhānu Gupta* [Bālāditya]
|	|
Pra[*kaṭāditya*] and *V*[*ajra*], his younger brother [I]	*Prakaṭāditya*
|	|
Rājyavardhana	*Rājyavardhana.*

It is thus clear that here we are dealing with a Bālāditya who flourished after, not before Kumāra Gupta II, i.e., Bālāditya II, and that this Bālāditya, father of Prakaṭāditya (Sarnath insc.) is to be identified with Bhānu Gupta, father of Pra. (*MMK*), and that Tathāgata Gupta came in between Budha Gupta and Bhānu Gupta (in the period *c.* 500 A.D. to 510 A.D.), that the Vajra of Yuan Chwang is identical with Prakaṭāditya's brother V. of the [T. MMK] or with Prakaṭāditya himself.

The line of Kṛishṇa Gupta and Ādityasena (7 generations before Harshavardhana) must have arisen about *c.* 500 A.D. According to the Deo-Barnārk inscription a gift made by *Parameśvara* Bālāditya was confirmed by "the presiding authorities for the time being" viz. by *Parameśvara* Śarvavarman and *Parameśvara* Avantivarman, and then finally by Jīvita Gupta II (*GI.*, 216). This shows that the Emperor Bālāditya whose gift was confirmed by another government, that is of Śarvavarman Maukhari and his successor, flourished just before the Maukhari Emperors, that is, he was Bālāditya II, and further, that Jīvita Gupta's and Ādityasena's ancestors were not rulers of Magadha in the time of Bālāditya and even in the Maukhari times. Their family in the Maukhari times was outside Magadha; for, the Maukharis were in direct possession of Deo-Barnārk. The so-called Guptas of Magadha appear to have been local rulers in Bengal—'the separatist Gauḍas', for Mādhava Gupta father of Ādityasena defeated Susthitavarman, king of Kāmarūpa, and Ādityasena's early inscription is found in Bhagalpur (*GI.*, 211) and Gauḍa officials are noticeable in his Secretariate (*GI.*, 201).

To return to the Magadha line. B ā l ā d i t y a has the imperial title in the Deo-Barnārk inscription (*Parameśvara*). Events connected with his life seem to have taken a course like this. Bhānu Gupta Bālāditya retired to Bengal under pressure from the Huns, in or following 510 A.D. His imprisoned son is set up as a pretender by Toramāṇa, but really he does not become king, in that very year Toramāṇa dies at Benares. There is some sort of peace between Bhānu Gupta and Mihirakula. Bhānu Gupta consolidates his power within the next fifteen years and then defies Mihirakula, and lures him into the swampy country of lower Bengal—the marshes and island of Yuan Chwang—and subjugates him. By his victory he keeps the tradition of his ancestors as the Emperor of India and confines Mihirakula in Kashmir which is included in Bālāditya's overlordship.

Soon after 526 A.D. Bālāditya dies. Mihirakula was still living and tyrannizing over his own countrymen in Kabul. At that time, on the imperial throne of Magadha, there was probably the ignominious son of Bhānu Gupta Bālāditya, once a vassal of the Hun. This was a signal for the Hindus, to usher in a new state of affairs for their safety from foreign conquest. This leads to the advent of Y ạ ś o d h a r m a n V i s h ṇ u v a r d h a n a of Thānesar with his Maukhari subordinates, about 530 A.D., i.e., before Mihirakula had had time to move towards the plains of India once more.

P r a k a ṭ ā d i t y a thus became a subordinate ruler under Yaśodharman-Vishṇuvardhana. According to the Sanskrit and the Tibetan Texts the interval between 606 A.D.—the end of the reign of P. or Pra. and the end of Rājyavardhana's reign—was as follows:

[King V[ajra]—7 days] }
[Ph., 3 years] } omitted in T.
V., his '*anuja*', 3 years according to both S. and T. MMK.
Rājyavardhana, 1 year.

That is, the interval was of 4 or 7 years. This V. (Vajra) was the last ruler of the line which is also implied by Yuan Chwang who places the Mid-India king i.e., Harsha after him. A.D. 602 or 599 is thus the last date for Prakaṭāditya. This fully agrees with the long reign assigned to Pra. by the MMK and the script of the inscription of Prakaṭāditya. In script, it agrees with the script of the Apsaḍ inscription of Ādityasena. The MMK gives the king a long age (94 years) and implies a long reign; he came to the throne about 533 A.D. on the end of the son of the H(un) king, at an early age. He was 17 in or about 510 A.D., and in 530 A.D. he must have been about 37, he died at the age of 94, i.e., about 587 A.D. A further test is to be found in the fact mentioned by the MMK that Soma or Śaśāṅka became Pra.'s rival. Pra. was a Buddhist and Soma a Brahmin. Śaśāṅka would be Pra.'s contemporary according to the above dates.

Prakaṭāditya saw many vicissitudes. First he came under the overlordship of Yaśodharman-Vishṇuvardhana (*c.* 530—540 A.D.) and his family (550 A.D.); then we see the Maukhari Emperor Śarvavarman confirming a pious grant at Deo-Barnārk (Shahabad) (about 570 A.D.), followed by his son Avantivarman, contemporary of Prabhākaravardhana. From *c.* 550 A.D. to 600 A.D. the Empire of Northern India was presided over by the Maukharis. The Maukharis may be dated approximately as follows:

Īśānavarman, 530—554 A.D.
Śarvavarman, 554—570 A.D. (coin dated, *GE.*, 234=554 A.D.).
Avantivarman, 570—600 A.D. (coin, 570 A.D.).
Grahavarman, 600—605 A.D.
[Suvrata, MMK, nominal].

The Maukharis who ruled from Kanauj on the unquestionable testimony of Bāṇa, seems to have superseded the family of Vishṇuvardhana about 550 A.D. in the time of Īśānavarman who was the first Maukhari to assume the dignity of the emperor of Āryavarta or Northern India, towards the end of his reign. Īśānavarman seems to have fought and defeated the Huns under Yaśodharman in Yaśodharman's northern campaigns. The reference in the Apsaḍ inscription (*GI.*, 203) to the Maukhari army which had defeated the Hūṇas, which killed Dāmodara Gupta, son of Kumāra Gupta (III) of the Later Guptas, and which had been successfully opposed by Kumāra Gupta (III) when Īśānavarman led them against him, is to these very victorious crack troops of the Maukhari king who had fought against the Huns. These Later Guptas, as the MMK positively asserts, were Kings of the Gauḍas who later on, from the time of Deva Gupta, (son of Ādityasena) (§ 26) became kings of Magadha, and were the gubernatorial family of Bengal and opposed the Maukhari invasion of the East on behalf of their overlord the main Gupta House in the person of Bālāditya. By the time of Śarvavarman, the fight was over, and the issue already decided. The Maukhari became the acknowledged *Parameśvara* (Emperor), as the Deo-Barnārk inscription of the Jīvita Gupta II attests. The Sone seems to have become the boundary of the direct rule of the Maukharis in the reign of Śarvavarman, and Magadha from Patna eastwards and Bengal remained Gupta possessions under the suzerainty of the Maukharis. We find Mahāsena Gupta, a contemporary of Śarvavarman or Avantivarman, victorious over Susthitavarman, king of Assam, where on the banks of the Lauhitya (Brahmaputra) songs were sung in later ages of Mahāsena Gupta's victory. The MMK gives the Lauhitya as the boundary of the kingdom of Pra(kaṭāditya), and probably after the Gupta defeat at the hands of the Maukharis there was a conflict between the old Gupta overlord and the king of Assam.

Īśānavarman succeeded to the prestige and position of Vishṇuvardhana-Yaśodharman, as being the next most successful military leader in crushing the Hun power and liberating India from its terrors. Īśānavarman definitely abolished the Imperial position of the Guptas in the reign of Prakaṭāditya (*c.* 550 A.D.) which had already been very effectively questioned a few years before by Vishṇuvardhana-Yaśodharman (530—33 A.D.). It is from Prakaṭāditya that the Later Guptas are to be counted. Up to his reign and the time of Rājyavardhana there were two lines—one in Magadha and the other in Bengal, and the latter, after Harsha, from the reign of Ādityasena, shifted to Magadha from Bengal and after the close of the House of Thānesar once more occupied the imperial position in northern India which is now made perfectly clear by our MMK. The recuperative power of the Guptas was phenomenal. Art of war and the secret of civil administration seem to have been hereditary monopolies of this race of Vikramādityas and this series of Hindu Napoleons. Ādityasena again became the *Sakalauttarāpatha-Nātha* once more and repeated the feat of Samudra Gupta in reaching the South, up to the Chola country.

The centre of Empire had, however, territorially changed from Eastern India to Madhyadeśa in 530 A.D. The imperial seat in Magadha was too far removed from the north which was exposed to the new danger, the Huns. Yaśodharman-Vishṇuvardhana evidently belonged to Thanesar itself, the seat of Lord Sthāṇu, to whom alone that hero bent his head. In any case, he must have belonged to some place in the neighbourhood of Thanesar, if not to Thanesar itself. Then in descending line, at Kanauj (Pañchāla) was seated the Maukhari hero. At Thanesar, the subordinate family of Rājyavardhana I (*c.* 530 A.D.) just a generation before, was certainly situated. From the time of Īśānavarman and Śarvavarman, Kanauj took the place of Pāṭaliputra and became the seat of the empire of Northern India and came to be so known to the whole of India when the Maukhari (Jaunpur inscription, *GI.*, 228)—either Īśanavarman or Śarvavarman—established his position up to Kathiāwāḍ in the West and at least up to Andhra in the South. The successor of the Maukharis, Harshavardhana, fully established the position of Kānyakubja which lasted up to the time of Mahmūd of Ghazni. In the generation following Ādityasena, the revivor of the Gupta Imperialism, Kanauj in the person of Yaśovarman contested the claim of the Gauḍa king of Magadha—i.e. the Later Guptas of Magadha then represented by Deva Gupta II; and it was re-questioned, with the final suppression of the Gupta dynasty, in the next generation by Lalitāditya of Kashmir who claimed to be the lord of Kanauj, which meant at the time the Emperor of Northern India. That struggle and rivalry between Kanauj and Pāṭaliputra or Magadha went down to the Pāla period when Dharma Pāla deposed and re-set up the king of Kanauj, and ended with the rise of the Pratihāra Empire of Kanauj a generation later.

The *MMK* proceeds to deal at great length with the kingdom of Pra(kaṭāditya) for whose reign the author seems to have had good material, like the details about the time of the dynasty of Harshavardhana.

It is a very important datum that after Rājyavardhana (that is, his House), the next emperor noted is Dha(rasena IV, 646—649 A.D.). He is called a descendant of (the family of) Rājyavardhana, evidently for the reason that he was the grandson and heir of Harshavardhana. His empire is described, and one more member of the latter's family, V.(?) is noted as the last emperor in this history. They are noted as All-India Emperors. The original caste of the dynasty was Kshatriya, according to the *MMK* (852).

Then in the Gauḍa system a branch of the family, to which Pra(kaṭāditya) belonged, i.e., the Guptas, is re-established. The first king of this revived line was with the name *Śrī,* probably Ādityasena of the Later Guptas. He is said to have reached the age of 80 and was killed by a subordinate ruler. This subordinate Y(aśovarman) became the unrivalled ruler for 8 years. The next king of the Pra. i.e., Later Gupta family, made a war and killed numerous men of this ex-feudatory. He himself, however, was worthless and was killed by his enemy who invaded him. This was probably Deva Gupta's son whose name is not recorded, for the latter's youngest brother *R.* ruled for 48 days. Vishṇu Gupta Chandrāditya's coins have *Ru.* His reign like that of Dvādaśāditya who according to § 26 ruled for a few months, was very short. Then comes the end of the dynasty, and the rise of a Śūdra king who was a cripple and ruled strongly and impartially and suppressed both Buddhist monks and Brahmins. He lived for 17 years. This ends the period and begins the rise of the Gopālas. The former Śūdra king who is called here Svāda in the Sanskrit text and Rājabhadra in Tibetan, is evidently the same Śūdra king who had been elected before Gopāla and ruled well but was a cripple, according to §§ 27—29, 47. His initial, however, here is *Bh.* which supports the Tibetan reading *Bhadra.*

After closing the Later Gupta dynasty the MMK records the fact that kings of this dynasty which was a branch distinct from that of Pra (kaṭāditya) that is, the main Gupta line, but which sprang from it, ceased to be independent with the end of *K.* i.e., Kumāra Gupta III. We know from the Apsaḍ and Deo-Barnārk inscriptions that Īśānavarman Maukhari took away the Imperial position from the Guptas. Prakaṭāditya was in Magadha at the time and Kumāra Gupta III was the king of Gauḍa under him. It seems that after Prakaṭāditya became subordinate to Īśānavarman, Kumāra Gupta III assumed full sovereignty in Bengal. He certainly defeated Īśānavarman and died a peaceful self-inflicted death at Prāyāga in token of his successful career. In his time therefore he proved to be the leading monarch in Northern India. Īśānavarman's imperial position is to be dated after Kumāra Gupta's death. Thus the MMK marks the end of the Gupta Empire with the death of Kumāra Gupta III.

In the history of Prakaṭāditya, the Francis Joseph of the Gupta Period, many changes happened in the history of the dynasty and the country, most of which we have already noticed. The remaining matter is the defection of the 'traitorous' prince of the Vindhya country—that is, Malwā. In Durga (which I am unable to identify) he, according to the Tibetan text, declared himself king. "The Gauḍa nation became split up". King Jaya, *mahāvisha,* set himself up in the South-East, then followed Kesarī (or Siṃha), then king Soma. *'Jaya the mahāvisha* (great poison)' seems to be the Jayanāga of Karṇasuvarṇa (*EI.*, XVIII, 60) who issued a copper-plate with the imperial title *mahārājādhirāja.* It seems that the gubernatorial family of Malwā noted in the Mandasor inscription of 533 A.D. had been ousted and Malwā had been recovered by the Guptas in the time of Prakaṭāditya.

Thus to sum up the history of the break-up of the Gupta Empire as gathered from the two sections of the MMK may be tabulated as below.

Table showing *the Disruption of the Gupta Imperial Dynasty, the rise and fall of the Gauḍa Dynasty of the Later Guptas,* and *the Succession of Empires.*

c. 500 A.D. Budha Gupta dies.
Succession of Tathāgata Gupta.
Foundation of the Gauḍa *'Separatist'* dynasty.

c. 500—510 A.D. Succession of Bhānu Gupta Bālāditya II.

510 A.D. Battle of Airakiṇa (Eran) between Bhānu Gupta (Bālāditya) and the Huns (predecessor of Toramāṇa or Toramāṇa himself).

c. 511—512 A.D. Fall of Malwā. Toramāṇa in Magadha. Retirement of Bālāditya to Bengal. Toramāṇa crowns the boy Prakaṭāditya at Benares as king of Magadha, and dies at Benares.

c. 512—526 A.D. Mihirakula emperor of Northern India.

c. 527 A.D. Defeat and capture of Mihirakula in Bengal. *Recovery of the Gupta Empire.*

c. 527—29 A.D. Bālāditya II builds a grand temple at Nālandā as a memorial to his victory (*EI.*, XX. 37; Nālandā inscription, verse 6).

c. 530 A.D. Bālāditya II retires as a Buddhist monk. Prakaṭāditya succeeds as Emperor.

PRAKAṬĀDITYA PERIOD

[*c.* 530—587 A.D.]

Succession of Empires

Imperial Dynasty of Vishṇuvardhana

c. 530—533 A.D. Digvijaya of Yaśodharman. Assumption of Imperial position by Vishṇuvardhana (Yaśodharman). Naravardhana of Thanesar. Īśānavarman takes a leading part in the battle with the Hun army (on the side of Yaśodharman).

c. 540—550 A.D. End of the Family of Vishṇuvardhana.

Gupta Imperial Revival

c. 535—550 Kumāra Gupta III defeats Īśānavarman and declares himself to be the Lord of the Three Oceans; burns himself about 550 A.D. at Allahabad.

The Maukhari Imperial Dynasty

550—554 A.D. Īśānavarman becomes Emperor.

554—570 A.D. Śarvavarman acknowledged emperor both in the North and the South. Rājyavardhana I at Thanesar.

570—600 A.D. Avantivarman. Gupta family of Malwā comes into existence. Prakaṭāditya dies. Ādityavardhana at Thanesar.

The Imperial Dynasty of Śrikaṇṭha [*Thanesar*]

c. 600—605 A.D. Prabhākaravardhana becomes Emperor.

605-606 A.D. Rājyavardhana II.

606—646 A.D. Harshavardhana.

The Imperial Dynasty of Valabhī

c. 646—649 A.D. Dharasena IV, grandson of Harshavardhana succeeds to the Imperial position in 645 A.D. He is called *chakravartin* [3 years according to *MMK*].

649 V. the youngest member of the family (*MMK*) succeeds [as Dhruvasena III] who was very old.

653 or 656 A.D. Dhruvasena III dies.

Revival and Fall of the Later Guptas of Gauḍa-Magadha

c. 656—700 A.D. Ādityasena of the Gauḍa Guptas re-establishes an All-India Empire.

c. 700—720 A.D. Deva Gupta; probably killed by Yaśovarman of Kanauj.

c. 720—728 A.D. Ya(śovarman) for 8 years [Emperor from Kanauj].

c. 728 A.D., c. 728—745 A.D. Chandrāditya Vishṇu Gupta in Magadha, 48 days. Dvādaśāditya in Magadha. Gupta Rule ends in Bengal where *Bhadra,* the elected Śūdra king, rules for 17 years. *D.* in Bengal, 10 days; *Bh.* in Bengal, 3 days.

c. 728—733 A.D., 733 A.D. Jīvita Gupta II in Magadha, probably taken prisoner by the king of Kashmir (Lalitāditya) claiming Paramountcy in India. End of the Gauḍa dynasty.

c. 745 A.D. Election of Gopāla.

745—772 A.D. Gopāla's reign.

772 A.D. Paramountcy of the Pāla Emperor.

We have thus a continuous Northern Empire up to the opening of the Pāla Period.

Text (*Continued*)

§ 39. *Later Imperial Guptas and the Later Gupta Dynasty of Magadha from Bhānu Gupta*

c. 500 A.D. — 550 A.D.

Bh(ānu Gupta)

His (Samudra Gupta's) descendant *Bh.* (Bhānu Gupta) settled in the East (Prāchī) (760).

Pra(kaṭāditya)

His son P. [*Pra.,* T.] was born in the Eastern countries. He has been described [*proktaḥ*] as the leading Kshatriya. He was imprisoned as a boy and remained in prison upto the age of 17 years. He had been imprisoned by king Gopa and was released at Bhagavat[pura].

Comments

The king called Gopa here is evidently the Goparāja, who fought so loyally by the side of Bhānu Gupta in a successful battle at Eran in 510 A.D., most obviously against Toramāṇa. He was a subordinate ruler under Bhānu Gupta, and Pra. must have been put into prison by an order of Bhānu Gupta, his father.

The Battle of Eran was between the Huns and Bhānu Gupta. He evidently gave the enemy battle there having gone from Magadha with Gopa-rāja.

§ 40. *Installation of Pra(kaṭāditya) by H. (Hūṇa)*

H. [T.] (Hūṇa) [S.—A], having come from the West, was a great king (mahānṛipaḥ). He occupied the banks of the Ganges upto the East. He was of Śūdra caste, a Mahārāja of large army and great power. From his base on the Ganges, from all sides he invaded the city of the Gauḍas called *Tīrtha* and remained there as a powerful king (763—65).

There that Kshatriya boy with a merchant (T.) entered at night, and was acknowledged at the dawn by the Śūdra king, who then retired to Nandapura (Pāṭaliputra) on the Ganges, and in Magadha installed that boy as king (766-67).

The powerful Śūdra king entered the Kāśī country (T.) and at Benares fell ill (768-69).

Comments

'*H.*' is the reading in the Tibetan text in place of '*A*' in S. MMK.

H., the Śūdra from the western country who invaded Magadha and Gauḍa, seems to have been the *Hūṇa* Toramāṇa. Later, in verse 777 he is described as having enjoyed kingdoms of others. By a writer of the time of Harshavardhana or rather of 700 A.D., the remnants of the Huns in India who had become part of the population and who have come down in several castes to our own times, would have been easily regarded as Śūdras. Mlechchhas resident in India have been classed amongst Śūdras.

Toramāṇa has a good hereafter according to MMK (772—776). He does not seem to have been obnoxious to the Buddhists.

According to verse 777 he enjoyed a kingdom which had been legally earned by others (*parairupārjitaṃ rājyam anubhoktā bhavishyati*).

§ 40-A. *The Planet* (*graha*) (=*Mihira*), *son and successor of the H. Śūdra*

H. falling very ill crowned his son *graha*, a minor, and died. (769—771).

[The king's future career and effect of Buddhism described up to verse 767].

The king will be the enjoyer of a kingdom which had been acquisitions of others. His son was established at Benares. The latter's kingdom will be lost on account of an attack from his neighbour. The kingdom will be full of Brahmins and will be attacked by enemies. This king marked as *'graha'* was an erring man and arbitrary; and without much delay he was struck by enemy and died (777—779).

Comments

All haters of Buddhism have their names translated or otherwise concealed in the MMK,—e.g., *Śaśāṅka* is *Soma, Pushyamitra* is *Gomi;* so *Mihira* is 'planet' (*graha*).

[See also Introduction to Part II above.]

§ 41. *Pra(kaṭāditya)* [*c.* 530—588 A.D.]

His Large Empire: Decline of the Gupta Empire

There will be mutual disunion in the Magadha monarchy in the East at the time of the rise of Soma. At that time on the Ganges up to Benares and beyond, there will be king P. (Pra, T.), the Kshatriya, who had been recognised by the Śūdra king [Hūṇa] at Nandanagara (Pāṭaliputra) on the Ganges (780—82).

His past birth, good effects of Buddhist faith and charity, pious explanation of the kingship of Pr. etc. described, (783—813).

Both in his previous birth and in this one his contemporary was Soma.

(Theological explanation of initial imprisonment and release, 820-21).

He rules for 55 years or 77 (822).

He will rule up to the sea in the East. Those situated in the valleys of the Vindhyas and the Mlechchha robbers on the frontiers will be under the control of P. All the provinces in the North and the valleys of the Himādri will be ruled by this Kshatriya king. (On account of his having raised unconsciously a toy-stūpa in childhood) he will be an unrivalled king of Magadha, in the East up to the sea and the Forest (Aṭavi), up to the Lauhitya (Brahmaputra river), and in the North up to the Himalayas.

His empire. Benares-Bihar and Bengal; Malwa; Punjab and hills.

Later, this Buddhist king will be at Benares and alternately at Śriṅgapura (814—818).

Having conquered Pañcha Kesarī he established his own government (in Orissa). He overthrew and uprooted the Siṃha dynasty (of Orissa). (819-20).

Conquest of Orissa.

Then he, the Kshatriya king, rules all the countries in the Himalayan valleys in the East up to the banks of the Daśānūpa. (821).

North-East.

The following passage (after verse, 829) omitted in the Sanskrit text is found in the Tibetan:

The traitorous ones of the interior of the Vindhyas [Mālwā ?] set themselves up as independent rulers in the middle tract called Inaccessible (*durga*) (829A).

Defection of Provinces.

Jaya the serpent (Jayanāga) conquered the people of the South-East.

Kesarī (Lion) and another named Soma (Śaśāṅka) became kings (829B). (This) led to the division of the Gauḍa nation. This is to happen in the time of that Kshatriya sovereign (829C).

Born in prosperity the king had luxuries up to his dotage. He will live for 94 years, and die of sheer old age (830-31). (Future career described, 832—840).

§ 42. *Successors of Pra.*

In that Low Age after *P.*, there was confusion by his servants (omitted in T.); *V.* was king for one week, he was killed (843; omitted in T.). After *P.*, *Bh.* became king for 3 years (844) (omitted in T.).

His (P's) younger brother (or, descendant) *V.* (Vajra) solemnly became king, he ruled for 3 years (845).

§ 43. *Rājyavardhana II (of Thanesar) as ruler of Magadha*

And Rājyavardhana will be king for 1 year (845).

Both these kings (V. and Rājyavardhana) had sudden and unnatural ending. (846).

§ 44. *Heir and successors of Rājyavardhana as ruler of Magadha (-Gauḍa)*

Emperors of Valabhī

His (Rājyavardhana's) descendant (*anuja*, heir, born after him) will be Dh(arasena IV), a Kshatriya (by caste), fond of *dharma* (Buddhism). He will be king for 3 years [847-48]. Then the youngest (in) his (family) will be king, the famous *V.* [T. MMK: *J.*]. He will be over the whole country an All-India Emperor (*Sārva-bhūmika-bhūpatiḥ*). He will possess (an army of), elephants, horses and chariots, and navy, everywhere.

He will conquer every enemy. He will decorate the whole empire with Buddha images, monasteries and relic-memorials. His original ancestry was Dvijāti Śākya (Ikshvāku) (449—52).

He was self-respecting, sharp, wise, humble, on account of Buddhist wisdom, with sense of honour, and in that low age attained happiness. He lives with care for 100 years and 5 (days) (853—55).

Comments on §§ 42—44

The Lauhitya country which was reconquered by Mahāsena Gupta had been annexed to Gauḍa under the reign of Prakaṭāditya.

The *Gauḍa-tantra,* rendered by me as *Gauḍa-system* seems to have been made up of Bihar-Bengal-Orissa-and-Assam.

On the decline see the Introduction above. The Vindhya country,

Karṇasuvarṇa and other parts of Bengal, Orissa, and Assam seem to have broken off in the latter days of Prakaṭāditya.

From the time of Kumāra Gupta III whose copper-plate of Damodarpur is dated *GE,* 224=544 A.D. (*EI.*, 17. 193) was a 'Separatist Gauḍa' to break off from Prakaṭāditya and to have set up his own independence and assumed imperial titles. It should be recalled here that the *MMK* regards him the only independent king among the Later Guptas. The Maukharis did not succeed to the Imperial position up to 554 A.D.

On §§ 43-44. Rājyavardhana is regarded as the direct ruler after the death of Prakaṭāditya and his successors (6 or 7 years). Hence Prakaṭāditya may have come to the throne about 10 years later than I have supposed and Vajra may have come before him. Or, Rājyavardhana might have been governor of Benares in his father's life-time. According to the Sarnath inscription Prakaṭāditya was a son of Bālāditya and according to Yuan Chuang, Vajra was son and successor of Bālāditya. According to the MMK, Pra.'s younger brother V. succeeded him, and that Pra. became king after the death of Graha (Mihira, i.e., after 533 A.D.). It is difficult to decide whether Vajra preceded or succeeded Prakaṭāditya.

Rājyavardhana had his successor in Harsha; and Dh., that is, Dharasena IV his grandson was really Harsha's *anuja* or descendant in which sense the MMK always uses the term. According to the Mitāksharā idea of Hindu Law, Dharasena IV would be considered a successor and descendant of Rājyavardhana. It is difficult to give value to the initial V. or *J.* (Tibetan version) of the successor of Dh. but the description leaves little doubt that it was Dhruvasena III, 'the youngest' of his grand-uncles, all elder to Dharasena's own grandfather. The long age (100 years) confirms the identification.

It is noteworthy that the Valabhī kings maintained a navy.

Dharasena IV in the year 546 A.D. issued two copper-plates; in the earlier of the two in the same Kārtikādi year (326 *GE.*) he is not *chakravartin* (*Emperor*), while a few months after he assumed that title (Bhandarkar's List, No. 1348, No. 1349). We should therefore conclude that his grandfather Harshavardhana died between the month of Māgha (5th, Dark Fortnight) and Āshāḍha (S., 10). By that title he claimed to be the heir to the Empire of Harshavardhana and something more, that is, as the Emperor of the South.

Evidently Dharasena IV sent governors to the East, or Mādhava Gupta or Ādityasena accepted the suzerainty of the Valabhī emperors. Ādityasena evidently started his reign as a subordinate to the Valabhī Emperor. Ādityasena who performed three Aśvamedhas and reached the shores of the seas must be taken to have broken the claim of the Valabhī Emperor to the title of *chakravartin*.

This record about the succession of the grandson of Harsha discounts the story of the usurpation of 'Arjuna', minister of Harsha of the Chinese account. The story is much exaggerated. 'Arjuna' seems to have set himself up as the local ruler of Tirhut and was easily defeated by a tiny army.

§ 45. *Later Guptas*

(*a*) King Śrī

After him, in the Gauḍa system there will be a king with the name *Śrī*, a *mahārāja*, and lover of dharma. His capital will be *V.*, a populous first class capital. Having conquered his neighbouring rivals he will rule there. Seven and eight monasteries he 'built' there. His minister was Śākaja, a Brahmin, with his help he ruled all around. He lived for 81 years. (856—59). He had a good career in heaven, as he was of religious soul, and whatever condition be brought about was only due to the fault of his servants. (860-61).

His feudatory (or servant) as sovereign *Y.* by name will have an unquestioned rule for 8 years. He was killed by women (853-54). Again (*b*) a Kshatriya dynast of the *P.-dynasty* will become king.

Comments

King *Śrī* with whom the family of '*Pa.-Vaṃśa*' begins is Śrī Ādityasena, son of Śrīmatī and Mādhava Gupta. This identity is established by his successors, who in § 26 are Deva Gupta, Vishṇu Gupta Chandrāditya and Dvādaśāditya, while here (§ 46) they are *R.*'s elder brother and *R.* who is identical with Vishṇu Gupta. In place of Deva Gupta here the rule of *Y*, a feudatory who became the master, is given. This seems to be Yaśovarman (see below). Yaśovarman's rule in Magadha is proved by the Nālandā stone inscription of his minister Mālāda (*EI.* XX. 43). Yaśovarman supplanted Deva Gupta who in § 26 is said to have been surrounded by his enemies and killed. The Nālandā inscription and the *Gauḍavaho*, composed in the reign of Yaśovarman, now read with the MMK, would indicate that the king who was killed in battle on the Sone and who is called here both the king of Gauḍa and the king of Magadha, was Deva Gupta of the Gauḍa dynasty of the Guptas.

The age of the king Śrī——, 81 years, shows that the king was the old king Ādityasena who had performed three *Aśvamedhas* and had a long reign. The later kings of the dynasty were all short-lived. The last apology for the king refers to his Brahmanic rule and sacrifices. The Buddhists were greatly pleased with Ādityasena. His capital bore the initial V.; was it *Vāruṇikā* (Deo-Barnārk) (*GI.* 216)?

The statement (§ 48) that Kumāra Gupta (III) was the last independent ruler of the dynasty would indicate that probably in his last days Ādityasena was defeated by the Chālukyas about 694 A.D. Vinayāditya who ruled up to 656 A.D. and in that year was succeeded by his son Vijayāditya (Kielhorn, *EI.* VIII. App. II. 2), defeated through his Crown-Prince Vijāyaditya between 680 A.D. (the date of his accession) and 694 A.D. (the date of his death) the Emperor of All-Northern India (cf. *I.A.*, Vol. VIII. 26). About 680—694 A.D. Ādityasena, the *aśvamedhin*, was undoubtedly the Emperor (Nātha) of *sakala-Uttarāpatha*. The description might as well refer to his son Deva Gupta as his imperial successor. That it refers to the king of Magadha is established by the fact that the imperial insignia of the *Gaṅgā* and *Yamunā* flags were captured from the Northern emperor. These emblems had belonged to the Vākāṭakas and are described as *pārameśvarya-chiñha*, 'emblems of imperialism', in the Chālukya documents. They descended to the Guptas from the Vākāṭakas.

The chronology proposed above in the Introduction is confirmed by the account of Hwui Lun (*IA.*, X. 110) who visited Magadha about 690 A.D. He found a temple under construction by Jih-kwan (*sun-army* = *Ādityasena*). In this temple the people from the South were to reside. It is remarkable that the temple mentioned before this was the Chālukya temple, which was probably raised as a memorial by the Chālukya Vijyāditya in the heart of his enemy's kingdom. It was about 40 stages west of Nālandā. Ādityasena was dead at the time and 'Devavarmā,' that is, 'Deva-Guṇpta' was ruling as '*the king of Eastern India*' (Prāchī). The approximate time of the visit of Hwui Lun may be gathered in this way. Itsing extracted this account. Itsing died in 713 A.D. Hwui Lun was sent out by the Chinese Emperor to follow the steps of and to attend on

Yüan-chau, a Chinese pilgrim, who had left for India a second time in 665 A.D. Yüan-chau had tarried in Dardistan for 4 years and then came to Magadha and died in Central India. Hwui Lun did not meet him, and lived for 10 years in a convent in the North and then came to Magadha. Thus if Yüan-chau died about 670 A.D., Hwui Lun reached Magadha later than 680 A.D. or later still. Deva Gupta had come to the throne and was reigning about 685—690 A.D. and he certainly flourished before 713 A.D., the date of the death of Itsing. The temple begun by his father was being finished and there had been no interruption in the dynastic régime up to that time.

The identity of Y. is established on the basis of the facts stated—to wit—that he was an outsider who interposed for 8 years, that Yaśovarman did rule in Magadha on the authority of the Nālandā inscription, and that he killed a king of Magadha-Gauḍa in the battle of the Sone, according to the *Gauḍavaho.* Under Ādityasena he must have been considered a subordinate to the Gauḍa (Later Gupta) Dynasty. According to Hwui Lun, Deva was reigning about 700 A.D. Yaśovarman's rise dates a little after 700 A.D. According to the other section (§ 26) Deva(Gupta) was surrounded by enemy forces and killed. We are therefore justified in placing DevaGupta immediately after Ādityasena, and treating him as the king killed by Yaśovarman.

It is to be marked that Y. is not treated as an Emperor. His attempt to establish himself as emperor did fail. He was defeated by Lalitāditya, but not slain as supposed by V. Smith (*EHI.*, 392) for Kalhaṇa says that Yaśovarman attended his court as a poet-courtier after his defeat. His sending an embassy to China in 731 A.D. seems to have followed his defeat at the hands of Lalitāditya, for Lalitāditya himself was under the acknowledged suzerainty of China and Yaśovarman would naturally seek the moral support of the Chinese Emperor after his defeat by his protégé.

It seems that Yaśovarman was ousted from Magadha before 731 A.D., probably at the time of his Kashmir defeat, which should be dated before 731 A.D.

§ 46. *P.'s dynasty* [*restored*]

He ['of the P.-dynasty'] killed the ministers (or, supporters of that feudatory) (863).

He was senseless on account of his prestige, taking steps in a hurry, unsteady, a drinker of wine, fond of rogues. He was lying on the ground drunk, and was killed by enemies (864—66).

(*c*) His only brother *R.* was king for 48 days (867). He gave money to Brahmins and passed time.

Comments

R.'s identity with Vishṇu Gupta Chandrāditya is already discussed in the Introduction above. The genealogy there is as following:—

Deva Gupta
- The unnamed king of *MMK.*
- Vishṇu Gupta (*Ru.*, coins)
  - Dvādaśāditya
  - Jīvita Gupta II

This section is not giving the name of Dvādaśāditya. Vishṇu Gupta (R.) is treated as the last king in Bengal proper. Dvādaśāditya, in any case, ruled only for a few months. It is evident that it was either Dvādaśāditya or Jīvita Gupta who was captured by Lalitāditya of Kashmir and taken there as a prisoner. It is more likely that it was Jīvita Gupta II, for Dvādaśāditya died as a boy, and the Gauḍa king captured by Lalitāditya had twice taken up arms against Lalitāditya. Lalitāditya was invested with royalty by the Emperor of China in 733 A.D. Lalitāditya undertook a *digvijaya* according to the *Rājataraṅgiṇī*, which was generally done on accession. This date agrees with the dates we approximately get from the MMK for the close of the Gauḍa Gupta Dynasty.

§ 47. *A Śūdra king in Gauḍa*

After him *Sva*, will be king (868). He will be a Śūdra by caste, a cripple, low, non-religious, ill-tempered, and quarrelsome. He destroys Brahmin feudal lords, recluses of good-conduct, and others. He will be always busy in maintaining law and order (*nigraha*). His administration will be sharp, he will be the killer of thieves, forbidder of all rascals practising religious hypocricy. He will be a freedom-giver and will be a donor. He will rule for 17 years. He dies of leprosy (869—73). [Then follows his future career in the hereafter (847-75)].

This is the history of the past Eastern kings, the '*lokavardhanas*', and known to every one. (875).

Comments

The *Sva.* is the same cripple as described in § 47 above, who had been a popular Bengali leader elected to kingship. He seems to have been a successful, impartial ruler, though peevish and inclined to be idealistic. With ill health, persistent executive capacity, and doctrinaire temperament this ancient Bengali politician served his country well for 17 years.

§ 48. *The constitutional position of the Later Guptas, the Gauḍa Dynasty*

A note on Emperor K(umāra Gupta III)

Under king P. (Pra.) there will be a king,—a descendent of another family branching off from the dynasty of P(ra).—a Kshatriya, very brave, an emperor of the three Seas. In this East Country he will be of large army and great power. He will beautify the earth with shining monasteries having relics of the Buddha, rest-houses and temples, with gardens, various stepped wells, wells, pavilions, roads, and free-kitchen hotels.

He was a devotee of the Buddhas, took to the good Yāna (Mahāyāna), and led the life of a Śākya monk, declining gifts, though making gifts. He was known by the name of K., a learned man and knowing tradition. He ruled for 21 years, and died of cholera. (876—82).

His descendants became subordinate rulers (874).

Comments

All what is said about *K's* position is verified from inscriptions about Kumāra Gupta III. The Gauḍa Guptas called themselves "the dynasty of Gauḍa". This is evident from contemporary records—the *Gaṇḍavaho* and inscriptions. Kumāra Gupta III and Ādityasena were the only truly paramount sovereigns in the line. Why Ādityasena is not counted in the line as a paramount king is probably due to his defeat by the Chālukyas. The Chālukya temple-hostel and his undertaking to build a temple-hostel for the Southerners imply the Chālukya domination in the last days of Ādityasena.

§ 49. *The Pāla Dynasty*

Then the Gopālas will be king who will be of the menial caste, and the people will be miserable with Brahmins. The Buddha's doctrine having been lost, the time will be irreligious (883-84). [Necessary mantras prescribed], [See next section].

§ 50. *Religious Practice in the East, South, Insulindia and Further India*

Then by mantra system (magical formulas) serve the people (884). [Directions

about Tārā worship etc. follow for the *East*, the *Dakshiṇāpatha* and *the Islands in the Sea*, for *Harikela*, *Karmaraṅga*, *Kāmarūpa* and *Kalaśa*, up to verse 894].

Comments

Insulindia and Further India come here in the Southern system. "*The Dvīpas in the middle of the Sea*" were inhabited by Mlechchhas and pirates (*taskara*) (899).

§ 51. *Madhyadeśa*

In Madhyadeśa there will be various Kings and Ministers, weak and of little intelligence. 'A brief notice of the main kings is being given as follows'. (903—912).

M. (Ś., in T.), N., P. (Pra., in T.), D., I., S. (not in T.), A.,
Graha (not in T.), Kīrti (not in T.), H., then Ś. (B. in T.).
J., B., L., Soma; H. (Dh., in T.), then A. (905—907).
S. and L. and Strī. (will be) haters of the people;
S. (A. in T.) and M. will be lords of men (or causing prosperity to men):
they will be respectively Kṛimi, Brahmins and Vaiśyas, doers of irreligious deeds, hated, and fond of women (909). The kings will have large numbers of dependants (relations) in that low age, in Madhyadeśa (910).

The middlings, best ones, intermediary ones, and the lowest have been mentioned. They will be of short life (912).

§ 52. *Miscellaneous Tracts*

On the river Ganges, on the table-land of the Himalayas and in Kāmarūpa, there will be similar kings (913).

The kings of Aṅgadeśa for the periods first, middle and last are now related. In the beginning there (will be) Vṛita-sudhāna; he (will be called *Karmarāja*. The last Aṅga king will be Subhūti-Bhūti, an Āṅga (914-15).

In Kāmarūpa the kings will be Sadaha and Bhavada, the casteless (915).

At Vaiśālī there will be Subhū, Mṛiga and Kumāra as the last ones and the two Vs' (916).

At Kapilapura where the Sage was born there (were) the pure-minded Śākyajas, descending from Āditya-Iksha (that is *Sūryavaṃśa* Ikshvākus). The last (was) Śuddhodana the Śākya, amongst the Śākyavardhanas (917).

(The magical matra's appropriate for Madhyadeśa are mentioned up to 924).

§ 53. *The Scheme of Royal History summed up*

Numerous kings have been related, belonging to Madhyadeśa, North,

West, East, South and minor directions (*vidikshu*)—everywhere, and outside, the Islands—divided into four (825-26).

Numerous kings and *mantra*-processes have been related according to quarters (927).

(According to time, place and rulers, Mantras have been prescribed (928—31).

All the kings have been described according to the quarters (924).

Comments

This ends the dynastic history. Then follow the notices of political monks, Brahmins and other citizens, and religious and social leaders.

PART III

RELIGIOUS AND SOCIAL LEADERS

§ 54. *Monks (Yatis) connected with the State*

The Buddhist recluses connected with the state (rājyavṛittinaḥ) will be these (935): Mātṛichīna (Matṛicheṭa, T.); Kusumāra (Kusuma, T.); *M.;* Kukura (Kumāra, T.), an extreme lover of dharma;

Nāga (Nāgārjuna) whose name was Ratnasaṃbhava;

G.; Kumāra; *V.* the dharma-thinker; *A.* the high-souled, who was unapproachable in Buddhism; *L.* the qualified, the wise; *R.* (not in T.); and *N.* (not in T.); (937-38).

Under king Buddhapaksha was the light of Buddhism, *A*(Aśvaghosha) the Buddhist recluse Brahmin of Saketa, who lived for 80 years (938—940);

A, the loving Bhikshu in the South, of 60 years, the wise, of Kāśi [T.] city;

South.

Th. [*Dh.,* T.] the recluse of the South, who prohibited criticism of others, and who had powers from mantra (940—42).

Apara, the excellent recluse of Ceylon; and the Ceylonese non-Hindu monks

Ceylon.

with Hindu names who condemn criticism of others and tolerant of the Tīrthikas will arise at the end of the Yuga in that terrible time.

V., L., R. [*D.,* T.], and *Vi.* [*V.,* T.], will be devoted to the Buddha's doctrine. (943—45).

Under king Bālāka (Kāla, T.), there will be the monk S. (*M.,* in T.) and

Heretical Buddhists.

monasteries, gardens, chaityas, reservoirs, wells, Buddha images, symbols, bridges, paths—all different from orthodox Buddhism (946-47).

There will be *M.* (S. in T.), *K., N.,* [*R., Gh.*—in T.] Sudatta, Sushena, Senakīrti, Dattaka, and Dinaka who will carp at the theories of others (850-49).

There will be a monk, formerly a Vaṇik (merchant) and another, formerly a

Philanthropists.

Vaidya (physician) who will think of the interest of the poor.

There will be *Ch.; R.; Bh.;* and Pratitha-Śrāddha who will explain the

Image-philosophers.

meaning of the Buddha images; M. the intelligent; and the monk Srāddha (950-51). There will be these and many others who will be light unto Buddhism, and when Buddhism will decay, beautiful

Artist monks.

Buddha images will be made by them (953).

'Amongst the future monks, the first place will be held by the Southern monks (945). They will win fame by mantra and tantra practices (955).

Leading class in the 8th century.

Comments

The time of N ā g ā r j u n a is indicated by placing him above A ś v a g h o s h a who is noted to have been a contemporary of *Buddha-paksha,* the Yaksha king—partial to Buddhism, that is, Kadphises (§ 11).

A more specific date of Nāgārjuna is given in § 9 above.

The notice shows that there was a regular school of philosophers who gave meaning to various images of the Buddha, and that there was a school who specialised in producing beautiful images.

§ 55. *Brahmins and others connected with the State*

Brahmins.

"Now I shall mention to you the religious Brahmins practising Mantra and Tantra, receiving maintenance from the State" [or, 'who took to politics, T.] (956).

V., the rich Brahmin, who went across the Vedas, in this whole country went round for controverting and went over all the three Oceans (to the Islands and Further India), and engaged himself in controversies. He practised the 16-syllable mantra (958, etc., 959).

(There will be) J a y a and S u j a y a the famous Ś u b h a m a t a of good family; U d y a t a the religious; M ā d h a v a the good; M a d h u S u m a d h u; S i d d h a; and N a m a (960-61).

§ 56. *Śūdras and Śakas*

R ā g h a v a the Śūdra, and others, (who will be) Ś a k a-b o r n (T.-Kaśa), will be repeaters [of mystic syllables] according to the prescription of [Mañju-Śrī] Kumāra, miracle-workers, wise and learned (962). They will be supported by the State on account of their knowledge of mantras (903).

§ 57. *Brahmins again*

Vishṇugupta

Then *V.*, the Brahmin, at Pushpapura: He will be angry, a miracle-worker, and will cause chastisement amongst kings on account of his poverty and feeling of insult (964). He is called '*the king of anger*' and '*Yamāntaka*'. He was a pacifier of the wicked, and was for removing what was harmful and for augmenting what was good.

But that fool of a poverty-stricken Brahmin, misled by anger threw his anger at the king's life (967).

S. (Subandhu)

After him was S. (S u b a n d h u?), the Brahmin, an expert in political counsel and Artha(śāstra), self-possessed, a lord, very famous. (He practised self-lessly mantras etc. 968-69).

Ś'.

Ś. will be in Mālava; he will control Brahmin goblins. He will be a Brahmin (970—72).

Southern Brahmins

V., an artist abroad

After this, V. will be a famous Brahmin in Dakshiṇāpatha. He will be a Buddhist. Reaching the two Seas he will decorate monasteries, gardens, chaityas and the Buddha images (974-75).

Bh.

After him, that good and very wealthy Brahmin *Bh.* [*N.* in T.] will be famous in the South (976).

Madhyadeśa Brahmins

In Madhyadeśa, there will Sampūrṇa the Brahmin; Vinaya and Suvinaya; Pūrṇa of Mathurā; and Bh. the chancellor of royal exchequer, a worshipper by mantra (977-78).

These are the Brahmin worshippers of Buddhism (979).

(Then follows a description of the Mahāyāna pantheon, and the work closes with Mahāyāna moral. T. has only up to verse 988 (half of 988).

Comments

The South, on the above data, was closely connected with Insulindia in the matter of Buddhist art.

It will be noticed that Vishṇugupta (Chāṇakya) who is also mentioned in the above section, is acknowledged here to be essentially a just man and as having great administrative capacity. Buddhist grievance is that he destroyed Nanda who was probably a Buddhist.

Subandhu, if my identification is correct, was essentially a politician.

INDEX

H

N

T

THE
TEXT OF THE MAÑJU-ŚRĪ-MŪLAKALPA

CORRECTED WITH THE HELP OF THE TIBETAN TEXT BY

VEN. RĀHULA SĀNKṚITYĀYANA

Tripiṭakâchārya, Mahāpaṇḍita

मञ्जुश्रीमूलकल्पे

अथ त्रिपञ्चाशः पटलविसरः

[I. Madhya-deśa—Imperial]

§ 1. Biography of the Buddha and Śaiśunāka Dynasty

G. ५७९ अथ खलु भगवां शाक्यमुनिः तस्मात् समाधेर्व्युत्थाय महासागरोपमायां पर्षन्मण्डलं धर्मं देशयमानः सर्वसत्त्वानां सर्वभूतगणानामग्रतः सन्निषण्णाः तत्र वज्रपाणिप्रमुखानामनेकबोधिसत्त्व-(1)सङ्ख्येयसहस्रां शारिपुत्रप्रमुखां अनेकासङ्ख्येयार्हत्सहस्रां वैश्रवणप्रमुखां असङ्ख्येयार्चचातुर्महाराजिकदेवपुत्रां शक्रप्रमुखां त्रायस्त्रिंशां असङ्ख्येयदेवपुत्रां सुयामसन्तुषितनिर्माणरतिपरनिर्मितवशवर्ति-ब्रह्मकायिकब्रह्मपुरोहितमहाब्रह्मपरीत्ताभाप्रमाणाभास्वरैर्यावत् पुण्यप्रसवाबृहत्फलातृहातपाकनिष्ठा देवानामन्त्रयते स्म । शृण्वन्तु भवन्तो देवसङ्घाः! सर्वबोधिसत्त्वार्यश्रावकाः !

अनित्याः सर्वसंस्कारा उत्पादव्ययधर्मिणः ।
उत्पद्य हि निरुद्ध्यन्ते तेषां व्युपशमः सुखम् ॥१॥
अविद्याप्रभावाः सर्वे उत्पद्यन्ते सहेतुकाः ।
सहेतुं दुःखमूलं तु स्कन्धा ह्युक्ताः समोदयाः ॥२॥
तेषां निरोधिनी विद्या सुखहेतुसुखक्रियाम् ।
T. 425 b. दुःखप्रहाणमित्युक्तं संक्षेपेण निवारणा ॥३॥
तदेव त्रिविधं यानं निर्दिष्टं च मया इह ।
अनित्यदुःखमानात्मानो क्षणिकं सर्वसंस्कृतम् ॥४॥
T. 426 a. शून्यं सदा सर्वदा सर्वं निर्दिष्टं भवबन्धनम् ।
तद्विरागा त्रिधा यान्ति ये सत्त्वा गोत्रनिसृता ॥५॥
बोधिसत्त्वास्तदा बुद्धा प्रत्येकां बोधिनिश्रिताम् ।
तथा परेऽर्हरहभो वीतरागा महर्द्धिका ॥६॥

---

२. प्रभवाः ।

श्रावकों बोधिनिसृत्य त्रिधा शान्तिगता हि ते ।
एष धर्मो समासेन निर्दिष्टो मे शुभाशुभम् ॥७॥
अशुभं वर्जयेन्नित्यं सर्वदा शुभमाचरेत् ।
अहिंसां सर्वभूतानां यथा धर्मो प्रकाशितः ॥८॥
एक एव भवेन्मार्गे धर्माणां गतिपञ्चके ।
अनाश्रवश्च यो धर्मो भूतकोटिसमाश्रृतः ॥९॥
G. ५८० स एप कथितो मार्गः आदिबुद्धैः पुरातनैः ।
मयापि कथितं सर्वं शान्तनिर्वाणगामिनम् ॥१०॥
धर्मकोटिं समासृत्य भूतकोटिं तु लभ्यते ।
अकोटी सर्वधर्माणां भूतकोटिमुदाहृता ॥११॥
एष धर्मः समासेन द्विविधैव प्रकाशितम् ।
शृण्वन्तु सर्वे देवा वै बोधिसत्त्वा महर्द्धिकाः ॥१२॥
अर्हन्तः श्रावका मह्यं निर्वाणं मे यदा भुवि ।
अभूत् सालवने मध्ये हिमवत्कुक्षिसम्भवे ॥१३॥
नद्यां हिरण्यवत्यायां *मल्लानामुपवर्तते* ।
यमकशालकवने मध्ये निर्वाणं मे भविष्यति ॥१४॥
T. 426 b. यावत् संज्ञी तथा नगरे चैत्ये *मकुटवर्धने* ।
नदीतीरे सदा रम्ये निर्वाणं मे तदा भुवि ॥१५॥
सर्वे वै बोधिसत्त्वास्तु श्रावकाश्च महर्द्धिकाः ।
देवा नागा तथा यक्षा लोकपाला महर्द्धिका ॥१६॥
शक्रब्रह्मसुयामाश्च अकनिष्ठाद्यास्तथा परे ।
सर्वेषां सन्निपाता वै तस्मिं स्थाने भविष्यति ॥१७॥
यमकशालकवने तत्र मल्लानामुपवर्तते ।
गङ्गायामुत्तरे तीरे महानद्यास्तथा परे ॥१८॥
हिमाद्रेर्दक्षिणे भागे अभूत् सालवने वने ।
अपश्चिमे मे तथा शय्या तस्मिं स्थाने भविष्यति ॥१९॥
नद्या तीरे तथा रम्ये *हिरण्याख्ये* शुभे तटे ।
सर्वदेवसङ्घानां सन्निपातो भविष्यति ॥२०॥

---

९. अनास्रवश्च । समाश्रितः । १०. एष । १४. वर्तने । १५. यावा-संज्ञे । मुकुट-वंधने । १८. वर्तने । नदी ।

मनुजैः नृपवरैः सर्वै(ः) मनुष्यामनुष्यसम्भवैः ।
सर्वभूतैस्तथा मर्त्यै(ः) बालिशाबालिशैस्तदा ॥२१॥
महोत्सवमहोत्साहं तस्मिं स्थाने समागमम् ।
कृतमन्त्रमहं दिव्यं मच्छरीरे तु सामिषे ॥२२॥
G. ५८१ निरामिषं तु तदास्थाप्य शान्तिमाप्नोति निर्वृतिम् ।
धर्मकोटिं परित्यज्य भूतकोटिं तु संविशेत् ॥२३॥
अपश्चिमा मे तथा जातिः नगरे कपिलवास्तुके ।
शाक्यानां च कुले मुख्ये जातोऽहं भवचारके ॥२४॥
ततोऽहं त्यज्य दुःखात्म्यं निर्यातोऽहं गृहात्तथा ।
बहुतीर्थीं तथासेव्य न च प्राप्तोमृतः पुनः ॥२५॥
T. 427 a. दुःकरं च मयाचीर्णं कायं सन्ताप्य तश्चैनम् ।
षडाब्दमुषितः भ्रष्ट देहं वापि विशुष्कतः ॥२६॥
न च किञ्चिन्मया लब्धं येन ज्ञानमवावृतम् ।
ततोत्थाय मया तत्र आहारं कृथ शुभोदनम् ॥२७॥
देवतासूचितं मार्गं गतोऽहं तत्र भूतलम् ।
नद्या नैरञ्जनातीरे वृक्षराजे सुशोभने ॥२८॥
नानापुष्पसमाकीर्णे तथेरण्येऽथ भूतले ।
महावनफलोपेते नानावृक्षसमुद्भवे ॥२९॥
महानदी परिवेष्टयान्ते तरुमूले ततो ह्यहम् ।
यो स्वकं दृष्टमात्रं तु भूभागं धृतिसंलभे ॥३०॥
तथैवाहं तं तरुं दृष्ट्वा पर्णशाखोपशोभितम् ।
महावृक्षं महाच्छायं मूलगूढोपशोभितम् ॥३१॥
अश्वत्थेऽश्वत्थतां गच्छेत् तरुमूले निषद्य वै ।
धृतिं तत्राभिविन्दामि ध्यानं चापि समाधिकम् ॥३२॥
प्राप्तं तत्र अनाशां वै रात्र्यन्ते जातिरन्तकम् ।
मारेण बहुधा विघ्ना अनेकाकारसुयोजिताः ॥३३॥
भग्नसैन्यपरावृत्य गतोऽसौ स्वभवनं पुनः ।
तदर्थे मन्त्रतन्त्रा वै भाषिता बहुधा पुनः ॥३४॥
अनेकाकारप्रयोगाश्च ध्याना ज्ञानाश्च भाषिताः ।
त्रिधा यानं पुनस्तत्र चरितं सर्वसेवितम् ॥३५॥

---

२४. तदा । २७. मपावृतम् ।

T. 427 b. G. ५८२ प्रतिपक्षा हि दोषाणां त्रिधा चैव प्रकाशितः ।
ततोत्थाय पुनर्गत्वा बुरुबिल्वां शुभोदकाम् ॥३६॥
स्नात्वाम्भसे तत्र ऋषिं प्रव्रज्य सशिष्यकाम् ।
सत्त्वार्थं बहुधा कृत्वा प्रक्रान्तोऽहं ततः पुनः ॥३७॥
पुनः काशिपुरीरम्यां अनुपूर्व्या समाविशेत् ।
तत्र स्थाने तु गत्वा वै परा बुद्धा महर्द्धिकाः ॥३८॥
तत्राहं स्थितो देशे जने काशिजने स्वयम् ।
प्रवर्त्यं चक्रं साधर्म्यं शान्ति निर्वाणकारकम् ॥३९॥
ससुरासुरलोकानां गतिं पञ्चासु निसृताम् ।
सर्वभूतसुखार्थाय तत्र धर्म प्रकाशितः ॥४०॥
आदिबुद्धैः पुरा तत्र धर्मचक्रं प्रवर्तितम् ।
मयापि दिशि तत्र धर्मचक्रो ह्यनुत्तरः ॥४१॥
भवमुक्तिसुखार्थाय सत्त्वदोषनिवारणा ।
प्रवर्त्त्यं चक्रं ब्राह्मं वै क्षेमं शान्त परायणम् ॥४२॥
भवमार्गविनाशार्थं चतुःसत्यसमाधिजम् ।
आर्याष्टाङ्गिकं मार्गं चतुर्ब्राह्मविभूषितम्॥ ४३॥
सप्रतीत्यसमुत्पादं द्वादशाकारकारितम् ।
अविद्यानिरोधसंयुक्तं विद्यामुत्पादनेमिजम् ॥४४॥
आमिता कोटितत्थ्यं वै भूतकोटिसुकोटिजम् ।
अनुलोमविलोमाभ्यां गतिमाहात्मनेमिजम् ॥४५॥
T. 428 a. सम्प्रदेश शिवं चक्रं बहुसत्त्वा विमोच्च च ।
विमुञ्च्य काशिपुरीं रम्यां श्रावस्त्याहं तदा गमे ॥४६॥
तीर्थिकानां तथा वर्ज्या प्रातिहार्यैर्विकुर्वतैः ।
शंकश्ये तथा कृत्वा ऋद्धिर्जनपदे तदा ॥४७॥
बहुतीर्थायतनांस्थानां सम्प्रतोष्य तदा पुनः ।
अग्निभाण्डे जने कृत्वा देवावतरणं शुभम् ॥४८॥
G. ५८३ त्रायस्त्रिंशेषु देवेषु शक्र(-क्रं) संयोज्य धर्मताम् ।
अकनिष्ठाद्यां* तथा देवां ब्रह्मादी शपुरन्दराम् ॥४९॥

---

३६. उरु बिल्वं । ३८. पुरा । ३९. सद्ध । ४१. देशितः । ४२. ब्राह्मयं ।
४७. प्रातिहार्ये विकुर्वणैः । ४८. यतनस्थानी । ४९. ब्रह्मादीन् स-पुरन्दरान् ।

* द्वितीया बहुवचनान्त-मकारस्थाने प्रायेणाऽनुस्वारो मकारो वेह प्रयुक्तः ।

उत्थातु भगवां क्षिप्रं बुद्धवेलानुवर्तनैः ।
महासागरेचलेवोल्लङ्घ्या मुनितद्गतैः ॥७८॥
न चावमन्यां बहूं सत्त्वां चिरकालं समोभिजे ।
ध्यानं विमोक्ष संसेस्तुशान्तनिर्वाणमार्गे ॥७९॥
निषेप्तुं वा भूततो मुनिः ।
एवम्प्रकारं ह्यनेकां बहुप्रलापां प्रलपवंचूरे ॥८०॥
तूष्णीम्भूताथ सर्वे वै देवसङ्घा महर्द्धिका ।
आक्रन्दमतुलं कृत्वा सप्रणामा ततस्थिरे ॥८१॥
चुकूचु विरःमुत्कोश्य साश्रुकण्ठा सगद्गदा ।
सशोकाचित्तमनसो ब्रह्माद्याः ससुरासुराः ॥८२॥
मनुजा नराधिपाः सर्वे निषण्णास्तत्र महीतले ।
अपरः शाक्यजो मुक्तः वीतरागो महर्द्धिकः ॥८३॥
ज्ञानिनो देवदेवस्य बुद्धस्यैव महात्मने ।
T. 430 a. अनिरुद्धो नामतो भिक्षुः अनुजोऽसौ मनुजः शुभः ॥८४॥
सुसूक्ष्म निपुणो व्यक्तः गीतनीतिविशारदः ।
परिवारितोरह(न्)मुख्यैस्तु अनेकैश्चापि नराधिपैः ॥८५॥
स भाषे मधुरां वाचां निश्वसन्तः सुचेरिताम् ।
करुणार्द्रचेतसां क्षिप्रां मल्लानां सनराधिपाम् ॥८६॥
मा तावन्मार्षा ह्यत्र चितावग्नि प्रदायथ ।
यावद् भगवतः पुत्रः अग्रतो धर्मतोद्भवः ॥८७॥
G. ५८६ महाकाश्यपनामेन श्रावकोऽसौ महर्द्धिकः ।
महामुने अग्रधीजात ब्राह्मणोऽसौ निरामिषः ॥८८॥
मगधानां जने जातः पर्वते तत्र समाहितः ।
तिष्ठ ग्रह पिप्पले नगरे राजगृहे वरे ॥८९॥
स एवागमनं क्षिप्रं करिष्यति न चान्यथा ।
या तत्र देवता भक्ता स चेहोल्कां निवारयेत् ॥९०॥
मा तावचितिसन्दीपं करिष्यथ वृथा श्रमम् ।
यावत् सो महर्द्धिको ह्यग्रः श्रावको मुनिनौरसः ॥९१॥

---

७८. नुवर्तते । महासागरवेलेवोल्लंघ्य । ७९. न चावमान्य बहून् सत्वान् । समाभिजम् । संशास्तु । मार्गम् । ८२. चुकुशुः चिर । ८९. गुहा-पिप्पले ९०. देहोल्का । ९१. सन्दीपे ।

प्रदक्षिणीकृत्य गुरवे बुद्धत्रैलोक्यपूजिते ।
मूर्ध्ना प्रणम्य पादौ शास्तुनो लोकपूजितौ ॥९२॥
तदायं चितिदीपार्थं सर्वे तत्र करिष्यथ ।
आदीमा चैत्यभूताद् भविष्यति तदा इमा ॥९३॥
सर्वे मा वृथा कुर्व श्रमं केवल भो इह ।
T. 430 b. एवमुक्तास्तु ते सर्वे *अनिरुद्धेन* धीमता ॥९४॥
निषण्णा सर्व *मल्लास्तु* मानुषास्ते सनराधिपाः ।
मानुषाणामुत्पन्नोऽहं मानुषैश्चापि वर्धितः ॥९५॥
भोगैर्बहुविधा चान्यैः कलाशिल्पशुभोदयैः ।
मनुष्याणां बोधिलब्धा मे तरुमूले महीतले ॥९६॥
मनुष्याणां धर्म निर्दिष्टः सर्वसत्त्वोपकारकम् ।
अत एव मनुष्याणां चिता दीपार्थयोजिता ॥९७॥
मनुष्योऽहं सर्वभूतानां अग्रथत्वं च समागतः ।
मनुष्यलोके च शान्ति मे परिनिर्वाणं तु कल्पितम् ॥९८॥
ये केचित् सर्वबुद्धा वै अतीतानागतवर्तिना ।
सर्वे वै मनुष्यलोकेऽस्मिं मनुष्या देहमुद्भवा ॥९९॥
जातिबोधि तथा चक्रं साधर्म्यं चरितुं शुभम् ।
शान्तिं समाविशेत् सर्वे प्रत्येकामर्हतस्त्रिधा ॥१००॥
G. ५८७ मानुषीं तनुमाश्रित्य गता शान्तिमनुत्तराम् ।
उपकारं मया तेषु कृतं कल्पामचिन्तिकाम् ॥१०१॥
आपश्चिमं मया शान्ते शीतीभूते निरोदये ।
स्थापिता धातवस्तत्र शून्यीभूते महीतले ॥१०२॥
मनुष्याणां हितार्थाय पूजानुग्रहकाम्यया ।
ससुरासुरलोकानां ऋषियक्षगरुत्मताम् ॥१०३॥
राक्षसां प्रेतकूश्माण्डां पिशाचां प्रेतमहर्द्धिकाम् ।
T. 431 a. सर्वांश्चैव भूतानां स-ग्रहाश्चैव मातरान् ॥१०४॥
सर्वांश्चैव तथा लोकां धात्वाचिन्त्यामसङ्ख्यकाम् ।
सर्वप्राणिभृतांश्चैव पूजनार्थाय धातवः ॥१०५॥
स्थापिता ते तदा काले शून्यीभूते महीतले ।
केचि द्रव्यागतैः मर्त्यैः देवराजैश्च चापरैः ॥१०६॥

---

९९. लोके । १०२. अ-पश्चिमे ।

पातालवासिभिश्चान्यैः दानवेन्द्रैर्महर्द्धिकैः ।
नागराजैस्तथा दैत्यैः धातवो मे पृथक् पृथक् ॥१०७॥
अपहृत्य हृतार्था ये गुणवन्तोऽथ महर्द्धिकाः ।
करिष्यन्ति तदा पूजां नीत्वा स्वभवनं पुनः ॥१०८॥
भविष्यन्ति न सन्देहः सर्वबुद्धा महर्द्धिकाः ।
उत्तमाधममध्यस्था त्रिधा चित्तप्रसादतः ॥१०९॥
भविष्यन्ति ते त्रिधा लोके बुद्धखड्गरर्हद्गता ।
त्रिधा यानं तथा लोके त्रिप्रकारं समोदितम् ॥११०॥
महायानानुवर्णिनं मार्गं तत्कर्माश्र (? श्रि) तनिर्गता ।
भविष्यन्ति तदा लोके प्रत्येकां बोधिनिःश्रिताम् ॥१११॥
श्रावकाश्च परे तत्र वीतरागमहर्द्धिका ।
भविष्यन्ति तदा लोके त्रिधा गोत्रविभूषिता ॥११२॥
महीपाला महाभोगा महासौम्याथ चक्रिणः ।
T. 431 b. दिव्यां मानुषसम्पत्तीः अनुभूय चिरं तदा ॥११३॥
G. ५८८ कालमासाद्य अन्ते वै त्रिधा शान्ति गता हि ते ।
आदिमद्भिः पुरा बुद्धैः वर्त्तमानैर्ह्यनागतैः ॥११४॥
सर्वेषां एष मार्गो वै यथार्थं सम्प्रकाशितः ।
तत्र निर्वाणभूमा वै निषण्णाः सर्वदेवता ॥११५॥
विभिन्नमनसोद्विग्नाः सहगद्गदभाषिणः ।
एवमाह तदा सर्वे अहो कष्टं ह्यनित्यता ॥११६॥
बुद्ध महर्द्धिका लोके परिनिर्वाणासृतापि ते ।
एवमुक्तास्तु ते सर्वे देवराजा महर्द्धिका ॥११७॥
(स शोकहृदया भूत्वा) तूष्णीम्भूताथ तस्थिरे ।
मागधानां जने श्रेष्ठे *कुशाग्रपुरिवासिनाम्* ॥११८॥
पर्वतं तत्समीपं तु *वाराहं* नाम नामतः ।
तत्रासौ ध्यायते भिक्षुः गुहालीनोऽथ पैपले ॥११९॥
श्रावको मे सुतो ह्यग्रः औरसो धर्मतोद्भवः ।
महाकाश्यपनामासौ निषण्णो गुहवरे तदा ॥१२०॥

---

१०९. सर्वे । ११०. खड्गार्हद्गताः । ११३. महासौम्यार्थं ।
११७. सितापि । ११९. वैभारं (?) ।

पिण्डपातं तदा भुक्त्वा निषण्णश्चिन्तयेत् स्वयम् ।
बहुकालं मया बुद्धो वन्दितोऽसौ महामुनिः ॥१२१॥
साम्प्रतं गन्तुमिच्छामि स्वयम्भुवं तं नरोत्तमम् ।
कुत्र वा तिष्ठते भगवां शाक्यतो मुनिसत्तमः ॥१२२॥
समन्वाहरति तत्रस्थः महाकाश्यप विप्रराट् ।
एवं समन्वाहृतवां नु चित्तेनैव मुनिना मुनिम् ॥१२३॥
T. 432 a. दिव्येन चक्षुषा लोकं सर्वलोकांश्चावलोकयेत् ।
अकनिष्ठाद्यं तथा लोकां अवभास्या लोकधातवः ॥१२४॥
सर्वां समप्रसत्त्वाख्यां महासाहस्रोद्भवोद्भवाम् ।
श्रावकानां गोचरं यावत् पश्यते दिव्यचक्षुषा ॥१२५॥
शासनं निर्वृतं शान्तं शीतीभूतं निरामिषम् ।
परिवारितं समन्ताद् वै देवसङ्घैः महर्द्धिकैः ॥१२६॥
G. ५८९ मनुजैर्नराधिपैश्चापि असुरैर्यक्षराक्षसैः ।
सर्वभूतगणैश्चापि बोधिसत्त्वैर्महर्द्धिकैः ॥१२७॥
महायशैः श्रावकैश्चापि प्राज्ञः धूर्धरतां गतैः ।
सरागैर्वीतरागैश्च दिव्यार्यैर्मनुजैस्तदा ॥१२८॥
चितामारोपितं वीरं बुद्धमादित्यबान्धवम् ।
देवदेवं तदा श्रेष्ठं मुनीनां सत्तमं प्रभुम् ॥१२९॥
परिवारित समन्ताद् वै भूपालैर्द्वीपवासिभिः ।
तृणोल्कैर्गृहीतसंहस्तैः मल्लैश्चापि मनुजेश्वरैः ॥१३०॥
नादीपयितुं समर्था ते देवताभिर्निवारिता ।
व्रतिना चैवमुक्तेन अनिरुद्धेनैव भिक्षुणा ॥१३१॥
साश्रुकण्ठं स चोत्क्रुष्टां विघुष्टांश्चैव मेदिनीम् ।
हाहाकाररवं घोरं दुन्दुभीनां च नादितम् ॥१३२॥
T. 432 b. दिव्यं ऋषिगणाकीर्णं अप्सरां(-)गणसंस्तुतम् ।
सिद्धविद्याधरीगीतं किन्नरोद्गीतं च तद् वनम् ॥१३३॥
मधुराकूजितोद्घुष्टं पक्षिणां रुदितं शुभम् ।
चित्रं मनोज्ञवादित्रं दिव्यमानुष्यनादितम् ॥१३४॥
अप्सरागणसङ्कीर्णं सिद्धविद्याधरोषितम् ।
योगिभिः सर्वतः कीर्णं अभूत् सालवनं वनम् ॥१३५॥

---

१२८. प्रज्ञाधुरन्धरता ।

समन्तात् परिवृतं श्रेष्ठं शयानं मुनिपुङ्गवम् ।
ततोर्ध्वं निःश्वस्य सशोको वै वीतशोको ।।१३६।।
अश्रुबिन्दुं प्रमुञ्चं वै श्रमणः काश्यपस्तदा ।
अग्रश्रावको मह्यं पृथिव्यामावर्तते तदा ।।१३७।।
वाचं चाभाषते क्षिप्रं अहो कष्टं प्रवर्तते ।
यत्र नाम तथा बुद्धाः परिनिर्वर्त्य नाश्रवाः ।।१३८।।
अनित्यं दुःखशून्यं तु इह तेनैव भाषितम् ।
न दृष्टो मे शाश्वतो विश्वं अन्यजन्मानुवर्तिनम् ।।१३९।।
G. ५९० ततोत्थाय ततः क्षिप्रं मगधानां नृपति व्रजेत् ।
अजातशत्रुं दुःखार्त्तं पितृशोकसमर्पिम् ।।१४०।।
गृहं तस्य तदा गत्वा तमुवाच नराधिपम् ।
निर्वृतोऽसौ महाराज ! सम्बुद्धो द्विपदोत्तमः ।।१४१।।
क्षिप्र योजय मानं तु गच्छामो शास्तु मन्तिकम् ।
धरणिस्थं शयानं वै निर्ज्वरं गतचेतसम् ।।१४२।।
सर्ववैरभयातीतं सम्भोग्यं कायसममम् ।
T. 433 a. श्रुत्वा तद्वचनं क्रूरं सुदुःखी सौ नृपतिः पुनः ।।१४३।।
अन्तः प्रलापं क्रन्दन्तः वाचां भाषे तदा नृप ।
उभाभ्यामपि भ्रष्टोऽहं शास्तुनो पितरस्य च ।।१४४।।
सर्वैर्बान्धवै त्यक्त्वा अविश्वास्योऽहं तथा जने ।
पतितोऽहं घोरनरकं कः शरण्यं वृणोम्यहम् ।।१४५।।
परित्रायस्व महावीर श्रावकः शास्तुमग्रकः ।
महाकाश्यपो महातेजा नास्ति मे जीवितं इह ।।१४६।।
इत्येवमुक्त्वा तु नृपो मुख्यो मागधानां नराधिपः ।
प्रपतितः तत्क्षणामुर्व्यां अग्रश्रावकपादयोः ।।१४७।।
निश्चेष्टो मूर्च्छितस्तत्र सहसा शयते महीम् ।
त्वं कुमार तदा कालं मञ्जुघोष महर्द्धिक ।।१४८।।
समन्ताद् विचरसे लोकां सत्त्वानुग्रहकाम्यया ।
चितामारोपिते देहे मम स्थाने वने तदा ।।१४९।।
मन्त्र त्वं निषण्णोऽभूद् बोधिसत्त्वगणावृतः ।
मच्छरीरं हि पूजार्थं त्वया कृत्वेह महीतले ।।१५०।।

---

१३७. ब्राह्मणः ।   १४२. यानं । अन्तिकम् ।   १४३. सत्तमम् ।   १४५. कं ।

समन्ताद्वालोकयसे भूतां को हि दुःखी कमुद्धरेत ।
इत्यहं पतितो भूमौ कुमारो गम्भीरतथ्यधीः ॥१५१॥
मञ्जुश्रियाथ त्वया वश्य भूपालस्यातिदुःखिते ।
तत्रस्थोऽपि त्वया तस्य त्वयैव विनयिनोऽसौ ॥१५२॥
T.433b. G.५९१ बोधिसत्त्वावगम्यो यो न तच्छक्यं महर्द्धिकैः ।
दैवतै ऋषिभिश्चान्यैः प्रत्येकार्हश्रावकैः ॥१५३॥
तत्रस्थः स्वप्नवत्पश्येन्मञ्जुघोषं नराधिपम् ।
त्वयैव ऋद्धिमाविष्टः स राजा शोकमूर्च्छितः ॥१५४॥
पश्यतेऽसौ तदा स्वप्ने प्रत्यक्षं च बालिनम् ।
कुमारं विश्वमात्मानं मञ्जुघोष महर्द्धिकम् ॥१५५॥
विकुर्वन्तं तथा धर्मं बोधिसत्त्वं स बालकम् ।
विचित्रं अचिन्त्यतां ऋद्धि मञ्जुश्रीः त्वत्प्रसादतः ॥१५६॥
अवीचिगमनं नृपतेः उत्थानं च सत्त्वरम् ।
विविधां धर्मतांश्चैव अपायं नाशशोभनम् ॥१५७॥
गतिमाहात्म्यगुणांश्चैव सर्वश्रावकवर्जिताम् ।
विस्तरेण ततः कृत्वा सूत्र कौकृत्यनाशनम् ॥१५८॥
अजातशत्रोर्नृपतेः विनोदं चातिविस्तरम् ।
समासेन इदं प्रोक्तं विस्तरार्थार्थभूषितम् ॥१५९॥
वचनं सर्वबुद्धानां आदिमध्यावसायिनाम् ।
सर्वसत्त्वहितार्थाय भाषितः कल्पविस्तरः ॥१६०॥
त्वं कुमार तदा काले मञ्जुश्रीर्वच सर्वतः ।
विनेष्यसि महीपालां पापकर्मानुवर्तिनाम् ॥१६१॥
अचिन्त्यं ते ऋद्धिविषयं विनेयं चापि अचिन्तितम ।
सर्वभूतगणांश्चैव त्वं विनेता भविष्यसि ॥१६२॥
इत्येवमुक्त्वा महावीरो बुद्धानां च महाद्युतिम् ।
T. 434 a. मञ्जुघोषं तदा काले शुद्धावासोपरिस्थितम् ॥१६३॥
उवाच वदतां श्रेष्ठः सम्बुद्धो द्विपदोत्तमः ।
भविष्यसि त्वं सम्बुद्धः बहुकल्पाभिनिर्गतैः ॥१६४॥
अचिन्त्यैर्गणनासङ्ख्यैर्मानुषैर्गणनासमैः ।
मञ्जुध्वजोऽथ नामो वै बुद्धा लोके भविष्यसि ॥१६५॥

---

१५२. पश्य । १६५. बुद्धो ।

G. ५९२ बुद्धकृत्यं तदा कृत्वा ह्यनुपूर्वेण यो सदा ।
विमोच्यथ बहुं सत्त्वां परिनिर्वाणं ते भविष्यति ॥१६६॥
इत्युक्त कुमारो वै बालरूपी महर्द्धिकः ।
स दीर्घं निःश्वस्य संविग्नः करुणाविष्टचेतसा ॥१६७॥
चिरमालोक्य सम्बुद्धं साश्रुबिन्दून् मुमूचचु ।
सप्रणामाञ्जलिपुटः निषसाद ततः पुनः ॥१६८॥
ततो क्ष्मातलाधस्थः अजाताख्यो नृपोत्तमः ।
प्रणम्य शिरसा विप्रं महाकाश्यपमद्भुतम् ॥१६९॥
विबुद्धश्चेतनायातं पादौ वन्द्य अग्रणः ।
निःश्वस्य च चिरं कालं विस्तरार्थं निवेद्य च ॥१७०॥
निषण्णो नृपतेः पुत्रः अजाताख्यो मगधेश्वरः ।
महाकाश्यपं ततो वव्रे गच्छामो स्तं चितालयम् ॥१७१॥
पूजितं चैत्यबिम्बस्थं उपकारार्हमानुषाम् ।
तत्रस्थः श्रावको ह्यग्रः श्रद्धया चैवमुपागमम् ॥१७२॥
T. 434 b. तस्योत्वहृते चित्तं अयुक्तं मम श्रद्धिये ।
पद्भ्यां गन्तुमिच्छामि महाचैत्तं समागमम् ॥१७३॥
अपश्चिमे गतिः शास्तुः दर्शनार्थं तु मागमम् ।
ततोऽर्धपथे तस्थुः सङ्घाराते तु स व्रती ॥१७४॥
यावत् पश्यते तत्र सङ्घारामनिवासिनम् ।
महल्लं भिक्षुनवक मुमायसत्त्वं विमोहितम् ॥१७५॥
स दृष्ट्वा उपसङ्क्रान्त महल्लो तं चिरोषिणम् ।
महेशाख्यं महाभागं शुद्धसत्त्वनिरामयम् ॥१७६॥
उपसङ्क्रम्य तं विप्रं वन्दित्वा पादयोस्तदा ।
उवाच तं महाभागं स्वागतं ते किमागतम् ॥१७७॥
कुत्र वा यास्यते क्षिप्रं उद्विग्नो वा किं व तिष्ठसे ।
उवाच सो तं ऋषिं तं बालं आयुष्मं न श्रुतं त्वया ॥१७८॥
G. ५९३ शास्ता वै सर्वलोकस्य सम्बुद्धो द्विपदोत्तमः ।
पिता मे अग्रधीः बुद्धः प्रदीपार्चिरिव निर्वृतः ॥१७९॥

---

१६६. वै । १७०. अग्रतः । १७१. महेश्वरः । तं । १७३. तस्योपाहृतं
१७४. संसारस्थः । १७५. पापसत्त्वं ।

अस्तं गतो महावीरः शून्योभूता हि मेदिनी ।
सर्वशून्यास्तथा लोकाः शून्या भूताश्च मे दिशाः ॥१८०॥
ततः प्रहृष्टो महल्लोऽसौ विपरीतो बालचेतनः ।
प्रसह्य वचनं चाह निर्वृतोऽसौ प्रदीर्घकः ॥१८१॥
प्रलम्बबाहुरत्युच्चच्छत्राकारसमशिरः ।
अस्माकं नायको ह्यमः शिक्षाशिक्षसुवर्तिनः ॥१८२॥
यथेष्टं विचरिष्यामि साम्प्रतं तेन निर्वृते ।
T. 435 a. इत्येवमुक्तो महल्लेन प्रहृष्टोऽसौ महर्द्धिकः ॥१८३॥
भृकुटिं कृत्वा ततो वक्रे हुङ्कारोऽसौ प्रयोजयेत् ।
रुरुध्य तत्क्षणाद् विप्रः वासनाभावितो यतिः ॥१८४॥
हन्यान्महीतले तत्र पादाङ्गुष्ठेन तत्क्षणात् ।
सर्वं प्रचलिता उर्वी पर्वतोद्याः समो रवः ॥१८५॥
क्षुभिताः सागराः सर्वे सर्वे वृक्षाश्च पर्वताः ।
कन्दरा गुहविन्यस्ता नागराजाश्च देवता ॥१८६॥
नष्टालोका मही तस्मिं काले चन्द्रभास्करौ ।
निवाता वा ततस्तस्थुः उल्काश्चापि पपेतुरे ॥१८७॥
ततोऽसौ मन्त्रमिति ख्यातः श्रावकाणां कुलोद्भवम् ।
एकाक्षरः स हुङ्कारः सर्वकर्मकरः शुभः ॥१८८॥
असाधितोऽपि करोत्येष जापमात्रेण मन्त्रराट् ।
सर्वशस्त्रांस्तथा स्तम्भं विषं स्थावरजङ्गमम् ॥१८९॥
सर्वेषां दुष्टसत्त्वानां जापमात्रेण स्तम्भनः ।
करोति कर्मवैचित्र्यं अन्यांश्चैव विशेषतः ॥१९०॥
प्रपलानो महल्लकस्तत्र तूष्णीम्भूतो ह्यतो गतः ।
श्रद्धया चावर्जितस्तेन विनयित्वा च तत्क्षणात् ॥१९१॥
G. ५९४ श्रावकेण तदाग्रेण नीतोऽसौ चितिसन्निधौ ।
पञ्चथां गतो हि सो भिक्षुः वीतरागो महर्द्धिकः ॥१९२॥
T. 435 b. गत्वासौ पश्यते तत्र मुनिनो देहचिताश्रिताम् ।
अनेकधा दैवसङ्घैस्तु महापूजां प्रवर्तिताम् ॥१९३॥
विविधाकारवरोपेतां सर्वाकारसुभूषिताम् ।
चितामारोपितं देहं मुनिनो गौतमस्य वै ॥१९४॥

---

१८४. वक्रे । रुरोध ।

दृष्ट्वा तु तं महाभागं *महाकाश्यप*मद्भुतम् ।
सर्वे ते वीतदोषा वै भिक्षवश्च महर्द्धिकाः ॥१९५॥
सर्वे देवगणा भूताः हाहाकारं प्रमुच्य च ।
आक्रन्द्य च महच्छब्दं रवं चापि सुशोकजम् ॥१९६॥
प्रत्युद्गम्य ततः सर्वे देवनागा महर्द्धिकाः ।
उवाच तं महाभागं वन्दस्व द्विपदोत्तमम् ॥१९७॥
तवैचोदीक्षणंतं विश्वा देवसङ्घा समानुषाः ।
सर्वे भूतगणाश्चैव ऋषयश्च नराधिपाः ॥१९८॥
पितादीपनतं निष्ठा अशक्ता दीपयितुं चिताम् ।
ततोऽसौ वीतदोषस्तु महाभोगो महर्द्धिकः ॥१९९॥
कृत्वा प्रदक्षिणं बाहु बहुधानुस्मृत्य तथागतम् ।
चितान्ते अन्तिमे भागे वन्दतेऽसौ महर्द्धिकः ॥२००॥
आयसीं च तदा द्रोणीं भित्वा पादौ विनिर्गतौ ।
वन्दित्वा पादयोर्मूर्ध्ना परामृश्य पुनः पुनः ॥२०१॥
उद्वीक्ष्य बहुधा तत्र चरणौ मुनिवरे वरौ ।
प्रविष्टा भूयसस्तत्र आयसीं द्रोणिमाश्रितौ ॥२०२॥
T. 436 a. निषण्णोऽसौ ततोत्थाय वीतरागो महर्द्धिकः ।
परिवारोऽथ अर्हन्तैः वीतरागैर्महर्द्धिभिः ॥२०३॥
राजा *मागधो* मुख्यः आगतोऽसौ चितान्तिके ।
अनुपूर्व्या तथा यानैः हस्त्यश्वरथवाहनैः ॥२०४॥
G. ५९५ महासैन्याथ भूपालाः सर्वे स-बलवाहनाः ।
आगता वन्दितुं तत्र मुनिं शाक्यमुनिं तदा ॥२०५॥
शयानं भूतले शान्ते प्रान्तेऽरण्ये (च निर्वृतम्) ।
नद्या *हिरण्यवती*तीरे चैत्ये *मकुटबन्धने* ॥२०६॥
शान्तधातुसमाविष्टे भूतकोटिसमासृते ।
मागधो नृपतिस्तत्र महासैन्यसमागतः ॥२०७॥
सोऽपि पश्यति तं दिव्यं विविधाकारचेष्टितम् ।
महानुशंसं प्रभावं च आश्चर्यं भुवि मण्डनम् ॥२०८॥

---

१९९. चिता ।   २०७. समाश्रिते ।

चैत्तदेहजं तत्र चितामारोपितं मुनिम् ।
आनन्दो नामतो भिक्षुः सुशैक्षे परिचारकः ॥२०९॥
यमेव मनुजं श्रेष्ठं वत्सलो मे सदा रतः ।
भविष्यति तदा काले आर्त्तो विक्लवमानसः ॥२१०॥
महाकाश्यपं ततो गत्य पादयोर्निपतितो भुवि ।
एवं चोवाच दुःखार्तः वेपथुन्ते सगद्गदः ॥२११॥
अद्य मे निर्वृतः शास्ता अनाथोऽहं स साम्प्रतम् ।
सति मे लयनं त्राणं त्वमेव परिकीर्त्तितः ॥२१२॥
T. 436 b. तेनैव मुनिचन्द्रेण व्याकृतोऽहं तवान्तिके ।
सर्वक्लेशप्रहाणां तु अर्हत्वं त्वमन्तिके ॥२१३॥
रात्र्यां पश्चिमे यामे निर्दिष्टं तेन जिनेन वै ।
म्रियते तुभ्य नित्यं वै मयैव परिनिर्वृतः ॥२१४॥
बुद्धकृत्यार्थं तुभ्यं वै कृतं तेन हितैषिणा ।
मयापि दुःखितः त्यक्त्वा शान्तियातो महामुनिः ॥२१५॥
अनिरुद्धो नामतो धीमां समाश्वासयति तं यतिम् ।
मा रोदन्तथा शोचं मा शोकं च समाविश ॥२१६॥
मा व्रज कुत्र वस्थानं एतमेव समाश्रय ।
एष एव भवेच्छास्ता निर्वृते लोकचक्षुषे ॥२१७॥
G. ५९६ मुनिना व्याकृतो ह्यत्र बुद्धकृत्यं करिष्यति ।
वयं च भवता सार्धं अनुयास्याम् काश्यपम् ॥२१८॥
ऋद्धिमाश्चं महाभागं तेजवन्तं महद्युतिम् ।
द्वितीयमिव शास्तारं प्रतिबिम्बं महीतले ॥२१९॥
*महाकाश्यप*मुख्यं तु श्रावकाणां महर्द्धिकम् ।
तिष्ठन्तं ध्रियमाणं वै मा शोकं चेत्तु वै कृथा ॥२२०॥
एवमालापिनः सर्वे करुणाविष्टा महर्द्धिका ।
वीतरागा महायोगा मुनिपुत्रा निषण्णवाम् ॥२२१॥
चितामादीपितो तैस्तु मल्लैश्चापि नराधिपैः ।
आदीप्ते तु समन्ता वै भस्मीभूतं तु तं चितम् ॥२२२॥
T. 437 a. तं दृष्ट्वा देवसङ्घा तु भोगवन्तो महोरगाः ।
शान्तये तच्चितास्थानं चन्दनोदकवारिणा ॥२२३॥

---

२१३. प्रहाणं । २१८. भगवता ।

महावर्षं प्रमुञ्चन्ता स्थिता भूयोऽथ तत्क्षणात् ।
महापुष्पौघमुत्सृज्य पुनरेव महीतले ॥२२४॥
आगता तत्क्षणात् सर्वे जिनधातुं सुपूजना ।
सर्वे परस्परं युद्धं कर्तुमारब्ध तत्क्षणात् ॥२२५॥
ब्रह्माद्या शक्र-यामाश्च सर्वदेवगणास्तथा ।
निवारिता वीतरागैस्तु श्रावकैश्च महर्द्धिकैः ॥२२६॥
महाकाश्यपेन विभज्यं वै धातवो जिनमूर्तिजा ।
स्तोकस्तोकानि दत्तानि पूजनार्थाय सर्वतः ॥२२७॥
त्रिधा यानपरावृत्तिं निष्ठाशान्ति च कारणात् ।
महाकाश्यपस्तदा योगी वीतरागो महर्द्धिकः ॥२२८॥
चिन्तयामास तं बोध्यं महल्लकस्य अभाषितम् ।
माहैव प्रवचनं कृत्स्नं द्वादशाङ्गं सुखोदयम् ॥२२९॥
सूत्रविनयाभिधर्मे वै धूमकालिकतां व्रजेत् ।
अस्तं याते महवीरे विप्रलोपो भविष्यति ॥२३०॥
G. ५९७ सङ्गातव्यमिमं कृत्स्नं वचनं बुद्धभाषितम् ।
गच्छामः सहिताः सर्वे वीतरागा महर्द्धिकाः ॥२३१॥
मागधानां पुरं श्रेष्ठं *राजाख्यं* नगरं शुभम् ।
T. 437 b. *कुशाग्रपुरे* रम्ये पर्वते सुशिलोच्चये ॥२३२॥
वैशाल्यां च शुभे देशे चैतस्थाने सुशोभने ।
एवम्प्रकारा ह्यनेकांश्च शासनार्थं तु कारणात् ॥२३३॥
मल्ला पलायिनः सर्वे चक्रिरे स महर्द्धिका ।
तस्मिं काले युगान्ते वै अस्तं याते मया तु वै ॥२३४॥
महीपाला भविष्यन्ति परस्परविधे रता ।
भिक्षवो बहुकर्मान्ता सत्वा लोभमूर्च्छिता ॥२३५॥
अश्राद्धा युगान्ते वै उपासकोपासिकास्तथा ।
परस्परवधासक्ताः परस्परगवेषिणः ॥२३६॥
छिद्रप्रहारिणो नित्यं सव्रणा दोषदस्तथा ।
भिक्षवो ह्यसंयतास्तत्र मुनिरस्तं गते युगे ॥२३७॥
स्थापिता रक्षणार्थाय शासनं भुवि मे तदा ।
अष्टौ महर्द्धिका लोके वीतरागा निराश्रवाः ॥२३८॥

---

२३०. नभधूमकता । २३४. संक्षेप-वचनं सर्वं उवाच स महर्द्धिकः ।

अर्हन्तः सदा ज्येष्ठा राहुलाद्या प्रकीर्त्तिता ।
तेषां दर्शनं नास्ति तस्मिं काले युमाधमे ॥२३९॥

अमोघं दर्शनं तेषां सिद्धिकाले तु मन्त्रिणाम् ।
मयात्र स्थापिताः सर्वे ऋद्धिमन्त्रो महर्द्धिकाः ॥२४०॥

प्रणिहितं मया तेषां दण्डकर्ममहायशाम् ।
आज्ञोल्लङ्घनं तेषां किञ्चिच्छिष्या व्यतिक्रमे ॥२४१॥

तिष्ठध्वं यावत् सद्धर्मं भूतकोटिं निरामिषम् ।
T. 438 a. मम वाक्यमिदं पुण्यं यावद् घुष्यते तले ॥२४२॥

ततः शान्ताः निरात्म(ा)नः परिनिर्वाथ निराश्रवाः ।
भविष्यति तदा काले शासनान्तर्हिते मुनौ ॥२४३॥

G. ५९८ भिक्षाभिक्षुकाः सर्वे भिक्षुण्यश्च सुमत्सराः ।
तर्कुकाः कुत्सिता नित्यं परिभूता तदा युगे ॥२४४॥

सुस्थिता शासने मह्यं गृहदारगवेषिणः ।
उपासकाश्च तदा काले परदारसदारताः सदा ॥२४५॥

चिह्नमात्रं तदा संज्ञा परिशेष्वेव चतुर्विधे ।
वैराभ्यासरताः सर्वे परस्परविहेठकाः ॥२४६॥

तीर्थिकाक्रान्तभुयिष्ठा सर्वाक्रान्ता च मेदिनी ।
भविष्यन्ति तदा काले द्विजवर्णरता जना ॥२४७॥

मिथ्याचारा तथा मूढा प्राणिहिंसारता नरा ।
मया तु परिनिर्वाणो व्याकृतोऽयं कलौ युगे ॥२४८॥

बहुनार्या नराश्चैव परदाररताः सदा ।
अकुशलेषु रताः सर्वे कुशलार्थार्थवर्जिताः ॥२४९॥

बहुसत्त्वा भविष्यन्ति मयि शान्तगते भुवि ।
ममैतच्छरीरपूजा तु देवसङ्घा महोजसा ॥२५०॥

मनुष्याश्चैव महात्मानो यक्षभूतगणास्तथा ।
T. 438 b. असुरा अथ गन्धर्वा किन्नराश्च महर्द्धिकाः ॥२५१॥

गरुडा अथ गन्धर्वा राक्षसा ऋषयस्तथा ।
सिद्धा योगिनश्चैव (ब्रह्माश्चैव) महोजसा ॥२५२॥

---

२३९. युगाधमे । २४०. मंत्राः । २४६. परिशेषैव । २४७. देवाक्रान्ता ।
२४९. र्थ-थि ।

विविधाकारसत्त्वास्तु विविधां गतियोनिजाः ।
भवसूत्रनिबद्धास्तु च्छिन्नबन्धनधीमता ॥२५३॥
करिष्यति तदा पूजां शरीरेऽस्मिं गतिज्वरे ।
नदी*हिरण्यवती*तीरे यमकशालवने वने ॥२५४॥
चैत्ये *मकुटबन्धे* तु *मल्लानामुपवर्तने* ।
परिनिर्वृते च तत्राहं शान्तिं गच्छेद् भयवर्जिताम् ॥२५५॥
ममैतद् धातु सङ्गृह्य ह्रयमाणैः परैस्तदा ।
देवैश्चासुरैश्चापि सर्वभूतगणैस्तथा ॥२५६॥
G. ५९९ विभज्य स पृथग् भागेषु व्यस्तं कारिता अभूत् ।
मनुष्यराजा महासैन्यः *अजाताख्यो मागधस्तदा* ॥२५७॥
प्र (ा) र्थयामास सर्वेषां श्रावकां सुमहर्द्धिकाम् ।
ममाप्यकृतपुण्यस्य पितुर्मरणकारिणः ॥२५८॥
अभ्युद्धरथ महात्मानं दुःखितं पतितं तु माम् ।
ततोऽग्र्यः श्रावको धीमां बुद्धस्य सुतमौरसः ॥२५९॥
महाकाश्यपेति विख्यातः प्रजानां हितकारकः ।
तं तु दृष्ट्वाथ वैक्लव्यं अजाताख्यास्य धीमतः ॥२६०॥
समन्वाहरति तत्कालं ऋद्धया चैवमधिष्ठयेत् ।
T. 439 a. भागैकं गृह्णयामास स धातूनां जिननिःश्रिताम् ॥२६१॥
अन्येदपहृतादन्यैः भोगिभिश्च महाबलैः ।
अन्योन्यरभसात् क्षोभं कृत्वा चैव परस्परम् ॥२६२॥
नीत्वा धातुं तदाकाशैः स्वगृहं चापि तस्थुते ।
महाकाश्यपो तदा भिक्षुः अग्रश्रावकः तदा मुनिः ॥२६३॥
चिन्तयामास
अहो कष्टं मनुष्येषु शून्योऽयं भुवि मण्डले ॥२६४॥
बुद्धैः प्रत्येकबुद्धैस्तु श्रावकैश्च महर्द्धिकैः ।
आलोकहीना सत्त्वा वै भवचारकचारिणा ॥२६५॥
ते दुःखां विविधां तीव्रां अनुभविष्यति ते चिरम् ।
धातुं पूजयित्वा तु लोकनाथस्य तापिने ॥२६६॥

---

२५३. गत । २५६. ह्रियमाणैः । तथा, दैवैश्चैवा । २५९. महात्मानो । २६०. ही ।
२६१. धातून् । नू । २६३. मुनेः चिन्तयामास । २६६. तायिनः ।

अनुभविष्यन्ति ते सौख्यं देवलोकमनल्पकम् ।
राज्यं च मथ भोगांश्च मन्त्रसिद्धिसुदुर्लभाम् ॥२६७॥
प्राप्स्यन्ति विविधाकारां विचित्रगतिचेष्टिताम् ।
लोकस्याग्रा सम्पदामिष्टां त्रिधा मोक्ष (वि)भूषिताम् ॥२६८॥
पूजयित्वा तु धातूनां प्राप्नुयात् सिद्धिमुत्तमाम् ।
एवं चिन्तयित्वा तु ब्राह्मणः लोकविश्रुतः ॥२६९॥
G. ६०० श्रावको मुनिवरे ज्येष्ठः *काश्यपो* नाम नामतः ।
सङ्गृह्य च तदा धातुं संबिभर्त्ति तदा भुवि ॥२७०॥
स्तोकं दत्वाजाताख्ये *मागध*स्यैव यत्नतः ।
एवं नराधिपेषु सर्वेषु अष्टेष्वपि महाद्युतिः ॥२७१॥
T. 439 b. सर्वेभ्यः सर्वतो दद्याच्छ्रावकोऽसौ महात्मनः ।
पुनरेव भवस्तस्था अनित्यसंज्ञमभावत ॥२७२॥
शोचयामास सत्त्वानां करुणाविष्टेन चेतसा ।
रोदिष्यन्ति चिरं सत्त्वा कल्पां बहुविधां तथा ॥२७३॥
सद्धर्मिन्तर्धिते लोके शास्तुनो शाक्यपुङ्गवे ।
सङ्गातव्यमिमं वाच्यं माहैवं धूमकालिकम् ॥२७४॥
ततोऽभ्युत्थितवां वीरः प्रभावामृतचेतसः ।
आमन्त्रयामास मन्त्रजेन्द्रं *अजाताख्यं* नराधिपम् ॥२७५॥
गच्छामो *राजगृहं* नगरं शास्तुशासनसत्कथा ।
गाथकुम्भसुविन्यस्तां धातुं प्रक्षिप्य यत्नतः ॥२७६॥
तेऽत्र पूर्वेण आयाता क्षिप्रं *राजगृहं* तदा ।
स्थानं *वेणुवनं* प्राप्य स्थापयामास जिनोद्भवाम् ॥२७७॥
स्तूपं महाद्भुतं कृत्वासौ लोकनाथस्य तापिने ।
पूजयामास तं स्तूपं विविधाकारभूषणैः ॥२७८॥
माल्यचीवरच्छत्रैश्च चूर्णगन्धैस्तु धूपनैः ।
ध्वजैः पताकैर्विचित्रैश्च घण्टामाल्यविलेपनैः ॥२७९॥

---

२६७. चैवाथ । २७०. वरो । विभज्य । २७२. स्मा । २७४. वाक्यं । सद्धर्मेऽन्तर्हिते । २७५. मञ्जुजेन्द्रं (मि-यि-यूवइ्-पो) । भित । २७६, कारणात् । यात । २७७. धातुकान् । २७८. तायिनः ।

अनेकाकारविचित्रैस्तु दीपमालाभि रश्मिभिः ।
पूजां कृत्वा महीपाल प्रणामगतचेतसः ॥२८०॥
मूर्ध्ना प्रणम्य तं स्तूपं प्रणिधिं चक्रिरे तदा ।
लोकाग्रं पूजजित्वा तु यन्मया कुशलं बहु ॥२८१॥
अनेकताथागतीपूजां प्राप्नुयाहमचिन्तिया ।
उत्थाय ततो राजा *महाकाश्यप*मब्रवीत् ॥२८२॥
T.440a. G.६०१ अश्रु सम्परामृज्य बाष्पाकुलितलोचनः ।
कृपाविष्टहृदयः पितरं संस्मरेत् तदा ॥२८३॥
आर्यो मे महाप्राज्ञः साक्षिभूतो भवस्व माम् ।
यन्मया कारितं पापं नियतावीचिपरायणम् ॥२८४॥
तादृशं धर्मराजं तु शास्तुर्वचनपथे स्थितम् ।
घातयित्वा तु तं पितरं न शक्नोमि विनोदितुम् ॥२८५॥
कल्याणमित्र आर्यो मे धमार्थं देष्टुमर्हति ।
एवमुक्तो महात्मासौ अग्रश्रावकौ जिने ॥२८६॥
काश्यपो नामतः धीमां इमं वाचमुदीरयेत् ।
मा भैष्ट महाराज कृतं ते कुशलं बहु ॥२८७॥
अस्ति ते जन्मिनोऽभ्यासः अनेकशतधा पुरा ।
बुद्धानामनुत्पादा प्रत्येकजिनसम्भवः ॥२८८॥
नगर्यां *वाराणस्यां* श्रेष्ठिपुत्र अभूत् तदा ।
अज्ञानाद् बालचापल्याद् रथ्यायां निर्ययौ तदा ॥२८९॥
स एव भगवं तत्र प्रत्येकजिनमागतः ।
भिक्षार्थी हिण्डते तत्र लोकानुग्रहकाम्यया ॥२९०॥
(अहं) बालस्य दृष्ट्वा तं प्रसन्नगतमानसम् ।
पादयोर्निपत्य पप्रच्छ किं करिष्यसि तैर्भिक्षु ॥२९१॥
तूष्णीमेव स्थितो भगवां खड्गकल्पमसम्भव ।
तदा तेन तु बालेन चीवरे गृह्यमस्थित ॥२९२॥
गच्छ गच्छ इमं श्रेष्ठं मन्दिरं ध्वजभूषितम् ।
T. 440 b. अस्माकमेतदावासं पादौ प्रक्षाल्य भोक्षसे ॥२९३॥
भुंक्ष्व क्षिप्रं यथाकामं क्रीडिष्यामो यथेष्टतः ।
ततोऽसौ वीतदोषस्तु त्रिमलान्तकघातकः ॥२९४॥

---

२८६. धर्मार्थं । २९१. त्वं भिक्षुः ।

अनुपूर्वेण ययौ तत्र परानुग्रहतत्परः ।
गत्वा द्वारमूलेऽस्मिं स्थित एव महाद्युतिः ॥२९५॥
G. १०२ ततस्तेन तु बालेन प्रविशित्वा अम्ब उच्यते ।
देहि भक्त मया अम्ब भिक्षांश्च विविधां बहूम् ॥२९६॥
मित्रो मे ह्यागतो ह्यत्र पांसुक्रीडनकश्चिरात् ।
मोदिष्यसि चिरं तेन तिष्ठते द्वारमागतः ॥२९७॥
तदा स त्वरमाना तु द्वारं निर्ययु तत्क्षणात् ।
पश्यते तं महाभागं शान्तवेषं महर्द्धिकम् ॥२९८॥
तदा सा क्षिप्रमागत्य गृहीत्वा भाजनं शुभम् ।
सुप्रक्षाल्य ततो हस्तौ (पुष्पधूपसुवासितम्) ॥२९९॥
गृहीत्वा ओदनं चौक्षमनेकरसभूषितम् ।
विविधाकारभक्षांश्च भाजने न्यस्य राजते ॥३००॥
आगम्य च तदा क्षिप्रं पात्रे निवेश्य च ।
पादयोर्निपतिता सा तु ससुता धर्मवत्सला ॥३०१॥
गृहीत्वासौ पिण्डपातं तु आकाशे अभ्यगच्छत ।
ततोऽसौ ज्वलमानस्तु दीपमालेव दृश्यते ॥३०२॥
तेन तेषां वाचिको धर्मे विद्यते खड्गचारिणाम् ।
T. 441 a. प्रभाव ऋद्धिसत्त्वानां दर्शयन्ति महात्मनः ॥३०३॥
अतिकारुणिका तेऽपि सत्त्वेभ्यो गतमत्सराः ।
परलोकार्थं तु सत्त्वेभ्यः ऋद्धिं सन्दर्शयन्ति ते ॥३०४॥
तेन कर्मविपाकेन मात्रया सह बालकः ।
पञ्चजन्मसहस्राणि देवत्वमथ कारयेत् ॥३०५॥
देवानां देवराजासौ सा एव जननी अभूत् ।
अमनुष्याणां चक्रवर्त्तित्वं मनुजेश अभूत् तदा ॥३०६॥
अनुभूय चिरं सौख्यं *बिम्बासारसुतो* इह ।
यस्ते आकर्षितो भगवां चीवरान्तेऽथ गृह्य च ॥३०७॥
वाचा दुर्भाषिता उक्ता भिक्षुवादेन चोदितः ।
पांसुक्रीडनको मह्यं भवस्वेति पुरा तदा ॥३०८॥
G. १०३ वाचो गतस्य कर्मस्य अनिष्टस्य कटुकस्य च ।
तीव्रं प्रतापनादुःखं अनुभूय चिरं बहु ॥३०९॥

---

२९८. महात्मानं । ३००. शुक्ल । ३०७. बिंबसार ।

नरके पतितो घोरे अनीप्सको दुःखदुःसहम् ।
कर्मपाशानुबद्धास्तु सत्त्वा गच्छन्ति दुर्गतिम् ॥३१०॥
हसद्भिः क्रियते कर्म रुदद्भिरनुभूयते ।
पूर्वं बालिशभावेन प्रत्येकजिनतापिने ॥३११॥
वाचा निश्चारिता दुष्टा तस्य कर्मस्य ईदृशम् ।
नरकेभ्यः व्यसित्वा तु मनुष्यत्वमिहागतः ॥३१२॥
नारके चेतना ह्यासीद् विपाकजाते नराधिप ।
T. 441 b. तेन तीव्रेण रोषेण जीविता ते द्रुतपूर्विकाम् ॥३१३॥
पूर्विकां वासनां स्मृत्वा प्रत्येकजिनचारिणीम् ।
सम्मुखं दर्शितो बुद्धः पूज्यश्चैवमकारिता ॥३१४॥
तेनैव हेतुना ह्यासीद् राज्यत्वमिह कारय ।
एवं वेणुवने तेषां अन्योन्या संलपेद् भुवि ॥३१५॥
एकश्च अग्रशिष्यो मे द्वितीयः स नराधिप ! ।
प्रणम्य शतधा स्तूपं स्वगृहेणैव ययौ तदा ॥३१६॥
ततोऽसौ शिष्यमुख्यैर्मे *पिप्पलागुह*वासिनः ।
सन्निपात्य मुनि सर्वां वीतरागां महर्द्धिकाम् ॥३१७॥
द्वादशाङ्गं प्रवचनं कृत्स्नं विनयं चैवमगायत ।
तन्मया कथितो धर्मः पूर्वं जिनवरैस्तथा ॥३१८॥
स तेन शिष्यवराग्रेण त्रिप्रकारं समादिशेत् ।
प्रथनं सूत्रभेदेष विनये वाभिधर्मतः ॥३१९॥
तृबन्धान्मोचयेत् सत्त्वां त्रिदोषां चापि शोषयेत् ।
तृदुखान्मुक्तवां धीरः त्रियानं स्थापयेत् तदा ॥३२०॥

Śaiśunākas

शासनार्थं तु बुद्धानां कारयिष्यति अग्रधीः ।
महाराजाजातविख्यातो *मागधेयो* नराधिपः ॥३२१॥
G. १०४ यावदादङ्कपर्यन्तं *वाराणस्या*मतत्परम् ।
उत्तरेण तु *वैशाल्यां* राजा सोऽथ महाबलः ॥३२२॥

३११. तायिने । ३१२. वसित्वा । ३१३. पिता हतः । ३१७. मुख्यो मे ।
३१९. भेदेन विनयेनाऽभिधर्मतः । ३२१. ह्यजुरिति । ३२२. यावन्मगधाङ्ग । अतः परम् ।

T. 442 a. भविष्यति न सन्देहः शासनार्थं करिष्यति ।
त्वया कुमार ! निर्दिष्टः व्याकृतः शान्तिमुत्तमे ॥३२३॥
तस्यापि सुतो राजा उकाराख्यः प्रकीर्त्तितः ।
भविष्यति तदा क्षिप्रं शासनार्थं च उद्यतः ॥३२४॥
तदेतत् प्रवचनं शास्तु लिखापयिष्यति विस्तरम् ।
पूजांश्च महतीं कृत्वा दिक्समन्तान्नयिष्यति ॥३२५॥
न चास्य दुर्गतिं चास्य देवेषूपपत्स्यते ।
विंशाद् वर्षाणि त्रिंशाच्च पितृणा सह जन्मिनः ॥३२६॥
वेलायामर्धरात्रे तु पञ्चत्वं यास्यते तदा ।
गोत्रजेनैव रोगेण अभिभूतोऽसौ भविष्यति ॥३२७॥
महारोगेण दुःखार्त्तः दिवसानि षड्विंशति ।
समस्तव्याधिग्रस्तोऽसौ विविधाकारमूर्छितः ॥३२८॥
च्युतोऽसौ नरपतिः क्षिप्र देशेषूपपत्स्यते ।
नियतं प्राप्स्यते बोधि सोऽनुपूर्वेण यत्नतः ॥३२९॥
एते चान्ये च बहवः अतीता येऽप्यनागता ।
कृत्वा तु विविधां कारां प्रत्येकजिनतापिषु ॥३३०॥
इष्टां विशिष्टां सम्पत्तिं दिव्या मानुषिकांस्तथा ।
तेऽनुपूर्वेण गच्छन्ति शान्तिं निर्जरसम्पदम् ॥३३१॥
हीनोत्कृष्टराजानो मध्यमाश्च नराधिपाः ।

§ 2. Ancient Kings [before the Buddha]

आद्ये तु युगे कथिता नहुषाद्या पार्थिवादयः ॥३३२॥
बुधशुक्रोदयो नित्यं मन्त्रसिद्धा नराधिपा ।
शान्तनुश्चित्र-सुमित्रश्च पाण्डवा सनराधिपाः ॥३३३॥
यातवा वारयस्याश्च रिषिशापास्तभिन्ना तदा ।
कार्त्तिकः कार्त्तवीर्योऽसौ दशरथदाशरथी पुरा ॥३३४॥
अर्जुनः सिद्धमन्त्रस्तु द्विद्रोणसुतोऽपरः ।
अश्वात्थामा परो मन्त्री साधयामास मन्त्रराट् ॥३३५॥
G. १०५ शास्तुमूर्जितमन्त्रार्थैः क्ष्मापत्यं कारयेत् तदा ।
समन्तात् त्रिषु द्वीपेषु जम्बुद्वीपगता तदा ॥३३६॥

---

३२७. बलनगरेऽ(मोङ्-क्येद्-सुलोष्-कूदम्-मूछन्-प्येद्-दु)। ३२९. देवे।
३३०. तापिषु।

देवकाराश्चैव मन्त्राणि पार्थिवादयः ।

T. 442 b. तेऽपि ताथागतीं पूजां अनुमोद्या दिवं गताः ॥३३७॥

बुद्धत्वनियता तेऽपि केचित् प्रत्येकयानिका ।

श्रावकत्वनियता केचित् सर्वे ते मोक्षपरायणाः ॥३३८॥

कालव्य(व)स्थानुरूपेण आयुषश्च विकल्पते ।

उत्तमा दीर्घमानुष्ये मध्या मध्यमके तथा ॥३३९॥

अन्तिमे तु युगे कष्टे कलिप्राप्ते युगाधमे ।

(अपरे हीनशासनाः) पार्थिवा तु कलिप्रियाः ॥३४०॥

अन्योऽन्य-वैरसंसक्ता परस्परविहेढकाः ।

नीचोत्पत्तिमायाताः शस्त्रसम्पातमृत्तवः ॥३४१॥

शस्त्रप्रवृत्तिसमुत्साहा परदाराभिरतस्तदा ।

भविष्यन्ति न सन्देहः भूपाला लोककुत्सिताः ॥३४२॥

धूर्ता निकृष्टकर्माणः अनार्या मत्सरिणस्तथा ।

भविष्यन्ति तदा काले मध्ये द्वापरयो कलौ ॥३४३॥

संक्षेपेण तु वक्ष्यामि कुमारस्त्वं निबोधत ।

§ 3. Kings of the time of the Buddha

वर्तमाने तु यत्काले पार्थिवा भुवि मण्डले ॥३४४॥

तेषां तु रूपचिह्नानि वर्णतश्च निबोधताम् ।

प्रसेनजित् कोसलो राजा *बिम्बिसारस्तथापरः* ॥३४५॥

उदयनः क्षत्रियश्रेष्ठः *शतानीकसमुद्भवः* ।

*सुबाहु सुधनख्यातो महेन्द्र*चन्द्रसमस्तथा ॥३४६॥

T. 443 a. *लिच्छवीनां* तथा जातः सिंहो वैशाल्यमुद्भव ।

उदाविद्योतमुद्योतमहासेनश्च कथ्यते ॥३४७॥

उज्जयन्यां तथा चण्डः *कपिलाह्वे* पुरे नृपः ।

राजा *शुद्धोदनश्चैव* वैराटाख्यो महाबलः ॥३४८॥

G. ১০১ इत्येते क्षत्रियाः प्रोक्ता महीपालाः शास्तुपूजकाः ।

सम्मुखं बुद्ध पश्यन्ति शाक्यसिंहे नरोत्तमम् ॥३४९॥

---

३३९. दीर्घ । ३४१. विहेठकाः । ३४६. चमसस्तथा । ३४७. शाक्यवंशिकः । उदायि । प्रद्योत । ३४८. उज्जयिन्या । वीराख्यो । ३४९. शाक्यसिंह ।

धर्मं श्रुत्वा ततस्तेऽपि चिरं प्राप्स्यन्ति सम्पदाम् ।
नियतं मोक्षकामास्तु शान्तिं प्राप्स्यन्ति तेऽपि ताम् ॥३५०॥
इत्येते लोकविख्याता भूपाला क्षितिमण्डले ।
वर्णतः क्षत्रियः प्रोक्तः चिह्नतो नामसंज्ञितः ॥३५१॥
पूजयिष्यति ते वाक्यं मयैव कथितं भुवि ।
त्वयैव व्याकृतो लोके कुमारो बालरूपिणः ॥३५२॥
*अजाता*ख्यो नामसौ नियतं बोधिपरायणः ।

§ 4. "Hundred years after the Buddha"

मयि वर्षशते परिनिर्वृते भुवि मण्डले ॥३५३॥
निरालोके निरानन्दे अज्ञानतमसा वृते ।
भविष्यति तदा शून्या मेदिनी जिनवर्जिता ॥३५४॥
तस्मिं काले महाघोरे *कुसुमाह्वे* नगरे तदा ।
अशोको नाम विख्यातः पार्थिवो भुवि पालकः ॥३५५॥
तीव्रकारी सरोषी च निर्घृणोऽसौ भवेत् तदा ।
कल्याणमित्रमागम्य वीतरागं महर्द्धिकम् ॥३५६॥
भिक्षुं शीलसम्पन्नं निज्वरं गतचेतसम् ।
T. 443 b. पूर्ववासनहेतुं च पांशुदानं महर्द्धिकम् ॥३५७॥
नियतं क्षेत्रसम्पन्नं पार्थिवोऽसौ महाधनः ।
धर्माधर्मविचारी च सघृणी कारुणिको हि सौ ॥३५८॥
हेतुमुद्घाटयामास वीतरागो महर्द्धिकः ।
त्वया हि नृपतेः पूर्वं अज्ञानाद् बालचापलात् ॥३५९॥
जिने शाक्यसिंहस्य पांसु अञ्जलिना तदा ।
पात्रं भस्मे प्रतिष्ठाप्य प्राप्ता सम्पत्तयो दिवि ॥३६०॥
देवलोकं च्यवित्वा तु पितृलोकमिहागतम् ।
भुंक्ष्व राज्यं महीपाल ! जम्बूद्वीपं सकाननम् ॥३६१॥
G. ६०७ आराध्य मन्त्रं यक्षस्य जम्भलस्य महात्मने ।
ततो भूतरथः सिद्धः क्षितिपश्च महात्मनः ॥३६२॥
यक्षास्तस्य तिष्ठन्ते आज्ञो दीक्षितमानसाः ।
नागाश्चैव तिष्ठन्ते भव्याः किङ्करहेतवः ॥३६३॥

---

३५०. बोधिकामास्तु । ३५७. निर्ज्वरं । ३६०. भस्म । ३६१. च्यवित्वा । भूमिलोक ।

एवं महर्द्धिका धर्मात्मा बलचक्री अभूत् तदा ।
यथेष्टगमनं तस्य निषेद्धा न कश्चिद् भवेत् ॥३६४॥
पूर्वस्थापितकार्ये तु जिनानां धातुवरा भुवि ।
नगरे राजमुख्ये तु वने वेणुवने तदा ॥३६५॥
गृह्य धातुधरे धातुं कुशलालम्बनमानसः ।
पूजयामास तं स्तूपं यथा पौराणमकारय ॥३६६॥
गृह्यन्तं धातुकुम्भं तु विभज्य शतधा पुनः ।
T. 444 a. क्षणेनैकेन मेधावी यक्षाणामाज्ञा विनिर्दिशेत् ॥३६७॥
जम्बूद्वीप इमं कृत्स्नं स्तूपालङ्कृतभूषणम् ।
कारयन्तु भवन्तो वै धातुगर्भां वसुन्धराम् ॥३६८॥
आज्ञाप्रतीच्छते यक्षाः अर्धरात्रे तु यत्नतः ।
अमानुषेयं कृतिं कृत्वा शिलायष्ट्योच्छ्रितां भुवि ॥३६९॥
अनेकस्तम्भसहस्राणि रोपयामास ते तदा ।
पूजनार्थं तु चैत्यानां चिह्नभूतं च देहिनाम् ॥३७०॥
कृत्वा तु विविधां स्तूपां लोकनाथेभ्य तापिषु ।
क्षणेनैकेन ते यक्षा नृपतेऽन्तिकमागताः ॥३७१॥
प्रणिपत्य ततो मूर्ध्ना वाचा निश्चार गुह्यकाम् ।
यथाज्ञप्तं कृतं सर्वं किं न पश्यसि भू(प)ते ॥३७२॥
ततोऽसौ पार्थिवः क्षिप्रं आरुरोह रथं तदा ।
विविधाकारपूजार्थं अनेकाकारशोभनाम् ॥३७३॥
काञ्चनं राजतं ताम्रं विविधांस्तूपभूषणाम् ।
ततो भूतरथं क्षिप्रं पूरयामास पार्थिवः ॥३७४॥
G. १०८ क्षणेनेकेन तं देशं यत्र ते धातुधरा जिना ।
विचित्राकारपूजाभिः पूजयेत नराधिपः ॥३७५॥
शोभने मेदिनीं कृत्स्नां जिन धातुधरैस्तदा ।
प्रणिधिं चक्रिरे राजा *धर्मा*शोको महात्मवान् ॥३७६॥
T. 444 b. अनेन कुशलार्थेन बुद्धो भूमामनुत्तरः ।
एवं विदित्वा महात्मासौ *धर्मा*शोको नराधिपः ॥३७७॥

---

३६५. राजगृहे । ३६७. गृह्य तं । माज्ञां । ३७१. तायिषु । ३७५. पूजा ।
३७७. भूया ।

मृतोऽसौ देवतां याति नियतं बोधिपरायणः ।
अशीतिवर्षाणि सम्यं च पूजये धातुवरां भुवि ॥३७८॥
जीवेद् वर्षशतं सार्धं कृत्वा राज्यमकण्टकम् ।
स्वकर्मजनितास्तस्य व्याधिरुत्पन्नदेहजे ॥३७९॥
तेनैव व्याधितो दुःखी मृतः स्वर्गोपगो भवेत् ।
महतीं सम्पदं प्राप्य अनुभूय दिवौकसाम् ॥३८०॥
अनुपूर्वेण मेधावी बोधिं प्राप्स्यति दुर्लभाम् ।
मन्त्रा सिद्ध्यन्ति तत्काले वज्राब्जकुलयोरपि ॥३८१॥
जम्भलाद्यास्तथा यक्षा अस्मिं शासनवर्त्तिनः ।
यक्षिण्यश्च समाख्याता हारीत्याद्या महर्द्धिकाः ॥३८२॥
चक्रवर्तिसमुत्पादे मन्त्रा सिद्ध्यन्ति चक्रिणः ।
जिनैस्तु कथिता ये मन्त्रा विद्याराजा महर्द्धिकाः ॥३८३॥
उष्णीषप्रभृतयः सर्वे ये चान्ये जिनभाषिताः ।
उत्तमां साधनां कुर्यात् तस्मिं काले सुशोभने ॥३८४॥
उत्तमैर्नाधमाः साध्या उत्तमां गतिमाश्रृतैः ।

§ 5. Early Emperors [before the Buddha]

*दिलीपो नहुष*श्चैव *मान्धाता सगर*स्तथा ॥३८५॥
साधयित्वा तु ते मन्त्रां चक्रिणां जिनभाषिताम् ।
तेजोराशिस्तदा सिद्धः *नहुष*स्य महात्मनः ॥३८६॥
T. 445 a. राजा सितातपत्रस्तु सिद्धस्तु *सगर*स्य वै ।
*दिलीप*स्य तथा मन्त्रं सिद्धमेकमक्षरम् ॥३८७॥
G. ६०९ *मान्धात*स्य तथा लोके सिद्ध उष्णीषमुन्नतः ।
जयोष्णीषस्तथा सिद्धो *धुन्धुमारे* नृपोत्तमे ॥३८८॥
*कन्दर्प*स्य तथा राज्ञो विजयोष्णीष कथ्यते ।
*प्रजापति*स्तस्य पुत्रो वै तस्यापि लोचना भुवि ॥३८९॥
प्रजापतेः सुतो *नाभिः* तस्यापि ऊर्णा मुच्यति ।
लाभिनो *ऋषभ* पुत्रो वै स सिद्धकर्म दृढव्रतः ॥३९०॥
तस्यापि माणिचरो यक्षः सिद्धो हैमवते गिरौ ।
*ऋषभ*स्य *भरतः* पुत्रः सोऽपि मन्त्रान् तदा जपेत् ॥३९१॥

---

३८७. राज्ञः सितातपत्रस्य सिद्धस्य सगरस्य (= महाविपर्ययं) । काक्षरम् । ३९०. उच्यते । नाभेः । ३९१. मणिचरो ।

सोऽनुपूर्वेण सिद्धस्तु महावीरं भुविस्तदा ।
एते चाऽन्ये च बहवः पार्थिवा लोकविश्रुताः ।।३९२।।
साधयित्वा तु मन्त्राणां राज्यं कृत्वा दिवं गताः ।
जिनेन्द्रैर्ये तु उक्तानि विद्याराजा महर्द्धिकाः ।।३९३।।
ते सर्वे शोभने काले युगेऽशीतिसहस्रगे ।
सिद्धाः साधयिष्यन्ति मन्त्रतन्त्रार्थकोविदाः ।।३९४।।
एते चान्ये च बहवः पार्थिवा लोकविश्रुताः ।
ततोऽशीतिसहस्राणि वर्षाणां शतमेव वा ।।३९५।।
राज्यं कृत्वा ततः स्वर्गं नियतं बोधिपरायणाः ।

§ 6. Dynasty of Benares [before the Buddha]

मध्यमे तु तदा काले दिव्यामाश्चर्यमहर्द्धिका: ।।३९६।।
T. 445 b. मन्त्राः सिद्धिमेवासुरब्जपाणिसमोदिताः ।
मन्त्रिभिर्नरमुख्यैस्तु भूपालैः सार्धभूमिकैः ।।३९७।।
राजा च *ब्रह्मदत्तो* वै *वाराणस्यां* महापुरे ।
सिद्धः अब्जपाणिस्तु लोकोशो लोकविश्रुतः ।।३९८।।
महावीर्यो महात्मासौ अतिकारुणिको महान् ।
सत्त्वानां मन्त्ररूपेण दिदेश धर्मदेशनाम् ।।३९९।।
राज्ञा ब्रह्मदत्तेन अनुभूतं मानुषं सुखम् ।
ततोऽसौ सिद्धमन्त्रस्तु सदेहः स्वगमाविशेत् ।।४००।।
G. ६१० तस्यापि च सुतो धीमान् पुण्यकर्मा *दृढव्रतः* ।
तस्यापि सिद्धो महावीर्यो हर्याख्येति विश्रुतः ।।४०१।।
तेन मन्त्रप्रभावेन जितः शक्र अभूत् तदा ।
तस्यापि सुतः *श्वेताख्यो* राजाभूत् सर्वदस्तदा ।।४०२।।
तस्यापि वरदा मन्त्रा महाश्वेता नाम नामतः ।
साधयित्वा तु तां मन्त्रं जीवेद् वर्षशतत्रयम् ।।४०३।।
तेन मन्त्रप्रभावेन सुखावत्या स गच्छति ।
नियतं बोधिमेवास्य ये चान्ये व्याहृता मया ।।४०४।।
मध्यमे तु तदा काले मध्यमन्त्रां तु साधयेत् ।
अधमेऽतियुगे कष्टे मयि बुद्धत्वमागते ।।४०५।।

---

३९५. मंत्रान् सम्यग् जपित्वा वै । ३९७. जाति । भूपालैः सार्वभूमिकैः ।
३९८. लोकेशः । ४००. स्वर्ग । ४०१. हयग्रीवेति । ४०२. तान् मंत्रान् । ४०४. व्याकृता ।

मन्त्राः सिद्धिं प्रयास्यन्ति वज्राब्जकुलयोरपि ।
त्वया कुमार ! मन्त्रा वै ये पूर्वं कथिता भुवि ॥४०६॥
तेऽपि सिद्धिं प्रयास्यन्ति मन्त्रा वै भागहेतुताम् ।
T. 446 a. इतराणि तु मन्त्राणि लौकिकां विविधां तथा ॥४०७॥
करमला विकृतरूपाश्च अन्तरिक्षा तु खेचरा ।
भौम्या च मथ यक्षिण्यः पिशाच्या विविधास्तथा ॥४०८॥
गरुडाः किन्नराश्चैव प्रेता राक्षसभाषिता ।
पिशाचोरगरक्षाणां नागीनां च महर्द्धिका ॥४०९॥
मन्त्रा सिद्धिं प्रयास्यन्ति युगे कष्टे युगाधमे ।
कुमाररूपास्तु मन्त्रा वै कुमारिरूपास्तु सर्वदा ॥४१०॥
तेऽपि सिद्धिं प्रयास्यन्ति तस्मिं काले भयानके ।
त्रिविधास्तु तथा मन्त्रा त्रिप्रकारास्तु साधना ॥४११॥

§ 7. Magadha Kings and their Ministers, subsequent to Udāyin

त्रिविधेनैव कालेन त्रिविधा सिद्धिरिष्यते ।
संक्षेपेण तु वक्ष्यामि कथ्यमानमतिविस्तरम् ॥४१२॥
राज्ञे सौ शोकमुख्यस्य पृष्ठतेत भवे नृपः ।
विशोक इति विख्यातो लोके धर्मानुचारिणः ॥४१३॥
G. ६११. तस्य सिद्धा इमा मन्त्रा देवी पण्डरवासिनी ।
विशोकः साधयित्वा तु आजहार दिवौकसाम ॥४१४॥
नाकपृष्ठे चिरं सौख्यमनुभूय स महानृपः ।
पुनरेव गच्छन्मानुष्यं धर्मशीलो हि बुद्धिमाम् ॥४१५॥
राज्यं विविधसम्पत्तिं अनुभूय महाद्युतिः ।
पूजयेद् धातुवरां श्रीमां वर्षाणि षट्सप्तति ॥४१६॥
T. 446 b. ततो ज्वरेणाभिभूतोऽसौ भिन्नदेहो दिवं गतः ।
तस्याप्यनन्तरे राजा *शूरसेनः* प्रकथ्यते ॥४१७॥
विघुष्टो धर्मचारी च शासनेऽस्मिं सदा हितः ।
तेनापि साधिता मन्त्रा देवीस्तूपमहाश्रिया ॥४१८॥
तेनापि कारिता शास्तुः कारा सुमहती तदा ।
स्तूपैरलङ्कृता सर्वा समुद्रान्ता वसुन्धरा ॥४१९॥
तस्य कर्मविपाकेन व्याधिरुत्पन्नदेहजा ।
पक्षमेकं क्षयित्वासौ च्युतदेहो भविष्यति ॥४२०॥

---

४१३. राज्ञोऽशोक । ४१५. बुद्धिमान् ।

कृत्वा राज्यं वर्षाणि दश सप्त च मानवीः ।
च्युतोऽसौ स्वर्गमाविष्टो नियतं बोधिपरायणः ॥४२१॥
तस्याप्यनन्तरो राजा नन्दनामा भविष्यति ।
पुष्पाख्ये नगरे श्रीमां महासैन्यो महाबलः ॥४२२॥
तेनापि साधितो मन्त्र पिशाचो पीलुनामतः ।
तस्य मन्त्रप्रभावं तु महाभोगो भविष्यति ॥४२३॥
नीचमुख्यसमाख्यातो ततो लोके भविष्यति ।
तद्धनं प्राप्य मन्त्री सौ लोके पार्थिवतां गतः ॥४२४॥
भविष्यति तदा काले ब्राह्मणास्तार्किका भुवि ।
सिद्ध्याभिमानलुब्धा वै नगरे मगधवासिनः ॥४२५॥
भविष्यन्ति न सन्देहो गिथ्यागर्वितमानिनः ।
तेभिः परिवारितो राजा वै (तेषां दास्यति तद्धनम्) ॥४२६॥
T.447a. G.६१३ धर्मशीलोऽपि धर्मात्मा तेषां दास्यति तं धनम् ।
कल्याणमित्रमागम्य पूजे धातुवरानसौ ॥४२७॥
केवलं तु तदाभ्यासाद् दानाविक्कबहेतुना ।
विहारा कारिता तेन षोडशाष्टौ च धीमता ॥४२८॥
भविष्यति तदा काले नगरे पुष्पसाह्वये ।
मन्त्रिमुख्यो महात्मा वै घृणी साधु तथा द्विजः ॥४२९॥
स भविष्यति धर्मात्मा तस्या राज्ञोऽतिशाक्यिनः ।
सोऽपि सिद्धमन्त्रस्तु यक्षिणी वीरमती भुवि ॥४३०॥
तेनापि कारितं श्रेष्ठं जिनानां धातुवरो भुवि ।
अतिप्राज्ञो हि संवृतो यक्षिण्यास्तु प्रभावतः ॥४३१॥
तेन वासनकर्मेण पूर्ववासनचोदितः ।
अनुपूर्वेण मेधावी बोधिं प्राप्स्यति दुर्लभाम् ॥४३२॥
स्त्रीकृतेन दोषेण मृत्युं प्राप्स्यन्ति मानवाः ।
वररुचिर्नाम विख्यात अतिरागो अभूत तदा ॥४३३॥
नन्दोऽपि नृपतिः श्रीमां पूर्वकर्मापराधतः ।
विरागयामास मन्त्रीणां नगरे पाटलाह्वये ॥४३४॥

---

४२५. मिथ्या । ४२७. तैर्धनैर्बहुभिः । धरान । ४२८. ध्ययसय तस्याऽभ्यासात् (म-अद्रेस्-दे-क-गोमुस्-प-दक्) । ४३०. तसय । शायिनः । ४३१. धातुवरो । ४३२. माणवाः (मम्-से-विय-बु) । ४३४. नरान् (मि-र्नमुस्) ।

विरक्तमन्त्रवर्गिस्तु सत्यसन्धो महाबलः ।
पूर्वकर्मापराधेन महारोगी भविष्यति ॥४३५॥
महाज्वरेण दुःखार्तं अर्धरात्रे भविष्यति ।
आयुस्तस्य च वै राज्ञः षट्षष्टिवर्षा तथा ॥४३६॥
नियतं श्रावके बोधौ तस्य राज्ञो भविष्यति ।
T. 447 b. तस्याप्यन्यतमः सख्यः पाणिनिर्नाम माणवः ॥४३७॥
नियतं श्रावकत्वेन व्याकृतो मे भविष्यति ।
सोऽपि सिद्धमन्त्रस्तु लोकीशस्य महात्मनः ॥४३८॥
साधयेत् प्रज्ञाकामस्तु क्रोधं हालहलं द्विजः ।

§ 8. Maurya Dynasty

तस्य राज्ञोऽपर ख्यातः चन्द्रगुप्तो भविष्यति ॥४३९॥
G. ६१२ जपेन्द्रयत्नसिद्धस्तु कारयेद् राज्यमकण्टकम् ।
महायोगी सत्यसन्धश्च धर्मात्मा स महीपतिः ॥४४०॥
अकल्याणमित्रमागम्य कृतं प्राणिवधं बहु ।
तेन कर्मविपाकेन विषस्फोटैः स मूर्छितः ॥४४१॥
अर्धरात्रे रुदित्वासौ पुत्रं स्थापयेद् भुवि ।
बिन्दुवारसमाख्यातं बालं दुष्टमन्त्रिणम् ॥४४२॥
ततोऽसौ चन्द्रगुप्तस्य च्युतः कालगतो भुवि ।
प्रेतलोकं तदा लेभे गतिं मानुषवर्जिताम् ॥४४३॥
मन्त्राभ्यासात् तदा युक्तो गतिं त्यक्त्वा दिवि गतम् ।
मन्त्रहेतुसमुत्पादात् कुशलालम्बनचेतनाम् ॥४४४॥
प्रत्येकं बोधिमायाति सोऽनुपूर्वेण नराधिपः ।
राज्ञाथ बिम्बसारेण बालेनाव्यक्तचेतसा ॥४४५॥
पुरा कारितं चैत्यं सिंहदत्तेन भवान्तरे ।
तस्य कर्मप्रभावेन दिवं यातो ह्यनिन्दितः ॥४४६॥
पञ्च जन्म सहस्राणि अमरेभ्यो भुक्तवान् सुखम् ।
स्वर्गलोकाच्च्यवित्वा तु मनुष्येन्द्रोपपद्यते ॥४४७॥

---

४३५. वर्ग । ४३६. पंचपंचाश । (? मरिष्यति) । ४३९. हालाहलं । ४४०. अलेन्द्र । भोगी । ४४१. सं । ४४२. विन्दुसार । ४४५. श्रावकबोधि । बिम्बु । ४४६. वालुकया (विप-म-लस्) । ४४७. अमरेषु ।

T. 448 a. जातो (नन्द-) राजकुले चन्द्रगुप्तस्य धीमतः ।
बाल एव ततो राजा प्राप्तः सौख्यमनल्पकम् ॥४४८॥
प्रौढो धृष्टश्च संवृत्तः प्रगल्भश्चापि प्रियवादिनम् ।
स्वाधीन एव तद् राज्यं कुर्याद् वर्षाणि सप्तति ॥४४९॥
मन्त्रा केशिनी नाम सिद्धा तस्य नराधिपे ।
कुमार ! त्वदीयमन्त्रे तु सिद्धिं गच्छेयु ते तदा ॥४५०॥
भविष्यति तदा काले मन्त्रसिद्धिस्त्वयोदिता ।
कुमाररूपी विश्वात्मा लोकानां प्रभविष्णवः ॥४५१॥
भविष्यति न सन्देहो मन्त्ररूपेण देहिनाम् ।
(मंत्रस्त्वयोदितो यो वै सत्त्वानां) हितकाम्यया ॥४५२॥
G. ६१४ तस्मिं काले सदा सिद्धिर्भविष्यन्ति पठिता भुवि ।
मन्त्री तस्य राज्ञस्य *बिन्दुसारस्य* धीमतः ॥४५३॥
चाणाक्य इति विख्यातः क्रोधसिद्धस्तु मानवः ।
यमान्तको नाम वै क्रोधः सिद्धस्तस्य च दुर्मतेः ॥४५४॥
तेन क्रोधाभिभूतेन प्राणिनो जीविताद्धता ।
कृत्वा तु पापकं तीव्रं त्रीणि राज्यानि वै तदा ॥४५५॥
दीर्घकालाभिजीवी सौ भविता द्विजकुत्सितः ।
तेन मन्त्रप्रभावेन स देहमासुरीं भजेत् ॥४५६॥
आसुरीं तनुमाविष्ट दीर्घकालं स जीवयेत् ।
T. 448 b. ततोऽसौ भिन्नदेहस्तु नरकेभ्यो विगच्छतः ॥४५७॥
ततोऽसौ नारकं दुःखं अनुभूयेह दुर्गतिः ।
विविधा नारकां दुःखां अनिष्टां कर्मजां तदा ॥४५८॥
कल्पमेकं क्षयित्वासौ क्रोधमन्त्रप्रचोदितम् ।
च्युतोऽसौ नरकाद् दुःखात् तिर्यग्भ्योपपद्यते ॥४५९॥
नागयोनिं समापद्य भीमरूपी भविष्यति ।
नागराजो महाक्रोधी महाभोगी विषदर्पितः ॥४६०॥
दारुणं कर्मचारी च ।
च्युतोऽसौ दुष्टकर्मा तु यमलोकमगच्छत ॥४६१॥
सुनिदा यमराजासौ प्रेतराजो महर्द्धिकः ।
एवं दुःखसहस्राणि अनुभूय पुनः पुनः ॥४६२॥

---

४५१. बाकानी । ४५४. माणवः । ४५५. त्रयो राजानो । ४६२. संभूतो ।

सोऽनुपूर्वेण दुर्मेधा भुविमायात माणवः ।
मानुष्यं जन्ममायातः भोमरूपी भविष्यति ॥४६३॥
दरिद्र क्रोधनश्चैव अल्पशाख्यो भविष्यति ।
प्रत्येकबुद्धा ये लोके निराशाः खड्गचारिणः ॥४६४॥
हीनदीनानुकम्प्यास्तु विचरन्ति महीतले ।
सत्त्वानां हितकाम्यर्थं प्रविष्टा पिण्डचारिकाम् ॥४६५॥
G. ६१५ ते तं दुर्मतिं दृष्ट्वा वै परचित्तविदोस्तदा ।
ते तत्र मनुबद्धास्तु कारुण्यान्नान्यहेतवः ॥४६६॥
तेन कुल्माषखण्डास्तु गृहीता भक्तहेतुना ।
क्रोधमन्त्राभिभूतेन हेतुमुद्घाटिता तदा ॥४६७॥
T. 449 a. तेषां निर्यातयेद् भिक्षं तत्रैकस्य महात्मनः ।
इदं भोः प्रव्रजिताः ! सर्वे ! भक्षयध्वं यथासुखम् ॥४६८॥
तस्यानुकम्पा बुद्धेभ्यः ऋद्धिं दर्शितवां तदा ।
ततोऽसौ विस्मयाविष्टः प्रभावोद्गतमानसः ॥४६९॥
प्रपतेत् सर्वतो मूर्ध्ना बुद्धेभ्यः खड्गकल्पिषु ।
आकाशेन गताः सर्वे वीतदोषा यथेष्टतः ॥४७०॥
तेनापि कुशलार्थेन प्रत्येकां बोधिचिन्तिताम् ।
यादृशा हि महात्मानः शान्तवेषा महर्द्धिकाः ॥४७१॥
तादृशोऽहं भवेल्लोके मा दुःखी मा च दुर्गतिः ।
क्षीणकर्मावशेषस्तु च्युतः स्वर्गोपगः सदा ॥४७२॥
सोऽनुपूर्वेण धर्मात्मा प्रत्येकं बोधि लप्स्यते ।
तस्मान्न कुर्यान्मन्त्रेभ्यः साधनमाभिचारुकम् ॥४७३॥
बुद्धैर्बोधिसत्त्वैश्च प्रतिषिद्धमाभिचारुकम् ।
अतिकारुणिका बुद्धा बोधिसत्त्वास्तु महर्द्धिकाः ॥४७४॥
प्रभावार्थं तु मन्त्राणां दर्शितं सर्वकर्मिणः ।
चिन्तामणयो मन्त्रा भाषितास्तु तथागतैः ॥४७५॥
बालरूपा मूढचित्तास्तु क्रोधलोभाभिभूतयः ।
परस्परं प्रयोज्यन्ते ये मन्त्रा आभिचारुके ॥४७६॥
T. 449 b. प्रतिषिद्धं तथा बुद्धैर्बोधिसत्त्वैस्तु धीमतैः ।
सर्वप्रकार तु मन्त्राणां सत्त्वेभ्यो भोगवर्धनम् ॥४७७॥

---

४६९. प्रत्येकबुद्धाः । ४७३. श्रावकबोधिं । ४७५. देशितं ।

उत्तिष्ठमथ राज्यं वै मदारत्नां धन्यहेतवः ।
आकर्षणं तु सत्त्वानां विविधां योनिमाश्रिताम् ॥४७८॥

§ 9. Buddhist Saints and Teachers

G. ६१६ साधनीयास्तु मन्त्रा वै न जीवमुपरोधतः ।
तस्मिं काले भविष्यन्ति भिक्षवो मे बहुश्रुताः ॥४७९॥
मातृचीनाख्यनामास्तु स्तोत्रं कृत्वा ममैव तु ।
यथा भूतगुणोद्देशैः यथाकारमभाषत ॥४८०॥
प्रसाद्य सर्वतश्चित्तं बुद्धानां शासने रतः ।
मन्त्रसिद्धस्तु दुर्लङ्घ्यः मञ्जुघोषस्तवैव तु ॥४८१॥
गुणवां शीलसम्पन्नः धर्मवादी बहुश्रुतः ।
पुरा तिर्यग्गतेनैव इमां स्तोत्रमभाषत ॥४८२॥
नृपाख्ये नगरे रम्ये खण्डाख्ये च वनेवतु ।
सार्धं शिष्यगणेनैव विहरामि यथासुखम् ॥४८३॥
तत्रस्थो वायस आसी मां चित्तं सम्प्रसादयेत् ।
प्रसाद्य च मयि चित्तं भिन्नदेहो दिवं गतः ॥४८४॥
देवेभ्यश्च च्यवित्वा तु मनुष्येभ्योपपत्स्यते ।
मनुष्येभ्योपपन्नस्तु प्रव्रजेच्छासने मम ॥४८५॥
प्रव्रजित्वा महात्मासौ यथाभूतं हि मां तदा ।
T. 450 a. स्तविष्यति तदा काले मातृचीनाख्य सव्रती ॥४८६॥
स्तोत्रोपहारं यथार्थं च नानादृष्टान्तरहतुभिः ।
प्रकर्ता सर्वभूतानां हितायैव सुभाषितम् ॥४८७॥
अनुग्रहार्थं तु सत्त्वानां स्तोत्रचोदनतत्परः ।
भविष्यति तदा काले युगान्ते लोकनिन्दिते ॥४८८॥
तेन कर्मविपाकेन भिन्नदेहो दिविं गतः ।
सोऽनुपूर्वेण मेधावी अनुभूय विविधां सुखाम् ॥४८९॥
बोधिं प्राप्स्यति सर्वज्ञि उत्तमार्थमचिन्तियाम् ।
चतुर्थे वर्षशते प्राप्ते निर्वृते मयि तथागते ॥४९०॥
नागाह्वो नाम सौ भिक्षुः शासनेऽस्मिं हिते रतः ।

४७८, उत्तमोऽथ राजा । मद्दा । ऐश्वर्यं । आकर्षणार्थं । ४८०. मातृचेटा (म-ख्योल्) ।
४८३. राजगृहे । वेण्वाख्ये । ४८६. मातृचेटाख्यः ।

मुदितां भूमिलब्धस्तु जीवेद् वर्षशतानि षट् ॥४९१॥
G. ६१८ मायूरी नामतो विद्या सिद्धा तस्य महात्मनः ।
नानाशास्त्रार्थधात्वर्थं निःस्वभावार्थतत्त्ववित् ॥४९२॥
सुखावत्यां चोपपद्येत यदासौ त्यक्तकलेबरः ।
सोऽनुपूर्वेण बुद्धत्वं नियतं सम्प्रपत्स्यते ॥४९३॥
(अ) संग नामा तदा भिक्षुः शास्त्रतत्त्वार्थकोविदः ।
सूत्रनीतार्थनेयानां विभज्य बहुधा पुनः ॥४९४॥
लोकाभिधायी युक्तात्मा तुच्छशीलो भविष्यति ।
(विद्या ह वै) तस्य सिद्धा शालदूतीति कथ्यते ॥४९५॥
T. 450 b. तस्य मन्त्रप्रभावेन बुद्धिरुत्पन्न श्रेयसी ।
सङ्ग्रहे सूत्रतत्त्वार्थं शासनस्य चिरस्थिते ॥४९६॥
जीवेद् वर्षशतं सार्धं त्यक्तदेहो दिविं गतः ।
अनुभूय चिरं सौख्यं दीर्घसंसारसंसरम् ॥४९७॥
अनुपूर्वेण चात्मासौ बोधिप्राप्तो भविष्यति ।
एवं बहुविधाकारो भिक्षवो मयि शासने ॥४९८॥
प्रज्ञा धर्मशीलास्तु भविताभूत् तदा युगे ।
अपश्चिमे तु तदा काले नन्दनामतः ॥४९९॥
सोऽपि मन्त्रार्थयुक्तात्मा तन्त्रज्ञोऽथ बहुश्रुतः ।
तस्य भद्रघटः सिद्धः यक्षमन्त्रप्रचोदितः ॥५००॥
महायानाग्रसूत्रे तु मया च कथिता पुरा ।
तस्मि काले घटे तस्मिं उज्जहार महातपा ॥५०१॥
तस्य दृष्टसदा तत्र पुस्तकेऽस्मिं मन्त्ररूपिणे ।
रक्षा न कारिता तत्र घटेऽस्मिं यक्षसाधिते ॥५०२॥
अनप्रमादात् स्मृतिभ्रंशा घटो मूर्ध्नटके हृतः ।
ततोऽसौ सिद्धमन्त्रस्तु भिक्षुर्मन्त्रतपी अभूत् ॥५०३॥
घटं निरीक्षयामास नाभिपश्येत तत्र वै ।
ततोऽसौ क्रोधरक्ताक्षः विस्फूर्जन अभाषत ॥५०४॥
G. ६१९ आग्रब्रह्मस्तम्बपर्यन्तं शक्राद्यां समहेश्वराम् ।
T. 451. a. मन्त्रेनाकृष्यमानेयं नाहं मन्त्री न मन्त्राराद् ॥५०५॥

---

४९२. महामायूरी वै । ४९५. ङङ्-हुङ् । ४९८. महात्मा । ४९९. पश्चिमे । अर्हद्भिक्षु ।

ये मन्त्रा बुद्धपुत्रैस्तु मन्त्रा जिनवरैस्तथा ।
भाषिता निग्रहार्थाय दुर्दान्तदमकापि वा ॥५०६॥
ते तु सर्वे भुविर्नास्ति यदि नाकृष्यामि चोरीणाम् ।
ततोत्थाय ततो मन्त्री सिद्धकर्मदृढव्रतः ॥५०७॥
यथा तु विहिते मन्त्रे प्रयोगाकृष्टहेतवः ।
प्रयोजयामास तं दिक्षु क्षिप्राकर्षणतत्परः ॥५०८॥
क्षणेना स्मृतमात्रेण क्षिप्रकर्मायति ह्यसौ ।
हुङ्कारेणैकेण मात्रेण ब्रह्माद्यामानयेद् भुवि ॥५०९॥
आकृष्टा सर्वदेवावास्तु ब्रह्माद्याः सशक्रका ।
हाहाकारं प्रमुञ्चाना आर्त्ता भैरवनादिनः ॥५१०॥
किं करोम किमानीता नाम यं मन्त्रापराधिनः ।
शीघ्रं च त्वरमाणस्तु भिक्षुर्धीमां विशारदः ॥५११॥
दिवौकसां मन्त्रयामास घटं प्रत्यर्पयथ इतो इह ।
अन्योन्यं वै सुराः सर्वे स भिक्षुः सम्प्रभाषत ॥५१२॥
क्षिप्रं वदत भद्रं वो येनेनापहृतो घटः ।
निरीक्षयामास ते देवाः न दास्यन्तेऽथ समन्ततः ॥५१३॥
ससन्वाहरति देवेशः केनायं घटकोऽपहृतः ।
पश्यते वज्रिणः श्रीमां बोधिसत्त्वो महाद्युतिः ॥५१४॥
T. 451 b. तस्यास्ति सुतो घोरः महारोषी सुदारुणः ।
निर्मितो विघ्नरूपेण विचेरुः सर्वतो जगत् ॥५१५॥
तेनासौ घटो नीत देवेशः सम्प्रभाषितम् ।
अस्ति वज्रकुले विघ्नः क्रीडते लीलया भुवि ॥५१६॥
पूजितोऽहमिमेनेति तेनासौ घटको हृतः ।
एतमुक्त्वा तु देवेशः पुनरेव दिविं गताः ॥५१७॥
G. ६१९ सर्वे विसर्जिता देवाः स्वमन्त्रेणैव ते तदा ।
क्षणेनैव तु तत्रैकः मुहूर्तसुतरानपि ॥५१८॥
आनयामास तं विघ्नमवशात् सघटं तदा ।
ततस्तेन तु विघ्नेन प्रेतानां घटमाददे ॥५१९॥
ततो नीतेन तु विघ्नेन इमां वाचामभाषिता ।
प्रेतलोके घटो नीतः न वयं तत्र दोषिणः ॥५२०॥

---

५१४. समन्वाहरति ।

रुष्टो सोऽपि महामन्त्री तं विघ्नमभ्यभाषत ।
गच्छ गच्छ महाविघ्न ! मा भूयो एवमाचरेत् ॥५२१॥
ततस्तेन तु प्रेते ता आनीतास्तत्क्षणादपि ।
क्षुभिताक्रान्तमनसः दीनाः सूचीमुखा हि ते ॥५२२॥
आर्तस्वरं च क्रन्देयुर्महाघोरतमा हि ते ।
चुक्रुतुः करुणां वाणीं परित्रायस्व महात्मन ॥५२३॥
घटं वो इह आनीता यथेष्ट कुरुते वयम् ।
महाकारुणिको मन्त्री वेपथु सम्प्रजायताम् ॥५२४॥
करुणार्द्रेण मनसा इमां वाचामभाषत ।
T. 452 a. किं दुःखं भवतां लोके सम्प्रभाषथ मा चिरम् ॥५२५॥
ते ऊचुर्दीनमनसा बुभुक्षास्मत् सम्प्रधावते ।
त्रिषिताः प्रेतलोकेऽस्मिं चिरं कालं महात्मनः ॥५२६॥
महाकारुणिको भिक्षुस्तेषामेव प्रददौ घटम् ।
ततस्ते तुष्टमनसाः सत्त्वरामालयं गताः ॥५२७॥
तेषां चिन्तितमात्रेण अन्नपानं भवेदु घटे ।
भविता चन्दनमालेऽस्मिं भिक्षुर्नन्दको भुवि ॥५२८॥
तस्मिं कालाधमे प्राप्ते जीवेदु वर्षशतत्रयम् ।
महात्मा बोधिनिम्नस्तु क्षिप्रं प्राप्स्यति दुर्लभाम् ॥५२९॥

§ 10. Low period—Kings after the Mauryas

भविष्यन्ति न सन्देहः तस्मिं काले युगाधमे ।
राजा गोमिमुख्यस्तु शासनान्तधपको मम ॥५३०॥
G. ६२० प्राचिं दिशिमुपादाय कश्मीरेद्वारमेव तु ।
नाशयिष्यति तदा मूढः विहारां धातुवरांस्तथा ॥५३१॥
भिक्षवः शीलसम्पन्नां घातयिष्यति दुर्मतिः ।
उत्तरां दिशमाश्रित्य मृत्युस्तस्य भविष्यति ॥५३२॥
अमानुषेणैव क्रुद्धेन सराष्ट्रापशुबान्धवः ।
आक्रान्तोऽद्रिखण्डेन पातालं यास्यति दुर्मति ॥५३३॥
अधो अथ गतिस्तस्य नरकान्नरकतरं भृशम् ।
दुःखा दुखतरं तीव्रं सम्प्रपत्स्यति दारुणम् ॥५३४॥
T. 452 b. अवीचिर्नाम विख्यातं नरकं पापकर्मिणा ।
मुच्यतेऽसौ महाकल्पं गोमिषण्डो दुरात्मनः ॥५३५॥

---

५३०. गोमिनामा तु । ५३१. कश्मीर । धातुधरां । ५३३. स-राष्ट्र ।

अकल्याणमित्रमागम्य कृतं पापसुदारुणम् ।
तस्मात् सर्वप्रयत्नेन शासनेऽस्मिं तथागते ॥५३६॥
प्रसाद्यमखिलं चित्तं सम्प्रभोक्ष्यथ सम्पदाम् ।
बुद्धत्वनियतं मार्गम् अष्टाङ्गपथयायिनम् ॥५३७॥
गमिष्यथ सदा सर्वे अशोकं निर्जरसं पुरम् ।

§ 11. Yaksha Dynasty

तस्यानन्तरे महीपालः बुद्धपक्ष इति श्रुतः ॥५३८॥
महायक्षो महात्यागी बुद्धानां शासने रतः ।
भविष्यति न सन्देहः तस्मिं काले युगाधमे ॥५३९॥
अतिप्रीतो हि नृपतिः शास्तुः शासनतत्परः ।
विहारारामचैत्यांश्च शास्तुर्बिम्बाननुत्तमाम् ॥५४०॥
वाप्यः (तडाग-) कूपाश्च (सरांसि चैव) अनेकधाः ।
कारयित्वा महाराजा दिवं गच्छेद् गतायुषः ॥५४१॥
तस्य सिद्धो महावीर्यः अब्जकेतुर्महोतले ।
पृथिवां पालनां प्रार्थे बोधिसत्त्वस्य महात्मने ॥५४२॥
तस्य मन्त्रप्रभावेन जीवेद् वर्षशतत्रयम् ।
तेन कर्माविशेषेण क्षिप्रं बोधिमवाप्नुयात् ॥५४३॥
G. ६२१ तस्यापि च सुतो राजा महासैन्यो महाबलः ।
गम्भीरयक्षो विख्यातः पृथिवीमखिलोदिताम् ॥५४४॥
सोऽपि राजाथ युक्तात्मा तस्मिं काले भविष्यति ।
T. 453 a. विहारावसथचैत्यांश्च वापीकूपांश्च नैकधा ॥५४५॥
कारयिष्यति न सन्देहो भूपतिः स महाद्युतिः ।
तेनापि साधितं मन्त्रं मञ्जुघोषस्य धीमतः ॥५४६॥
षडक्षरं नाम यद् वाक्यं महार्थं भोगवर्धनम् ।
तस्य मन्त्रप्रभावेन महाभोगी भवेद्यसौ ॥५४७॥
अनुपूर्वेण मेधावी क्षिप्रं बोधिपरायणः ।
विविधाकारकारांस्तु शासनेऽस्मिं तथागते ॥५४८॥

---

५३८. तदा । ५३९. महापक्षो । ५४२. पृथिव्या । ५४४. गम्भीरपक्षो । पृथिवीं नगरोदिताम् । ५४७. भवेत्यसौ ।

II. Provincial History: §12. North: §12*a*. Nepal

भविष्यति तदा काले उत्तरां दिशिमाश्रितः ।
नेपालमण्डले ख्याते हिमाद्रेः कुक्षिमाश्रिते ॥५४९॥
राजा मानवेन्द्रस्तु लिच्छवीनां कुलोद्भवः ।
सोऽपि मन्त्रार्थसिद्धस्तु महाभोगी भविष्यति ॥५५०॥
विद्या भोगवती नाम तस्य सिद्धा नराधिपे ।
अशीतिवर्षाणि कृत्वासौ राज्यं तस्करवर्जितम् ॥५५१॥
ततः प्राणात्यये नृपतौ स्वर्गलोके जजग्मसु ।
तत्र मन्त्राशु सिध्यन्ति शीतला शान्तिक पौष्टिका ॥५५२॥
तारा च लोकविख्याता देवी पण्डरवासिनी ।
महाश्वेता परहितोद्युक्ता अखिन्नमनसां सदा ॥५५३॥
इत्येवमाद्यो प्रोक्ता बहुधा नृपतयोस्तदा ।
अनेकधा बहुधाश्चैव नानारूपविवर्णिताः ॥५५४॥
शास्तुपूजकास्तेऽपि म्लेच्छराजा न है ।
T. 453 b. वविषः सुवृषश्चैव भावसु शुभसुस्तथा ॥५५५॥
भाक्रमः *पदक्रम*श्चैव *कमल*श्चैव कीर्त्यते ।
भागुप्तः *वसक*श्चैव (भास्वांश्चैव) पश्चिमः ॥५५६॥

§ 12*b*. Fall of Nepal

G. ६२२ उदयः जिह्नुनो ह्यन्ते म्लेच्छानां विविधास्तथा ।
अम्भोधेः भ्रष्टमर्यादा बहिः प्राज्ञोपभोजिनः ॥५५७॥
शस्त्रसम्पातविध्वस्ता *नेपाला*धिपतिस्तदा ।
विद्यालुप्ता लुप्तराजानो म्लेच्छतस्करसेविनः ॥५५८॥
अनेका भूपतयो प्रोक्ता नाना चैव द्विजप्रिया ।

§ 13. Tibet [China]

भविष्यन्ति तदा काले चीनं प्राप्य समन्ततः ॥५५९॥

---

५४९. देववन् (ल्ह-ल्दन्) । ५५०. मानवदेवस्तु । ५५४. नृपतयस्तदा । ५५५. हिमवद्वासिनः । वृषः । भूभासः सुभूभासस्तथा । ५५६. पराक्रमः (फ-रोल्-ग्नोद्-मिद्) । भूगुप्तः (स-ब्सुङ्=भूपालः) । ५५७. ल्ह-लुङ् (शीली, जिष्णुः) । ततः परं (दे-ऽोग्) । परपुरुषोपसेविनः (फिय-रोल्-स्क्ये-बुगुस्-मे-वद्-स्प्योद्) । ५५८. विलुप्तास्तत्र राजानो । ५५९. देव-द्विज-प्रियाः ।

राजा हिरण्यगर्भस्तु महासैन्यो महाबलः ।
विस्तीर्णश्च तन्त्रश्च प्रभूतजनबान्धवः ॥५६०॥
म्लेच्छप्रणतो विजयी च शास्तुः शासनतत्परः ।
तेनापि साधितो मन्त्रः कुमारस्यैव महाद्युतेः ॥५६१॥
(महाबलेन युक्तश्च) विद्याराजामश्च अक्षरम् ।
महावीरं नाम विख्यातं सम्पदानां महास्पदम् ॥५६२॥
तेन बालधियो राजा राज्यहेतोः समाहितः ।
यस्य स्मरितमात्रेण बुद्धत्वं नियतं पदम् ॥५६३॥
सोऽल्पकार्यनियुञ्जानः राज्यहेतो नराधिपः ।
आकांक्षमानयद्येवं वरदानमनुत्तमम् ॥५६४॥
आज्ञाद्या देवतां कृत्स्नामाज्ञापयति सर्वदा ।
T. 454 a. किं पुनर्मानुषां लोके इतरां भावकुत्सिताम् ॥५६५॥
जीवित्वा वर्षशतं सार्धं दिवं गच्छन्महानृपः ।
सोऽनुपूर्वेण धर्मात्मा उत्तमां बोधिमाप्नुयात् ॥५६६॥
तस्मिं देश इमा विद्या ये कुमारेण भाषिता ।
सत्वरा तेऽपि सिद्ध्यन्ते नान्ये विद्या कदाचन ॥५६७॥
बोधिसत्त्वो महाधीरः मञ्जुघोषो महाद्युतिः ।
तस्मिं देशे तु साक्षाद् वै तिष्ठते बालरूपिणः ॥५६८॥

§ 14. Balkh to Kashmir: Turushka [Kanishka]

सिद्धिक्षेत्राऽथ परं दिव्यं मानुष्यैः साधयिष्यति ।
तुरुष्कनामा वै राजा उत्तरापथमाश्रृत ॥५६९॥
G. ६२१ महासैन्यो महावीर्यः तस्मिं स्थाने भविष्यति ।
कश्मीरद्वारपर्यन्तं बष्कलोद्यं सकाविशम् ॥५७०॥
योजनशतसप्तं तु राजा भुंक्तेऽथ भूतलम् ।
सप्तसप्ततिसहस्राणि लक्षौ द्वौ तस्य भूपतेः ॥५७१॥
भविष्यति न सन्देहो तस्मिं काले युगाधमे ।
सोऽपि सिद्धमन्त्रस्तु जीवेद् वर्षशतत्रयम् ॥५७२॥

---

५६०. वसुगर्भ (वृडियग्-गि-स्ञिङ्-पो) । मंत्रिक । ५६१. कुमारस्य महात्मा वै । ५६३. स्मरणमात्रेण । ५६४. सोऽनल्पकल्पजातो वै (दे. नि-बुस्कल्प-मि-शुङ्-ऽग्युर) । आप्नोति (थोब्-प-यिद्) । ५६५. कुदेवान् । ५६६. महायशाः । ५६८. महावीरः । ५७०. शिन्-ग्रुन् ग्योन्-शुङ्-सब्-पो (?)-यक । थान-सकाशिकम् (क-शिडि-बूबस्) । ५७१. सप्तशतं ।

साधिता केशिनी विद्या नराध्यक्षेण धीमता ।
आत्मना श्रेयसार्थं तु विहारां कारयेद् बहून् ॥५७३॥
षडाशीतिसहस्राणि कुर्यात् स्तूपवरांस्तथा ।
महायानाग्रधर्मं तु बुद्धानां जननीस्तथा ॥५७४॥
प्रज्ञापारमिता लोके तस्मिं देशे प्रतिष्ठिता ।
T. 454 b. स राजा भिन्नदेहस्तु स्वर्गलोकं गमिष्यति ॥५७५॥
सोऽनुपूर्वेण क्षितीपेशः बोधिं प्राप्यस्यति मुत्तमाम् ।
तस्यान्तरे क्षितिपतेः *महातुरुष्को* नाम नामतः ॥५७६॥
धीमतः बहुमतः ख्यातो गुरुपूजकतत्परः ।
सदा सोऽपि साधे स मन्त्रं वै तारादेवीं महर्द्धिकाम् ॥५७७॥
सोऽपि प्रसिद्धमन्त्रस्तु राज्यहेतो थ भूतले ।
महायक्षा महासैन्यः महेशाख्योऽथ भूपतिः ॥५७८॥
सम्मतो बन्धुवर्गाणां राजा सोऽपि भविष्यति ।
अष्टौ सहस्रविहाराणां तस्मिं काले भविष्यति ॥५७९॥
तस्य मन्त्रप्रभावेन जीवेद् वर्षशतद्वयम् ।
यदासौ भिन्नदेहस्तु तुषितेभ्योपपद्यते ॥५८०॥
सोन्मत्तो देवपुत्राणां बोधिसत्त्वो महर्द्धिकः ।
सोऽनुपूर्वेण धर्मात्मा बोध्यङ्ग समभिपूरतः ॥५८१॥
प्राप्नुयामतुलां बोधिं सोऽनुपूर्वेण यत्नतः ।
तत्र देशे सदा कालं तिष्ठते प्रवरं बहु ॥५८२॥
G. ६२४ जिनैस्तु कथितं पूर्वं अधुना चर्यया भुवि ।
वीतरागैः समाक्रान्तं नागैश्चापि महर्द्धिकैः ॥५८३॥
लोकपालास्तथा यक्षाः शास्तु-शासन-रक्षकाः ।
भविष्यन्ति तदा काले सद्धर्मारक्षका भुवि ॥५८४॥
एवं बहुविधाः प्रोक्ताः भूपाला लोकविश्रुताः ।
कथिताः कथयिष्यन्ति तस्मिं काले सुदारुणे ॥५८५॥

---

५७४. एकाशीति । ५७७. पुण्यक्षेत्र (पूगे-बडि-श्रिङ्) । पूजायां रतः (मछोद्-क-बूगऽ) तस्या मंत्रं प्रसाधते । ५७८. महापक्षा । महेशाख्यो । ५८१. सम्मतो । ५८२. प्रवचनं (गृसुङ्-रब्) । ५८३. अधुनाऽपि कथितं मया ।

Provincial History—Western India §. 15. Valabhi Dynasty

T. 455 a. पश्चाद्देशपर्यन्तं <u>उज्जयन्यामतः</u> परे ।

समुद्रतीरपर्यन्तं *लाडानां* जनपदे तथा ॥५८६॥

शीलाह्वो नाम नृपतिः बुद्धानां शासने रतः ।

पुरीं *वलभ्य* सम्प्राप्तो धर्मराजा भविष्यति ॥५८७॥

विहारां <u>धातुवरां चित्रां</u> श्रेयसां प्राणिनांस्तथा ।

कारयिष्यति युक्तात्मा भूपतिर्धर्मवत्सलः ॥५८८॥

पूजां च विविधाकारां जिनबिम्बां मनोरमाम् ।

पूजयेद्धा<u>तुवरां</u> अर्घ्यां लोकनाथेभ्यो यशस्विषु ॥५८९॥

नासौ मन्त्रसिद्धस्तु <u>केवलं</u> कर्मजोत्तमः ।

तत्र देशे समाख्यातो भिक्षुः पिण्डचारिकः ॥५९०॥

शीलवां बुद्धिसपन्नो बुद्धानां शासने रतः ।

कालचारी महात्मासौ प्रविष्टो पिण्डचारिकम् ॥५९१॥

पश्यते राजकुलं श्रेष्ठं विस्तीर्णं च जनावृतन् ।

प्रविष्टो तत्र भिक्षार्थी क्षुधया च समन्वितः ॥५९२॥

तृषितो क्लान्तमनसो न लेभे पिण्डकं तदा ।

गृहीत्वासौ पुरुषैः क्षिप्रं निर्ययुः तद्गृहात् परम् ॥५९३॥

ततो सौद्विग्नमनसो रक्षितो राजभटैस्तदा ।

निर्ययुर्नगरात् तस्मात् स्वालयं तत्क्षणाद् गतः ॥५९४॥

क्षुधितो तृषितश्चैव दुःखी च दुर्मतिं गतः ।

T. 455 b. ततोऽसौ भक्तच्छिन्नस्तु अर्धरात्रे समुपस्थिते ॥५९५॥

G. ६२५ प्राणत्यागं तदा चक्रुः यती सौ लघुचेतसः ।

प्रणिधिं च तदा चक्रे *लाडानामधिपतिर्भवेत्* ॥५९६॥

ततोऽसौ कालगतो भिक्षु<u>र्ध</u>*राख्ये* नृपतौ कुले ।

उत्पद्येत महात्मासौ शास्तुः शासनपूजकः ॥५९७॥

दशवर्षाणि विंशं च राज्यं कृत्वा मकण्टकम् ।

लुब्धः स्वजनप्रयोगेण अजीर्णयतिमूर्छितः ॥५९८॥

भिन्नदेहो <u>ततो</u> राजा कालं कृत्वा दिविं गतः ।

देवा तुषितवरा नाम मैत्रेयो यत्र तिष्ठति ॥५९९॥

---

५८६. उज्जयिन्यां । ५८८. लोके चित्रां । ५८९. धातुधरान् (मूछोद्-र्तेन्) ।
५९०. राजा (ग्र्यल्-पो) । ५९७. धुराख्ये । ५९९. तदा ।

धर्मश्रावी महात्मासौ तत्रासौ उपपत्स्यते ।
धर्मं शृण्वन्ति सत्कृत्य मैत्रेयस्य महाद्युतेः ॥६००॥
सोऽनुपूर्वेण बोधिं च प्राप्स्यति दुर्लभाम् ।
शीलाख्ये नृपतौ वृत्ते चपलस्तत्र भविष्यति ॥६०१॥
वर्षार्धपञ्चमेकं तु पञ्च मासां तथैव तु ।
राज्यं कृत्वा विभिन्नोऽसौ शस्त्रिभिः शस्त्रजीविभिः ॥६०२॥
स्वोकृतेनैव तु दोषेण शस्त्रभिन्नो अधो गतः ।
तस्याप्यनुजो *ध्रुवाख्यस्तु* ध्रुवः स्थावरतां गतः ॥६०३॥
सेवकः कृपणो मूर्खः *लाडानामधिपतिर्भवेत्* ।
शेषा नराधिपाः सर्वे मूर्धान्तास्तु सेवकाः ॥६०४॥

§ 16. Yādava Republic

T. 456 a. तेषां च पूर्वजा वंशाः शीलाह्वोपरते तदा ।
भविता भूपतयः सर्वे अम्भोजे तीरपर्षगाः ॥६०५॥
नृपः इन्द्रो सुचन्द्रश्च धनुः केतुस्तथैव च ।
पुष्पनामो ततः प्रोक्ता *वारवत्यां* पुरोद्भवः ॥६०६॥
वलभ्यां पुरिमागम्य आद्यमस्यानुपूर्वका ।
प्रभनामा सहस्राणि *विष्णुप्रभनामा* तथैव च ॥६०७॥
अनन्ता नृपतयो प्रोक्ता *यादवानां* कुलोद्भवाः ।
तेषामपश्चिमो राजा *विष्णुनामा* भविष्यति ॥६०८॥
G. ६२६ ऋषिशापाभिभूतस्तु सपौरजनबान्धवः । ~
अस्तं गते नृपो धीमां उदके प्लाविता पुरी ॥६०९॥
द्वारवत्या तदा तस्य महोदधिसमाश्रिता ।

Imperial History, Madhya-deśa—§ 17. Śaka Dynasty

उत्तरां दिशि सर्वत्र नानारम्भनितम्बयोः ॥६१०॥
अनन्ता नृपतयः प्रोक्ता नानाजातिसमाश्रिताः ।
शकवंशा तदा त्रिंशत् मनुजेशा निबोधता ॥६११॥

---

६०१. चपलो नाम । ६०२. वर्षान् पंचपंचाशत् । ६०३. असौ मृतः । ६०४. प्रजानां चैव । ६०५. धीरा अम्भोधिपारगाः । ६०६. पुष्पधन्वा च राजपुत्रः । ६१०. धार-रेस्-पूत्स्, गिरि । ६११. एकविंशा ।

दशाष्ट भूपतयः ख्याता सार्धभूतिकमध्यमा ।

§ 18. The Nāga-Senas

अन्ते *नागसेना* तु विलुप्ता ते परे तदा ॥६१२॥

Post-Guptan Imperial Rulers of Madhyadeśa—§ 19. Vishṇu [Vardhana]—§ 19*a*. Maukhari, § 19*b*. Vaiśya Dynasty of Thanesar

ततो *विष्णु* हरश्चैव *कुन्तनामाजितः* परः ।
ईशान-सर्वपंकिश्च ग्रह-सुव्रत (श्र)थापरः ॥६१३॥
ततस्ते विलुप्तराजानः भ्रष्टमर्याद सर्वदा ।

Thanesar Dynasty

T. 456 b. *विष्णुप्रभवौ* तत्र महाभोगो धनिनो तदा ॥६१४॥
मध्यमात् तौ *भ*काराद्यौ मन्त्रिमुख्यौ उभौ तदा ।
धनिनौ श्रीमतौ ख्यातौ शासनेऽस्मिं हिते रतौ ॥६१५॥
जप्तमन्त्रौ तथा मन्त्रे कुमारस्त्वयि मन्त्रराट् ।
ततः परेण भूपालो जाताना मनुजेश्वरौ ॥६१६॥
सप्तमष्टशता त्रीणि *श्रीकण्ठा*वासिनस्तदा ।
*आदित्य*नामा वैश्यास्तु *स्थानमीश्वर*वासिनः ॥६१७॥
भविष्यति न सन्देहो अन्ते सर्वत्र भूपतिः ।
हकाराख्यो नामतः प्रोक्तो सार्वभूमिनराधिपः ॥६१८॥
तत्र देशे इमे मन्त्रा सिद्धिं गच्छेयु वै तदा ।
धर्मराजेन ये प्रोक्ता विद्या शान्तिकपौष्टिका ॥६१९॥
विविधां भोगविषयां सम्पदां विविधांस्तथा ।
नाना च रूपधारिण्यो यक्षिण्यश्च महर्द्धिकाः ॥६२०॥
भविष्यन्ति तत्र वै सिद्धा तस्मिं काले युगाधमे ।

Southern India—§ 20. Sātavāhanas

दक्षिणां दिशिमाश्रित्य ससमुद्रां वसुन्धराम् ॥६२१॥
G. ६२७ राजा श्वेत (:) सुचन्द्रश्च *सातवाहन* एव तु ।

§ 21. Southern contemporaries of Harsha-vardhana

महेन्द्रं शकरश्चैव वल्लभोऽथ महीपतिः ॥६२२॥

---

६१२. सर्वभूपतिमध्यमा । ६१३. हरः । ६१४. ब्राह्मण-प्रभवौ । ६१६. मंत्री भूपालौ जातौ मनुजेश्वरौ । ६१७. सप्तत्यष्टौ तथा । स्थानेश्वर । ६२२. सातवाहन । महेन्द्रः ।

(भोगी) सुकेशि-केशिश्च विख्याता दक्षिणां दिशि ।
मंगलो वल्लभः प्रोक्तो गोविन्दः बृन्दखेतुः ॥६२३॥
मुत्पातः पोतश्चैव महेन्द्रः चन्द्रः एव तु ।
गोपेन्द्रो इन्द्रसेनश्च प्रद्युम्नो माधवस्तदा ॥६२४॥
T. 457 a. गणशंकरश्चैव व्याघ्रं सिंहो तथा बुधः ।
बुधः शुद्धस्तथा कुम्भः निकुम्भश्चैव कीर्त्यते ॥६२५॥
मथितः सुमितश्चैव ।
बलः पुलिनश्चैव सुकेशिः केशिनस्तथा ॥६२६॥
अनन्ता बहवो ख्याता भूपाला दक्षिणां दिशि ।
अतीतानागता चापि वर्त्तमाना निबोधिता ॥६२७॥
नानामृत्युभवे ह्येते नानाव्याधिसमाप्लुता ।
शस्त्रसम्पातदुर्भिक्षै मृताः केचिद् दिवि गताः ॥६२८॥
इत्येते नृपतयः सर्वे कथिता विपुलस्तथा ।
महेन्द्रान्त नृपोताख्यातः तथासहतिस्तथा ॥६२९॥
भविष्यन्ति तदा अभूत् ।
तस्मिं काले तदा देशे मन्त्राणां सिद्धिमिच्छताम् ॥६३०॥
साधनीया इमा मन्त्राः क्रोधाद्याः कुलिशोचिताः ।
आभिचारुककर्मेषु वश्यार्थे च तथा हितम् ॥६३१॥
मञ्जुश्रियोऽथ माहात्मां वै कुमारो बालरूपिणः ।
सिध्यते च तदा देशे कलिप्राप्ते च तदा युगे ॥६३२॥
पर्वतविन्ध्यमाश्रितं सागरे लवणोदके ।
G. ६२८ कार्तिकेयेति समाख्यातः सत्त्वानां वरदायकः ॥६३३॥
आज्ञां भो बोधिसत्त्वेन मञ्जुघोषेण धीमता ।
सत्त्वानां हितकाम्यर्थं निवसेद् दक्षिणां दिशि ॥६३४॥

---

६२३. वृषकेतुः । ६२४. महापोतश्च पोतश्च । चन्द्रसेनश्च । कामदेवो मगधस्तथा । ६२५. व्याघ्रः । बुद्धग्रहः । बुद्धः । ६२६. सहितश्च सुमंगुश्च । ६२८. दिशा । ६२९. काञ्चिपुरे स्थिताः । तथा सहस्रं विख्याताः । ६३०. विधु । ६३२. महात्मा । ६३३. माश्रितं । षण्मुखेति विख्यातः ।

कार्तिकेयस्य ये मन्त्राः कथिता मञ्जुभाषिणा ।

T. 457 b. तस्मिं देशे तदा सिद्धिः भविष्यति न संशयः ॥६३५॥

श्रीपर्वते तदा देशे *विन्ध्य*कुक्षिनितम्बयोः ।

§ 22. Indian Archipelago and Further India

द्वीपेष्वेव च सर्वत्र कलिङ्गोद्रेषु कीर्त्यते ॥६३६॥

त्रैगुण्या म्लेच्छदेशेषु (*कोसलेषु*) समन्ततः ।

अम्भोधेः कुक्षितीरान्ताः नृपा ख्याता अनन्तकाः ॥६३७॥

कामरूप (:) कलाख्या हि *हिमाद्रेः* कुक्षिमाश्रिताः ।

बह्वो नृपतयो प्रोक्ता उद्रसन्धिषु सर्वदा ॥६३८॥

नानाम्लेच्छगणाध्यक्षा शास्तुपूजकतत्पराः ।

इन्द्रो सुचन्द्र महेन्द्रश्च भूपाल म्लेच्छवासिनः ॥६३९॥

क्षमापालौ उभौ तत्र षोडशार्द्धा शासने रता ।

पूजकाः शास्तुबिम्बानां त्वत्प्रसादा ॥६४०॥

भविष्यन्ति न सन्देहो प्रसन्ना शासने जिने ।

§ 23. East Gauḍa Dynasty

बह्वो नृपवराः प्रोक्ताः पूर्वायां दिशिमाश्रिताः ॥६४१॥

अतीतानागता ये तु वर्त्तमानाश्च सर्वदा ।

आद्यं नृपवरं वक्ष्ये *गौडानां* वंशजो भुवि ॥६४२॥

जातोऽसौ नगरे रम्ये वर्धमाने यशास्विनः ।

लोकाख्यो नाम सौ राजा भवति गौडवर्धनः ॥६४३॥

मामानुत्पन्नलोकेऽस्मिं भवितासौ धर्मचिन्तकः ।

बह्वः क्षितिपाः क्रान्ता विविधा जीवकर्मिणः ॥६४४॥

§ 24. Imperial Guptas

मध्यकाले समास्वासा मध्यमा मध्यधर्मिणः ।

अनन्ते व युगे नृपेन्द्रा शृणु तत्त्वतः ॥६४५॥

समुद्राख्यो नृपश्चैव *विक्रम*श्चैव कीर्त्तितः ।

*महेन्द्र*नृपवरो मुख्य *सकाराद्यो* मतः परम् ॥६४६॥

---

६३६. नानाद्वीपेषु । ६३८. सर्वतः (कुन्-नस्) । ६३९. म्लेच्छराजानः । पूजन । चन्द्रश्च नन्दश्च । ६४०. अष्टवर्ष । ततः सर्वेषु जन्मसु । ६४४. सदा वध्यवजीविनः (?) । ६४५. अन्ते कलौ युगे । ६४६. ततः ।

T. 458 a. देवराजाख्यनामासौ (भविष्यति) युगाधमे ।
निर्द्धाख्ये नृपः श्रेष्ठः बुद्धिमान् धर्मवत्सलः ॥६४७॥
G. २९१ तस्याप्यनुजो बलाध्यक्षः शासने च हिते रतः ।
प्राचीं समुद्रपर्यन्तां चैत्यालङ्कृतशोभनाम् ॥६४८॥
करिष्यति न सन्देहः कृत्स्नां वसुमतीं तदा ।
विहारारामवापीश्च उद्याना मण्डवकां सदा ॥६४९॥
करिष्यति तदा श्रीमां सङ्क्रमां सेतुकारकः ।
शास्तुर्बिम्बान् तदा पूजेत् तत्प्रसन्नांश्च पूजयेत् ॥६५०॥
कृत्वा राज्यं महीपालो निःसपत्नमकण्टकम् ।
जीवेद् वर्षा षट्त्रिंशत्त्रिंशाहं प्रव्रजे नृपः ॥६५१॥
ततोत्मानं घातयेद् राजा ध्यायन्तः सम्प्रमूर्च्छितः ।
पुत्रशोकाभिसन्तप्तः यतिवृत्तिसमाश्रुतः ॥६५२॥
ततोऽसौ भिन्नदेहस्तु नरकेभ्योपपद्यत ।
त्रीणि एकं च दिवसानि उषित्वा नरकं गतिम ॥६५३॥
(सो नरक-) देहमुत्सृज्य दिविं गच्छेत् सदा नृपः ।
देवानां सुकृतिनां लोकः शुद्धावास इति स्मृतः ॥६५४॥
देवराजा भवेत् तत्र शुद्धात्मा बोधिनिम्नगः ।
शतशः सहस्रशश्चैव अनुभूय दिविं सुखम् ॥६५५॥
पुनरेव मानुष्यं प्राप्य बुद्धो भूयो भवान्तरे ।
तेनैव कारितं कर्म अन्यजन्मेषु देहिनाम् ॥६५६॥
पुरीमुज्जयिनीं ख्याता मालवानां जने तदा ।
T. 458 b. तत्रायनी मुख्यः वणिजो यो महाधनः ॥६५७॥
बुद्धानामसम्भवे काले शून्ये लोके निरास्पदे ।
प्रत्येकबुद्धा लोकेऽस्मि विहरन्ति महर्द्धिकाः ॥६५८॥
सत्त्वानां हितकामाय विचरन्ति महीतले ।
पुरी उज्जयिनी प्राप्य प्रविष्टा पिण्डचारिका ॥६५९॥

---

६४७. विविधाख्यो । ६४८. बालाख्यः । ६४९. मंडपां । ६५०. पोतः । ६५१. त्रिंशतपर्यन्तं त्रिंशाहं । ६५२. परेण सत्रुणा जितः । ६५४. लोके । ६५७. तत्र भूत्वा । नाकपजो ।

वर्गचारिणो महात्मानः रथ्यायामवतरतत् ।
वाणयाजेयस्तुस्तदा सैव दृष्ट्वा तु संमुखां मुनिम् ॥६६०॥
G. ६३० निमन्त्रयामास तदा भक्तेन स्वगृहं चैव नयेत् तदा ।
नीत्वा मुनिवरां क्षिप्रमासनेन निमन्त्रयेत् ॥६६१॥
सन्नीभवध्व भवतः भक्तकालोऽयमुपस्थितः ।
तेऽपि तूष्णीं महात्मानो न वार्ता भाषिरे तदा ॥६६२॥
पात्रं च नामयामास वाणिजेयस्य सर्वदा ।
वणिजा इङ्गितज्ञाश्च बुद्धिमन्तो भवेत् तदा ॥६६३॥
पात्रं च पूरयामास विविधाकारभोजनैः ।
तदासौ स्वहस्तेनैव तेषां प्रायच्छ यत्नतः ॥६६४॥
गृहीत्वा तु ततः सर्वे प्रजग्मुः सर्वतो नभम् ।
दीपमालेव दृश्यन्ते व्योममूर्त्तिसमाश्रिताः ॥६६५॥
ततोऽसौ हृष्टरोमस्तु संवेगबहुलस्तदा ।
भूम्यां च पतितस्तत्र श्रद्धयावर्जितमानसः ॥६६६॥
प्रणिधिं च तदा चक्रे प्रव्याहार वर्भं यथा ।
अनेन कुशलमूलेन यन्मया प्राप्तमद्यतः ॥६६७॥
एषा मुनिवरा मग्र भवेद् बुद्धो ह्यनुत्तरः ।
दशजन्मसहस्राणि चक्रवर्त्ती तदा भुवि ॥६६८॥
T. 459 a. ततोऽसौ व्युक्तदेहस्तु कोटिषष्टिदिवौकसाम् ।
अनुभूय चिरं सौख्यं त्यक्त्वा जन्म दिवौकसाम् ॥६६९॥
मानुषाणां तदा जन्म प्राप्नुयात् परवशा इह ।
तस्य राजकुले जन्म भवतीह तु सर्वदा ॥६७०॥
बालाख्यो नाम सौ नृपतिर्भविता पूर्वदेशकः ।
आजन्मसहस्राणि चिरसौख्यमनावृतम् ॥६७१॥
प्राप्नुवन्ति या नृपतिः श्रीमां सर्वज्ञत्वं च पश्चिमम् ।
एवं बहुविधं मत्वा सम्पदो विपुलास्तथा ॥६७२॥
को नु कुर्यात् तदा शास्तुः पूजनाभ्येषणांस्तथा ।
कारांश्च श्रेयसीं युक्तां बोधिमार्गवियोजनीम् ॥६७३॥

---

६६०. अहा (? वाणिजो) वै तदा । संमुखं । ६६२. आमीय भगवन्तः । ६६३. तस्य वै । ६६७. वचो । ६६८. भवेयं । ६६९. मुक्तदेहस्तु । ६७२. सत्व । ६७३. क्रिया च । बोधिमार्गोपयोजिनीम् ।

G. ६२१ तस्यापरेण नृपतिः गौडानां प्रभविष्णवः ।
कुमाराख्यो नामतः प्रोक्तः सोऽपि रत्यन्तधर्मवाम् ॥६७४॥
तस्यापरेण श्रोमां उकाराख्येति विश्रुतः ।

§ 25. Break-up of the Empire

ततः परेण विश्लेष तेषामन्योन्यतेष्यते ॥६७५॥
महाविश्लेषणा ह्येते गौडा रौद्रचेतसः ।

§ 26. Later Guptas: Gauḍa Dynasty

ततो देव इति ख्यातो राजा मागधकः स्मृतः ॥६७६॥
सोऽप्यतहतविध्वस्त रिपुभिः समता वृतः ।
यस्यापरेण चन्द्राख्यः नृपतित्वं कारयेत् तदा ॥६७७॥
सोऽपि शस्त्रविभिन्नस्तु पूर्वचोदितकर्मणा ।
T. 459 b. तस्यापि सुतो द्वादश गणानां जोवेन्मासपरम्परम् ॥६७८॥
सोऽपि विभिन्नशस्त्रेण बाल एव अभूत तदा ।

§ 29. Bengal Election—Anarchy—Election of Gopāla

तेषा परस्परोपविघ्नचित्तानां रौद्राणामहिते रताम् ॥६७९॥
भविष्यति तदा काले भकाराख्यो नृपपुङ्गवः ।
अग्रणीगौडलोकानां महाव्याधिसमाकुलः ॥६८०॥
तेनैव व्याधिना आर्त्तः कालं कृत्वा अधो गतः ।
तस्यापरेण दकाराख्यः कतिपायां दिवसां दश ॥६८१॥
भविता गौडदेशेऽस्मिं गंगातोरसमाश्रृतः ।
तस्यापरेण भकाराख्यस्त्रीणि दिवसानि कारयेत् ॥६८२॥
ततो गोपालको राजा भविता सर्वदस्तदा ।
प्रियवादी च सो राजा घृणी चैव महाबलः ॥६८३॥
स्त्रीवशः कृपणो मूर्खः जितशत्रुर्भवेद् युवाम् ।
कल्याणमित्रमागम्य महात्यागी भवेत् तदा ॥६८४॥
विहारांश्चैत्यवरां रम्यामारामां विविधांस्तदा ।
वाप्योऽथ जलसम्पन्ना सत्रागारां सुशोभनाम् ॥६८५॥

---

६७४. शोक-संयुतः । अत्यन्तधर्मवान् । ६७५. श्रीमान् । ६७६. विध्वंसका । राजमार्गक्रियाविदः । वहत, समंताद् ६७८. जीवे- द्दर्षाहकम् । ६७९. सुतस्तदा । ६८०. तकाराख्यो । ६८१. कतिपयान् दिवसान् शवास । ६८२. सर्वतस्तदा ।

सेवतो बहवस्तस्य यशः कीर्त्यार्थमुद्यतः ।
देवायतनरम्यां वै गुणावसथकारिणः ॥६८६॥
G. १२२ पाषण्डोभिः समाक्रान्तं नानातीर्थिकवासिभिः ।
आक्रान्तः सो दिशः सर्वा समुद्रातीरचर्यगाः ॥६८७॥
क्रिपो भोगी प्रमादी च सं राजा धर्मवत्सलः ।
भविष्यति न सन्देहः स प्राचीं दिशि मूर्जितः ॥६८८॥
T. 460 a. सधातीसारसंयुक्तवार्द्धिक्ये समुपस्थितः ।
*गंगा*तीरमुपाश्रित्य राज्यं कृत्वा तु वै तदा ॥६८९॥
विंशद् वर्षाणि सप्तं च जन्मनाशीतिको मृतः ।
ततोऽसौ भिन्नदेहस्तु तिर्यगेभ्योऽपिपद्यते ॥६९०॥

Earlier History of Gauḍa. § 30. The Nāga Dynasty in Gauḍa

नागराजा ततः श्रीमान् (धर्मात्मा) धर्मवत्सलः ।
येनास्य कारितं चैत्य शास्तुबिम्बं मनोरमम् ॥६९१॥
विहारां कारितवांश्चात्र सङ्घस्यार्थे तदा भुवि ।
तेन कर्मविपाकेन अन्तिमे च भवे श्रिते ॥६९२॥
बुद्धत्वं नियतं मार्गं प्राप्नुयादचलं पदम् ।
ततः परेण गौडानां तीर्थिकाक्रान्तपुरं भुवि ॥६९३॥

§ 30 *a*. Emperor Prabha-Vishṇu and Gauḍa King

ता पूर्वदेशेऽस्मिन् नगरे तीर्थिकसमाह्वये ।
भगवाख्ये नृपे ख्यातः गौडानां प्रभविष्णव: ॥६९४॥
अभिषिक्तो दक्षिणात्येन प्रतिना प्रभविष्णुना ।
राज्यं कृत्वा तु वै तत्र पश्चिमां दिशिमागतः ॥६९५॥
प्रविश्य नगरीं रम्यां *साकेतां* तु यथेप्सितः ।
अरिणा भूतस्तु पुनरेव निवर्तते ॥६९६॥
प्राचीं समुद्रपर्यन्तां तस्करैश्च समावृतः ।
शस्त्रप्रहारविध्वस्त मृतोऽसो प्रेततां गतः ॥६९७॥

---

६८६. गुहावसथकारिणः । ६८८. अमितभोगी च स । ६८९. सदा । द्वंक्ये ।
६९०. त्रिंशद् (गुसुम्-त्तु) वर्षाणि सप्त च । पपद्यते । ६९४. मगवद्‌ाख्यो नृपः । प्रभविष्णुकः ।
६९५. दक्षिणास्येन प्रतिना । ६९७. अजीर्णेन (? अरिणा) परिभूतस्तु ।

त्रीणि वर्षाणि कृत्वासौ भूपालो राज्यमल्पकम् ।
ततो दस्युभिर्ग्रस्तः मृतः प्रेत महर्द्धिकः ॥६९८॥
T. 460 b. त्रीणि वर्षाणि तत्रैव प्रेतेभ्यो राज्यमकारयेत् ।
ततोऽपि सो त्यक्तदेहस्तु प्रेतलोकां सुदारुणाम् ॥६९९॥

§ 31. Emperor Samudra Gupta

G. ६२२ तस्मान्मुक्तजन्मानः स्वर्लोकं च सदा व्रजेत् ।
तस्याधरेण नृपतिस्तु *समुद्राख्यो* नाम कीर्त्तितः ॥७००॥
त्रीणि दिवसानि दुर्मेधः राज्यं प्राप्स्यति दुर्मतिः ।
तस्याप्यनुजो विक्यातः भस्ममाख्यो नाम नामतः ॥७०१॥
प्रभुः प्राणातिपातसंयुक्तः महासावद्यकारिणः ।
निर्घृणी अप्रमत्तश्च स्वशरीरे तु यत्नतः ॥७०२॥
परलोकार्थिने नासौ बलिसत्त्ववदिहैव तु ।
अकल्याणमित्रमागम्य पापं कर्म कृतं बहु ॥७०३॥
द्विजैराक्रान्ततद्राज्यं तार्किकैः कृपणैस्तथा ।
विविधाकारभोगांश्च मानुषा पितरास्तथा ॥७०४॥
विविधां सम्पदां सोऽपि प्राप्तवान् नृपतिस्तथा ।
सोऽनुपूर्वेण गत्वासौ पश्चिमां दिशि भूपतिः ॥७०५॥
कश्मीरद्वारपर्यन्तं उत्तरां दिशिमाश्रृतः ।
तत्रापि जितसङ्ग्रामी राज्यं कृत्वा तु वै तदा ॥७०६॥
द्वादशाब्दानि सर्वत्र मासां पञ्चदशास्तथा ।
पृथिव्यामार्तरोगोऽसौ मूर्छितश्च पुनः पुनः ॥७०७॥

§ 32. Condition of Bengal: Later Gupta Period

महादुःखाभिभूतस्तु भिन्नदेह अधोगतः ।
तेषां परस्परतो द्वेषे लुब्धानां राज्यहेतुनाम् ॥७०८॥
महाशस्त्रोपसम्पातं कृत्वा ते तु परस्परम् ।
T. 461 a. अभिषिच्य तदा राज्यं *सकराख्यं* बालदारकम् ॥७०९॥
चिह्नमात्रं तु तं कृत्वा पुनरेव निवर्त्तते ।
यैर्द्विजातिमुक्यानां भिन्नास्तेऽपि परस्परम् ॥७१०॥
मागधा जनपदां प्राप्य पुरे *उदुम्बराह्वये* ।
द्वे बालौ द्विजातिमुख्यश्च अभिषेच्य स्वयं भुवि ॥७११॥

---

७०१. वर्षाणि । विक्यातो भस्माक्यो । ७०७. पंच वै तथा । ७१०. मुख्यानां ।

ततोऽनुपूर्वेण गत्वासौ प्राचीं दिशिमाश्रृतः ।
गौडां जनपदां प्राप्य निःसपत्ना ह्य वै तदा ॥७१२॥
G. १२४ घातितौ बालमुख्यौ तौ कलिङ्गस्तु दुरात्मना ।
अकल्याणमित्रमागम्य कृतं प्राणिवधो बहुम् ॥७१३॥
पूर्वसम्मानिता ये तु नृपैर्विग्रहमानिभिः ।
घातयामास सर्वेषां *गौडानां* जनवासिनाम् ॥७१४॥

§ 33. Soma=Śaśāṅka

*सोमाख्यो*ऽपि ततो राजा एकवीरो भविष्यति ।
*गंगातीरपर्यन्तं वाराणस्या*मतःपरम् ॥७१५॥
नाशयिष्यति दुर्मेधः शास्तुर्बिम्बां मनोरमाम् ।
जिनैस्तु कथितं पूर्वं धर्मसेतुमनल्पकम् ॥७१६॥
दाहापयति दुर्मेधः तीर्थिकस्य वचे रतः ।
ततोऽसौ क्रुद्धलुब्धस्तु मिथ्यामानी ह्यसंमतः ॥७१७॥
विहारारामचैत्यांश्च निर्ग्रन्थावसथां भुवि ।
भेत्स्यते च तदा सर्वा वृत्तिरोधमकारक ॥७१८॥

§ 34. Rājyavardhana and Harshavardhana, and War with Śaśāṅka

T. 461 b. भविष्यते च तदा काले मध्यदेशे नृपो वरः ।
रकाराद्योतयुक्तात्मा वैश्यवृत्तिमचञ्चलः ॥७१९॥
शासनेऽस्मि तथा शक्त *सोमाख्य*ससमो नृप ।
सोऽपि याति तवान्तेन नग्नजातिनृपेण तु ॥७२०॥
तस्याप्यनुजो हकाराख्य एकवीरो भविष्यति ।
महासैन्यसमायुक्तः शूरः क्रान्तविक्रमः ॥७२१॥
निर्धारये हकाराख्यो नृपतिं सोमविश्रुतम् (:) ।
वैश्यवृत्तिस्ततो राजा महासैन्यो महाबलः ॥७२२॥
पूर्वदेशं तदा जग्मुः पुण्ड्राख्यं पुरमुत्तमम् ।
क्षत्रधर्मं समाश्रृत्य मानरोषमशीलिनः ॥७२३॥
घृणी धर्मार्त्थको विघ्नां कुर्यात् प्राणिवधं बहून् ।
सत्त्वानुपीडनपरो निग्रहायैव सो रतः ॥७२४॥

---

७१३. कलिंगेन्द्र-। ७१८. निर्ग्रन्थावस्थां । वृत्तिरोध-चिकीर्षकः । ७१९. रकाराख्यस्तु विद्यात्मा । ७२३. पुण्ड्राख्यं ।

पराजयामास सोमाख्यं दुष्टकर्मानुचारिणम् ।
ततो निषिद्धः सोमाख्यो स्वदेशेनावतिष्ठतः ॥७२५॥
G. १२५ निवर्तयामास हकाराख्यः म्लेच्छराज्ये मपूजितः ।
दुष्टकर्मा हकाराख्यो नृपः श्रेयसा चार्थधर्मिणः ॥७२६॥
स्वदेशेनैव प्रयातः यथेष्टगतिनापि वा ।
तैरेव कारितं कर्म राज्यहर्षीसमन्वितैः ॥७२७॥
अधुना प्राप्तवां भोगां राज्यवृत्तिमुपाश्रृताम् ।
पूर्वं प्रत्येकबुद्धाय भक्ताच्छादनदत्तवाम् (? न्) ॥७२८॥
T. 462 a. पादुकौ च तदा दत्तौ च्छत्रचामरभूषितम् ।
तस्य धर्मप्रभावेतौ महाराज्यतृदेवतो ॥७२९॥
भुक्त्वां भोगसम्पत्तीः देवमनुष्यसर्वदा ।
सोमाख्यो द्विजाह्वयो महाभोगी भवे ह्यसौ ॥७३०॥
भोगां द्विजातिषु दत्त्वा वै राज्यं कृत्वा वै तदा ।
सार्धं सप्तमं तथा ॥७३१॥
वर्षा दश सप्तं च मासमेकं तथापरम् ।
दिवसां सप्तमष्टौ च मुखरोगसमाकुलः ॥७३२॥
कृमिभिर्भक्षमाणस्तु कालं कृत्वा अधोगति ।
अमानुषाक्रान्तविध्वस्तं तत्पुरं च अभूत् तदा ॥७३३॥
(अ)मानुषेणैव दोषेण ज्वरार्तो व्याधिमूर्च्छितः ।
मृतो मन्त्रप्रयोगेण राजासौ कालगतस्तदा ॥७३४॥
अवीचिर्नाम विख्यातं नरकं पापकारिणा ।
तत्रासौ उपपद्येत पापकर्मान्तचारिणः ॥७३५॥
महाकल्पं तदा नरके पच्यतेऽसौ दुष्टचेतसः ।
ततो (ऽ)टटं हहवं चैव सञ्जीवं कालसूत्रं तु ॥७३६॥
असिपत्रवनं घोरं अनुभूय पुनः पुनः ।
तिर्यक्प्रेतलोकं च (यमलोकं) पुनस्तथा ॥७३७॥
एवं जन्मसहस्राणि संसारे संसरतः पुनः ।
नासौ विन्दति सौख्यानि दुःखभाजो भवेद् सदा ॥७३८॥

---

७२६. मपूजितः । ७२७. हर्षं । ७२९. कर्मप्रभावेन । नृदेवतौ । ७३३. अधोगतः ।

G. १२१ तस्मात् सर्वप्रयत्नेन शासनेऽस्मिं तथागते ।

T. 462 b. प्रसाद्यमखिलं चित्तं गच्छध्वं निर्जरसम्पदम् ॥७३९॥

बुद्धे कारापकारां च अनन्ता भवति कर्मता ।

बुद्धे प्रासादः कर्तव्यः धर्मसङ्घे च वै तथा ॥७४०॥

भवन्ति लोके अग्रस्तु त्रिरन्ते पूजका नृपा ।

महेशाख्यमहेराज्यं महाभोगा धनेश्वरा ॥७४१॥

प्राप्नुयाद् विविधां सोख्यां सम्पदां विपुलां नृपा ।

पूजयित्वा तु लोकाग्र्यां लोक ईश्वरतां व्रजेत् ॥७४२॥

शक्रत्वमथ याम्यत्वं ब्रह्मत्वं च पुनः पुनः ।

प्रत्येकबुद्धा बुद्धत्वं श्रावकत्वं च वै भुवि ॥७४३॥

प्राप्नुवन्ति त्रियानमग्रत्वं द्वौ यातौ निःस्पृहतां गतः ।

एवं ह्यचिन्तिया बुद्धा बुद्धज्ञानोपचिन्तियः ॥७४४॥

अचिन्तियो हि फलं तेषां विपाको भवन्त्यचिन्तियः ।

§§ 35-36. Condition of Bengal, Śaśāṅkas death and Revolution

अतः परेण सोमाख्यो नृपतौ अप्यस्तमिते भुवि ॥७४५॥

अन्योन्यक्षोभशीलस्तु गौडतन्त्रो भविष्यति ।

सदा उद्यतशस्त्रास्तु अन्योन्यापि नर्पेक्षिणः ॥७४६॥

दिवसा सप्तमेवं तु मासमेकं तथापरम् ।

गणराज्यं तदा तन्त्रे भविष्यति सदा भुवि ॥७४७॥

गङ्गातीरे एतस्मिं विहाराध्युषितमालये ।

ततः परेण सुतस्तस्य सोमाख्यस्य च मानवे ॥७४८॥

मासान्यष्टौ दिवसा पञ्च साधाहे सुनिशात्यन्तु ।

§ 37. Nāga kings and Prabha Vishṇu (repeated)

वैश्यवर्णशिशुस्तदा ॥७४९॥

T. 463 a. नगाराजसमाह्वयो गौडराजा भविष्यति ।

अन्ते तस्य नृपे तिष्ठं जयाद्यावर्णतद्विशौ ॥७५०॥

---

७३९. निर्जरसम्पदम् । ७४१. त्रिरन्तपूजका । महेशाख्यामहाराज्या । ७४२. सौख्य । ७४३. प्रत्येकबुद्धबुद्धत्व । ७४४. द्वे-याने । बुद्धज्ञानमप्यचिन्त्यम् । ७४६. अन्योऽन्यानपेक्षिणः । ७४७. सप्तमेकं । गणराज्यं । सदा । ७४८. चकार विहारावसथं । माणवः । ७४९. सार्धाहेषु जीवति । ७५०. समाह्वयो जयादिवर्णब्राह्मणः ।

वैश्यैः परिवृतो वैश्यं नागाह्वयो समन्ततः ।
दुर्भिक्षोपद्रवास्तेऽपि परचक्रोपद्रुतास्तदा ॥७५१॥
G. ६३७ तेषां राज्यमसम्प्राप्तं महातस्करमाकुलाः ।
ते तं भ्रष्टमर्यादा ॥७५२॥
वर्षा पञ्चकमेकं वै भुङ्क्ते तत्र समाकुलाम् ।
प्राणात्ययं तदा चक्रुः कृत्वा प्राणिवधं बहून् ॥७५३॥
पूर्वकर्मपराधेन ते जना वैश्यवृत्तयः ।
अन्योन्यक्षोभशीलास्तु भविष्यन्ति तदा अभूत् ॥७५४॥
प्रभविष्णुस्तदा तेषां क्षत्रवृत्तिसमाश्रितः ।

§ 38. Confusion in the East: reign of Siśu [Rudrasena], and rise of Samudra Gupta

भविष्यन्तिं न सन्देहः *गौडतंत्रे* नराधिपः ॥७५५॥
शस्त्रभिन्ना तथा केचिद् व्याधिभिश्च समाकुलाः ।
कालं कृत्वा ततो याता नरकेभ्यो नराधिपा ॥७५६॥
सोप्रधानं शिशुस्तत्र पुनरेव नराधिपः ।
पक्षमेकं तथा वै शस्त्रभिन्नो हतस्तदा ॥७५७॥
महादुर्भिक्षसम्पातं परचक्रसमाकुलम् ।
प्राच्या जनपदा व्यस्ता उत्रस्ता गतमानसा ॥७५८॥
भविष्यन्ति न सन्देहः तस्मिं देशे नराधिपाः ।
मधुरायां जातवंशाढ्यः वणिक् सुर्वो नृपो वरः ॥७५९॥
T. 463 b. सोऽपि पूजितमूर्त्तिस्तु *मागधानां* नृपो भवेत् ।

§ 39. Later Imperial Guptas and the East

तस्याप्यनुजो *भकाराख्य* प्राचीं दिशि समाश्रितः ॥७६०॥
तस्यापि सुतः पकाराख्यः प्राग्देशेष्वेव जायतः ।
क्षत्रियः अग्रणी प्रोक्तः बालबन्धानुचारिणः ॥७६१॥
दश वर्षाणि सप्तं च बन्धनस्थमधिष्ठितः ।
गोपाख्येन नृपतिना बद्धो मुक्तोऽसौ *मगधाह्वये* ॥७६२॥

---

७५१. विप्रैः परिवृतो वैश्यो नागाह्वयः । तथा । ७५३. ग्रासमाकुलम् । ७५७. च ते ।
७५९. मधुराजातो वैशाख्याः पूर्वी । ७६१. प्रकाराख्यः प्राग्देशेषु स जायते ।

§ 40. Installation of Pra(kaṭâditya) by H[ūṇa]

पश्चाद्देशसमायातः प्रकाराख्यो महानृपः ।
प्राचिं दिशिपर्यन्तं *गङ्गा*तीरमतिष्ठत ॥७६३॥
शूद्रवर्णो महाराजा महासैन्यो महाबलः ।
सो तं तीरं समाश्रृत्य तिष्ठते च समन्ततः ॥७६४॥
G. ६३८ पुरीं *गौडजने* ख्यातं तीर्थाह्वति विश्रुतः ।
समाक्रम्य राजासौ तिष्ठते च महाबलः ॥७६५॥
तत्रौ च क्षत्रियो बालः वणिना च तथागतः ।
रात्रौ प्रविष्टवांस्तत्र रक्ष्यन्ते च प्रपूजितः ॥७६६॥
शूद्रवर्णे नृपः ख्यातः पुनरेव निवर्तयम् ।
गङ्गातोरपर्यन्तं नगरे *नन्द*समाह्वये ॥७६७॥
मागधानां तदा राज्यं (? ज्ये) स्थापयामास तं शिशुम् ।
काशिनं पद प्राप्य *वाराणस्य*मतः पुरे ॥७६८॥
प्रविशेच्छूद्रवर्णस्तु महीपालो महाबलः ।

§ 40*a*. Graha [Mihira] son of H[ūṇa] and his father

महारोगेण दुःखार्तः अभिषेचे सतं तदा ॥७६९॥
अभिषिच्य तदा राज्यं *ग्रहा*ख्यं बालदारकम् ।
महारोगाभिभूतस्तु भूमावावर्त वै तदा ॥७७०॥
ततोर्ध्वं निःश्वस्य यत्नेन भिन्नदेहोऽपि तीर्यतः ।
तिर्येभ्ये वसं मासां अष्ट सप्तं च वै तदा ॥७७१॥
ततोऽसौ मुक्तजन्मान देवेभ्यो मुपपद्यते ।
विविधां देवसम्पत्तिं विंशजन्मानि वै तदा ॥७७२॥
ततोऽनुपूर्वेण धर्मात्मा प्रत्येकं बोधिमाप्नुयात् ।
तेनैवोपार्जितं कर्म पूर्वकालेषु जन्मनि ॥७७३॥
प्रत्येकबुद्धो महात्मा वै वस्त्रैः समभिच्छादितः ।
उपानहं नामयामास हस्त्यश्वरथहेतुना ॥७७४॥
भोजनं च तदा तस्य तस्मा दद्युः प्रयत्नधीः ।
तेन कर्मविपाकेन देवराजा शतक्रतुः ॥७७५॥

---

७६३. हकाराख्यो । ७६५. ह्वेति । ७६६. तत्र । वणिजा च सहागतः । ७६७. वर्णो । ७६८. काशिजनपदं ।७६९. सुतं । ७७०. भूमिं पश्यति । ७७१. तिर्यग् । तिर्यक्स्यो ।

भविता देवलोकेऽस्मिं त्रिंशत्कोट्यास्तु जन्मतः ।
भुविमायात राजासौ भविता इह जन्मनि ॥७७६॥
परैरुपार्जितं राज्यं अनुभोक्ता भविष्यति ।
तस्यापि च सुतो राजा *वाराणस्यां* तु प्रतिष्ठितः ॥७७७॥

[Garha's end]

G. ६२९ समन्ताद्धतविध्वस्तविलुप्तराज्यो भविष्यति ।
द्विजक्रान्तमभूयिष्ठं तद् राज्यं रिपुभिस्तदा ॥७७८॥
प्रमादो कामचारो च स राजा मद्दचिह्नितः ।
अपश्चिमे तु काले वै पश्चाच्छत्रुहतो मृतः ॥७७९॥

T. 464 b. *मागधो* नृपतिस्तेषां अन्योन्यावरोधिनः ।
सोमाख्ये नृपते वृत्ते प्राग्देशे समन्ततः ॥७८०॥
गंगातीरपर्यन्तं वाराणस्यामतः परम् ।
भविष्यति तदा राजा पकाराख्यः क्षत्रियस्तदा ॥७८१॥
योऽसौ शूद्रवर्णेन अकाराख्येन पूजितः ।
नगरे *नन्दसमाख्याते गंगा*तीरे तु समाश्रिते ॥७८२॥
भविता क्षत्रियो राजा पूर्वकर्मैस्तु चोदितः ।
तेनैव कारितं कर्म कृतं चाप्यनुमोदितम् ॥७८३॥
अतिक्रान्ते तदा काले कनकाह्वे शास्तुसम्भवे ।
वाराणस्यां महानगर्यां श्रेष्ठिरासीन्महाधनः ॥७८४॥
वणिजः स सुतो बालः बालिशैस्तु समावृतः ।
पांसुक्रीडनमर्थाय रथ्यायां प्रतिपद्यते ॥७८५॥
स्वगृहे स्तूपवरं दृष्ट्वा पितामात्राभिपूजितम् ।
तदेव मनसा वर्ते स्तूपं कृत्वा तु पांसुना ॥७८६॥
पूजां च कारयामास निर्माल्यकुसुमैस्तदा ।
संस्तवामास तं स्तूपं बुद्धत्वं श्राद्धगतिस्मृतिः ॥७८७॥
क्रीडते बालस्तत्र शिशुभिः परिवारितः ।
जिने कनकशास्तुस्य श्रावकाभो तदैकक: ॥७८८॥
वीतदोषस्तु युक्तात्मा त्रैधातुकमुक्तधीः ।
T. 465 a. तदासौ वीतदोषस्तु पिण्डपातमहिण्डत ॥७८९॥

---

७७६. नवकोट्यस्तु । ७७८. द्विजाक्रान्तभूयिष्ठं । ७७९. च्छत्रहतो । ७८०. मृते ।
७८१. प्रकाराख्यः । ७८२. हकाराख्येन । ७८५. वाणिजस्य । ७८७. बुद्धगतस्मृतिः ।

प्रविशते च तदा नगरीं *वारणस्यां* सुशोभनाम् ।
वीतरागस्तदादेशं यत्र ते बालिशा भुवि ॥७९०॥
G. ६४० यत्र ते शैशवः सर्वे समन्तात् परिवारिताः ।
एहि भिक्षु इहागच्छ वन्द स्त्वं शास्तुचैत्यकम् ॥७९१॥
अस्माभिः कारितं यत्नात् न त्वं पश्यसि शोभनम् ।
ततः श्रेष्ठिसुतो बालः गृहीत्वा तृणावर्तितम् ॥७९२॥
क्रीडया बन्धयामास वीतरागं महर्द्धिकम् ।
समन्वाहरति तत्रासौ वीतरागो महर्द्धिकः ॥७९३॥
पश्यते भुवि तत्रस्थं चैत्यं कारितकं हि तैः ।
बालिशं मूर्ध्नि मासृज्य एवं वोच महात्मधीः ॥७९४॥
मुञ्च दारक गच्छामो यत्र त्वं कारितं कृतिः ।
आगता च ततः सर्वे यत्र धातुधरं भुवि ॥७९५॥
वन्दित्वा वीतरागा महात्मासौ शिशुभिश्चैतदासमैः ।
पुनरेव प्रस्थितो वीरः पिण्डकार्थं यथेप्सतः ॥७९६॥
ततः श्रेष्ठिसुतो बालः गृहीत्वा चीवरान्तिकम् ।
स्वगृहं नीतवां ह्यासोद् भोजनार्थं च कारयेत् ॥७९७॥
ततः श्रेष्ठिमुख्योऽसौ दृष्ट्वा तं बालिशम् ।
गृहीत्वा चीवरान्ते तु वीतरागं महर्द्धिकम् ॥७९८॥
T. 465 b. भीतो हृष्टरोमश्च गृहं मे आगतोऽग्रजः ।
पादयोर्निपतितं क्षिप्रं मुञ्चापयति बालकम् ॥७९९॥
गृहीत्वा तु सुतं तस्य क्षमापयामास यत्नतः ।
पात्रं तु गृहीत्वा वै जिने अप्रजिते हिते ॥८००॥
पूरयामास तं पात्रं शालिव्यञ्जनभक्तकैः ।
सुतं चामन्त्रयामास गृह्य मन्त्र प्रयच्छ भोः ॥८०१॥
ततो बालोऽथ सम्प्रह्नो हस्तौ प्रक्षाल्य यत्नतः ।
गृहीत्वा पात्रपूरं तु वीतरागाय नामयेत् ॥८०१ अ॥
नामयित्वा तु तं क्षिप्रं पादयोर्निपतितो भुवि ।
वीतरागो गृहीत्वा तु (विहारं प्राप्य) भुक्तवाम् (? न्) ॥८०२॥

---

७९१. स्वं । ७९२. तृणवरत्राम् । ७९४. आमृज्य । ७९७. भिक्षुं ।
८००. पुष्पोत्तमो हितेरतः । ८०१. पात्रं (?) ।

G. ६४१ वीतरागो तदा ह्यासीत् सुखसंस्पर्शी च लब्धवाम् ।
अपरस्तत्र बालो वै मात्सर्याविष्टमानसः ॥८०३॥
केवलं रोषचित्तेन वीतरागो परेऽहनि ।
प्रभूतं खाद्यभोज्यं च गृहीत्वा तं प्रयच्छत ॥८०४॥
यद्यस्ति कुशलं किञ्चित् त्वयि दत्वा तु पिण्डकम् ।
अनेन श्रेष्ठिसुतस्याहं भविता आढ्यतमो भुवि ॥८०५॥
ततस्ते तीर्थिकाः सर्वे द्विजातिवनिता तदा ।
सन्निपत्य तदा सर्वे कलहं निन्दकं कृत्वा ॥८०६॥
बालिशस्त्वं न जानासि मुण्डकानां कुतो गतिः ।
T. 466 a. आत्मना अस्थिता ह्येते परेषां कुत्र निर्वृतिः ॥८०७॥
तस्य बालकसत्त्वस्य द्वेषमुत्पन्न तादृशम् ।
नाशयामास एतेषां शास्तारेणोपवर्णिताम् ॥८०८॥
धर्मसेतु सदा कीर्तिं विहारां चैत्यवरां भुवि ।
श्रेष्ठिमुख्यसुतस्यैव आघातं चैव कारयेत् ॥८०९॥
एतेषां मुण्डकानां तु दत्त्वा दानं कुतो गतिः ।
कुगतिग्रस्तचित्तानां विघातं कारयाम्यहम् ॥८१०॥
यो सौ वाद्यतमो बालो सोमाख्योऽपि नृपो ह्यसौ ।
अनुभूय चिरं दुःखं विपाकः तस्य नैष्ठिकम् ॥८११॥
श्रेष्ठिमुख्यस्य पुत्रोऽसौ भिन्नदेहो दिविं गतः ।
अनुभूय चिरं सौख्यं दिवौकसानां तदा तदा ॥८१२॥
च्युतोऽसौ देवलोकेऽस्मिम् ।
(अन्तिमे च) तदाजन्मे बन्धं सेत्स्यति सर्वदा ॥८१३॥
नृजन्मोपगतो मर्त्यः क्ष्मापतिः भविता पुनः ।
पुनश्च पतितः कर्मेण तत्र तत्र तदा तदा ॥८१४॥
भविता जन्मलोकेऽस्मिं नृपतित्वं कारयेद् भुवि ।
निर्माल्यदानं यस्स्तूपे निवेद्य सौ बालचापलात् ॥८१५॥
तेनास्य भोगा क्लिष्टा वै क्लिष्टादानस्य तत् फलम् ।
दुःखेन भोगांस्तु प्राप्तस्तु नम्रसन्धीव सौ नृपः ॥८१६॥

---

८११. बालतमो । ८१३. तदा तदा स च तत्र च्युतोऽसौ देवलोकादस्मात् ।
८१४. अन्यजन्मोपगतो । ८१६. क्लिष्टदानस्य । शासन एव ।

G. १४२ अस्थैर्या बालवस्त्वश्च चलचित्ततया च सदा ।
T. 466 b. कुर्वीत महतीं पूजां शास्तुर्धातुवरे भुवि ॥८१७॥
तेन कर्मविपाकेन राज्यैश्वर्यं चलतां व्रजेत् ।
भूत्वा भवति राजा अभूत्वा प्रतिगच्छति ॥८१८॥
उदीच्यप्रतीच्यमध्यौ सो नृपतित्वं कारयेद् भुवि ।
यो सौ मुक्तधीबन्धः पुनर्मुक्तश्च बालकः ॥८१९॥
तेन कर्मविपाकेन बद्धो मुक्तश्च बालकः ।
पञ्चजन्मशतानैव बद्धो मुक्तश्च बालकः ॥८२०॥
अपश्चिमे तु तदा जन्मे बन्धं छेत्स्यति सर्वदा ।
पञ्चपञ्चाशवर्षस्तु सप्तसप्ततिकोऽपि वा ॥८२१॥
प्राचीं समुद्रपर्यन्तां राजासौ भविता भुवि ।
*विन्ध्य*कुक्षिनिविष्टास्तु प्रत्यन्तम्लेच्छतस्कराः ॥८२२॥
सर्वे ते वशवर्ति स्यात् पकाराख्ये नृपतौ भुवि ।
हिमाद्रिकुक्षिसन्निविष्टा तु उत्तरां दिशिमाश्रृताम् ॥८२३॥
सर्वां जनपदां भुङ्क्ते राजासौ क्षत्रियस्तदा ।
पांसुना कृत्वा स्तूपं अज्ञानाद् बालभावतः ॥८२४॥
*मागधे*षु भवेद् राजा निःसपत्नमकण्टकः ।
सैमामटवीपर्यन्तां प्राचीसमुद्रमाश्रृतः ॥८२५॥
*लौहित्या*परतो धीमां उत्तरे *हिमवां*स्तथा ।
पश्चात् *काशिपुरी* रम्यां *शृंगाख्ये* पुर एव वा ॥८२६॥
अत्रान्तरे महीपालः शास्तुशासनदायकः ।
पञ्च केसरिनामानौ जित्वा नृपतिनौ सौ ॥८२७॥
स्वं राज्यमकारयत् ।
T. 467 a. सर्वास्तां सिंहजास्तेऽपि ध्वस्तोन्मूलिता तदा ॥८२८॥
हिमाद्रिकुक्षिप्राच्यां भो दशानूपः तीरमाश्रयेत् ।
सर्वा जनपदां भुङ्क्ते राजासौ क्षत्रियस्तदा ॥८२९॥

---

८१७. अस्थैर्याद् बालिकास्त्वाच्च । ८१९. कृत । ८२१. पश्चिमे । ८२३. प्रकाराख्ये । ८२७. गौडजितेव परनृपतिना जिताः । ८२८. सर्वे वै । ८२९. हिमाद्रिकुक्षौ प्राच्यां च दश सिंधुतीरमाश्रितः । सर्वान् जनपदान् ।

*(शठाः पर-शृत्तिकाश्चैव विन्ध्यकुक्षिनिवासिनः ।
दुर्गेति मध्यदेशे ते स्वयं राज्यं अकार्षुः ॥८२९A॥
महाविषजयो जित्वा प्रागुदक् सर्वतः स्थितान् ।
केसरिनामा तथाऽन्यः सोमाख्यो नृपो मृतः ॥८२९B॥
तदा गौडजना भिन्नाः क्षत्रियो राजा तदा ।
राजाऽभिवर्धमान जन्मेतिभविष्यति न संशयः) ॥८२९C॥
G. ६५१ अभिवर्धमानजन्मस्तु भोगास्तस्य च वर्द्धताम् ।
वार्धिक्ये च तदा प्रोक्ते भोगां निश्चलतां व्रजेत् ॥८३०॥
अशीतिवर्षाणि जीवेयुः सप्त सप्त तथा पराम् ।
ततो जीर्णाभिभूतस्तु कालं कृत्वा दिवं गतः ॥८३१॥
देवलोकेऽस्मिं चिरसौख्यमनुभूय तथा नृपः ।
पुनश्च्यवति कर्मेण पूर्वसङ्क्लेशितेन तु ॥८३२॥
तिर्यक्षु न्वसे मासं नागराजमहर्द्धिकः ।
ततोऽसौ भिन्नदेहस्तु मानुषेष्वोपपद्यते ॥८३३॥
क्षत्रियो धीमतो जतो वणिग्जीवी विशारदः ।
कल्याणमित्रमागम्य मोक्तासौ जिनशासने ॥८३४॥
साधयेद् विद्याराज्ञीं तारादेविं महर्द्धिकाम् ।
सिद्धमंत्रस्तु जिनो नासौ यथेष्टगतिचारिणः ॥८३५॥
विद्याधराणां तदा राजा भविता सुगतस्तदा ।
चक्रवर्तिस्तदा ख्यातो नाम्नासौ चित्रकेतवः ॥८३६॥
T. 467 b. विद्याधराणां तदा कर्म ख्यातोऽसौ मतिमांस्तथा ।
अशीतिवर्षकोट्यानि नवसप्तानि चैतदा ॥८३७॥
दिव्यमानुष्यमाद्येन भविता चक्रवर्त्तिनः ।
परिवारस्तस्य कन्यानां षष्टिकोट्यो मजायत ॥८३८॥

---

* (ग्.योन्-चन्-बृशन्-ल-तंन्-प-दक् । ऽविग्स्-क्येद्-मङ्-न-गूनस्-प-यि ।
दे-यङ्-रङ्-गि-ग्यंल्-पो-व्यस् । बृग्रोद्-बृकऽ-बोस्-क्यऽि-युल्-दबु-सु ॥
दुग्-छेन्-र्ग्यंल्-वल्-र्गम्-र्ग्यंल्-व्यस् । व्यङ्-शर्-कुन्-ल-गूनस्-प-यि ।
सेङ्-गे-शेस्-ब्य-दे-बृशिन्-गूशन् । स-वऽि-र्शस्-ब्यऽि-र्ग्यंल्-पो-ऽदस् ॥
दे-छे-गौ-डऽि स्क्येबो-ऽजिग् । दे-छे-र्ग्यंल्-रिग्स्-स-यि-बृदग् ।
ऽग्युर्-पर्-ऽग्युर्-नु-थ-छोम्-मेद् । र्ग्यंल्-पो-मूकोन्-ऽफेल्-स्क्ये-बोस्-ब्य ॥)

८३०. वार्धक्ये । प्राप्ते । ८३२. पुनश्च्यवति । ८३३. वसेद्धीमान् । ८३५. सिद्धमंत्रो वणिक् चासौ । ८३८. सौख्येन । अजायत ।

ततोऽसौ भिन्नदेहस्तु तारादेव्यानुचोदितः ।
देवानामधिपतिं गच्छेत् तत्र धर्मं च देशयेत् ॥८३९॥
सोऽनुपूर्वेण महीपाल क्षिप्रं बोधिपरायणः ।
(सोऽपि वर्षत्रयं राजैश्वर्यं वै कृत्वा ।)
पकाराख्ये च नृपतौ वृत्ते तदा काले युगाधमे ॥८४०॥

§. 42. Successors of Pra.

भिन्नं परस्परं तत्र महाविग्रहमाश्रिताः ।
भृत्यस्तस्य तु सप्ताहं राज्यैश्वर्यमकारयेत् ॥८४१॥
ततोऽनुपूर्वेण सप्ताहाद् वकाराख्यो नृपतिस्तथा ।
सोऽप्यहतविश्वस्तः प्रक्रमेत दिशास्ततः ॥८४२॥
G. ६४४ पकाराख्ये नृपतौ तत्र भकाराद्यो मतः परः ।
सोऽपि त्रीणि वर्षाणि राज्यैश्वर्यमकारयेत् ॥८४३॥
तस्याप्यनुजो वकाराख्यो व्रतिना समधिष्ठितः ।

§ 43. Rājyavardhana II as sovereign of Magadha

त्रीणि वर्षाणि एकं च भविता राज्यवर्द्धन ॥८४४॥
अजीर्णितौ उभावप्येतौ सद्यातीसारमूर्च्छितौ ।
कालगतौ लोके यद्देभ्योपपद्यते ॥८४५॥

§ 44. Heir and successors of Rājyavardhana

तेऽनुपूर्वेण धर्मात्मानो प्रत्येकां बोधिमाप्नुयाम् ।
तस्याप्यनुजो धकाराख्यः क्षत्रियो धर्मवत्सलः ॥८४६॥
भविता सोऽपि राजा वै त्रीणि वर्षाणि ।
भवितासौ नराधिपः ॥८४७॥
तस्यापि कन्यसो राजा वकाराख्योऽथ विश्रुतः ।
भविता तत्र देशेऽस्मिं सार्वभूमिकभूपतिः ॥८४८॥
हस्त्यश्वरथयानानि नौयानानि समन्ततः ।
जेता रिपूणां सर्वेषां समरे प्रत्युपस्थिताम् ॥८४९॥
T. 468 a. स इमां जनपदां सर्वां कृत्स्नां चैव वसुन्धराम् ।
शास्तुबिम्बैर्विहारैश्च जिनानां धातुधरैस्तथा ॥८५०॥

---

८४०. a. दे-यङ्-लो-नि-गृसुम्-दग्-तु । र्ग्यल्-पोडि-दुबङ्-फ्युग्-ब्येस्-मस्-बि । वृत्ते ।
८४६. पकाराख्यः । ८४८. कनीयान् । जकाराख्यो ।

शोभापयति सर्वां वै कृत्स्नां चैव वसुन्धराम् ।
नृपपूर्वी तथा तस्य द्विजातिः शाक्यजस्तथा ॥८५१॥
मानी तीक्ष्णोऽथ स प्राज्ञः बोधिनिम्नोऽथ मानधीः ।
सैवास्य सुखायतां याति तस्मिं काले युगाधमे ॥८५२॥
क्षत्रियः अग्रधीः प्रोक्तः राजा वै धर्मवत्सलः ।
जीवेद् वर्षशतं विंशत् सप्त चाष्टं च यत्नतः ॥८५३॥
स्त्रीकृतेनैव दोषेण कालं कृत्वा दिविं गतः ।
सोऽनुपूर्वेण मेधावी प्राप्नुयाद् बोधिमुत्तमाम् ॥८५४॥

§45. Later Guptas

ततः परेण विख्यातः श्री नामाथ महीपतिः ।
गौडतन्त्रे महाराजा भविता धर्मवत्सलः ॥८५५॥
G. ६४५ गौडानां च पुरे श्रेष्ठे वकाराद्ये च महाजने ।
कारयेत् तत्र राज्यं वै जितश ु समन्ततः ॥८५६॥
विहारां कारयामास सप्त चाष्टौ च तत्र वै ।
द्विजमुख्या तथा युक्ते शाकजेतिसमाश्रिते ॥८५७॥
तेन साहाय्यतां याते कुर्याद् राज्यं समन्ततः ।
अशीतिरेकं च वर्षाणि जीवेत् तत्र नराधिपः ॥८५८॥
भृत्यदोषेण धर्मात्मा कालं कृत्वा दिविं गतः ।
T. 464 b. अनुपूर्वेण तथा राज्यं देवानामपि कारयेत् ॥८५९॥
ततोऽसौ भिन्नदेहस्तु स्वर्गात् स्वर्गतमं व्रजेत् ।
परिपूर्य कुशलात् धर्मां बोधि ये तस्य हेतवः ॥८६०॥
तस्यैव भृत्यो राजा वै कुर्याद् राज्यमकण्टकम् ।
नाम्ना यकाराद्यस्तु महीपालो भविष्यति ॥८६१॥
सप्त चैकं वर्षाणि कुर्याद् राज्यं तदा युगे ।
सैव घात्यते स्त्रीभिः घातितश्च अधो गतः ॥८६२॥
पुनः पकारवंशास्तु राजा भविताथ क्षत्रियः ।

§ 46. Prakaṭâditya's family restored

तेनासौ भृत्यवर्गस्तु घातितोऽसौ निरन्तरः ॥८६३॥

---

८५२. सहायतां । ८५३. क्षत्रियाग्रः । वर्षान् विंशत् । ८५५. ततः ख्यातश्री नामा तथा वै महामतिः । उद्दियाने (अु-डि-यन्-न) । ८५६. उड्यानानां । महापुरे । जितशत्रुः । ८५७. अष्टानां तत्र वै तदा । शाक्यजातिसमाश्रिताः । ८६२. मरिष्यति । ८६३. स्वैरिकः ।

अकल्याणमित्रमागम्य कृतं प्राणिवधं बहून् ।
भविता सर्वलोकेऽस्मिं प्रतापोर्जितमूर्च्छितः ॥८६४॥
क्षिप्रकारी चपलस्तु मद्यपश्च शठप्रियः ।
मद्यप्रमादात् सम्मूढः तदासौ शयने भुवि ॥८६५॥
भिन्नोऽसौ शस्त्रघातैस्तु अरिभिश्च समुद्यतैः ।
ततोऽसौ भिन्नदेहस्तु कालं कृत्वा अधोगतः ॥८६६॥
तस्याप्यन्यतमो भ्राता रकाराद्यो नामतः स्मृतः ।
अष्टचत्वारिंशद्दिवसानि राज्यकर्त्ता सदा भुवि ॥८६७॥
दत्वा द्रविणं द्विजातिभ्यः कालं कुर्यान्न संशयः ।

§ 47-*a*. Śūdra King in Gauḍa

ततः परेण भूपालः स्वादाद्यो भविता तदा ॥८६८॥
G. ६४६ स एव शूद्रवर्णस्तु न्यङ्गः कुत्सित एव तु ।
T. 469 a. अधर्मभूयिष्ठः दुःशीलो विग्रहे च सदा रतः ॥८६९॥
द्विजातिगणसामन्तां संयतां प्रव्रजितांस्तथा ।
स ह्रापयति सर्वा वै निग्रहे च सदा रतः ॥८७०॥
तीव्रशासनकर्ता च तस्करां घातकस्तथा ।
निषेद्धा सर्वदुष्टानां पाषण्डव्रतमाश्रृताम् ॥८७१॥
विनिर्मुक्ता च दाता च राज्यं कृत्वा तु वै तदा ।
दशवर्षाणि सप्त च जीवेद् भूपतिस्तत्र वै ॥८७२॥
कुष्ठदुःखाभिभूतस्तु कालं कृत्वाथ तिर्यत् ।
तिर्यग्भ्यो नागराजस्तु महाभोगी विशारदः ॥८७३॥
मूर्त्तिमां परमबीभत्सी स्फुटाटोपी च वै तदा ।
अनुभूय चिरं दुःखं धर्मतस्तस्य नैष्ठिकम् ॥८७४॥
एवम्प्रकाराः कथिता भूपाला लोकवर्द्धना ।
विदिता सर्वलोकेऽस्मिं प्राच्या च स्थितदेहिनी ॥८७५॥

§ 48. Constitutional position of the Later Guptās of Gauḍa Dynasty; and Kumāra Gupta II

पकाराख्यस्य नृपतौ वंशाद् वंशजोऽपरः ।
क्षत्रियः शूरविक्रान्तः त्रिसमुद्राधिपतिस्तदा ॥८७६॥
भविता प्राच्यदेशेऽस्मिं महासैन्यो महाबलः ।
शास्तुधातुधरैर्दिव्यैर्विहारावसथमन्दिरैः ॥८७७॥

---

८६७. तदा । ८६८. राजमद्रो । ८७३. तिर्यंक् ।

उद्यानविविधैर्वाप्यैः कूपमण्डपसंक्रमैः ।
सत्रागारतथानित्यं शोभापयति मेदिनीम् ॥८७८॥
भक्तोऽसौ जिनवरां श्रेष्ठां उत्तमं यानमाश्रितः ।
T. 469 b. शाक्यप्रव्रजितेनैव स तदा निष्ठितो ह्यसौ ॥८७९॥
वर्जयेद् दक्षिणां सर्वां दक्षिणां चैव प्रभावयेत् ।
नाम्ना ककारविख्यातः स्मृतिमांश्चैव विशारदः ॥८८०॥
राज्यं कृत्वा तु भूपालः वर्षाण्येकविंशति ।
ततोऽसौ विषूचिकाभिश्च कालं कृत्वा दिविं गतः ॥८८१॥
G. ६४७ सोऽनुपूर्वेण मेधावी क्षिप्रं बोधिपरायणः ।
तस्यैव शेषवंशास्तु पराधीनायतनवृत्तनः ॥८८२॥

§. 49. The Pāla Dynasty

ततः परेण भूपाला गोपाला दासजीविनः ।
भविष्यति न सन्देहो द्विजातिकृपणा जना ॥८८३॥
अधर्मिष्ठ तदा काले निर्नष्टे शास्तुशासने ।

§ 50. Religious Practice in the East, South, Insulindia, and Further India

मन्त्रवादेन सत्त्वानां कुशलार्थां नियोजयेत् ॥८८४॥
कुमारेण तु ये प्रोक्ता मन्त्रा भोगवर्द्धना ।
साधनीया तदा काले राज्यैश्वर्येण हेतुना ॥८८५॥
न साध्या उत्तमा सिद्धिः तस्मिं देशे तु वै तदा ।
धर्मचक्रे तथा रम्ये महाबोधिवने तथा ॥८८६॥
यत्रासौ भगवां शान्तिं निरोपधिं च प्रविष्टवां ।
तत्र साध्यौ इमौ मन्त्रौ तारा भ्रूकुटी च देवता ॥८८७॥
समुद्रकूले तथा नित्यं विस्फूर्ज्यां सरितावरे ।
गङ्गातीरे तु सर्वत्र साधनीयाब्जसम्भवा ॥८८८॥
योऽसौ बोधिसत्त्वस्तु (दशभूमिप्रभुत्त्व प्राप्तः सत्त्वानां विनेयः)
चन्द्रनामाथ विश्रुतः ।
T. 470 a. स वै तारमिति प्रोक्तां विद्याराज्ञी महर्द्धिका ॥८८९॥
स्त्रीरूपधारिणी भूत्वा देवी विचेरुः सर्वतो जगतः ।
सत्त्वानां हितकाम्यार्थं करुणार्द्रेण चेतसा ॥८९०॥

---

८७९. मुनिवरान् । ८८२. पराधीनावालवृत्तयः । ८८६. महावेणुवने । ८८९. तारेति ।

सह्यं च लोकधातुस्थां तैम्भ्याख्यमिति वर्तते ।
महर्द्धिको बोधिसत्त्वस्तु दशभूम्यानन्तरप्रभुः ॥८९१॥
विनेयः सर्वसत्त्वानां तारा देवी तु कीर्त्यते ।
अयत्नसिद्धिमेवास्य रक्षावरणगुप्तये ॥८९२॥
यत्नेन साध्यते देवी भोगैश्वर्यविवर्द्धना ।
बोधिसम्भारहेतुं च ॥८९३॥
अनुबद्धा तदा देवी करुणाविष्टा हि देहिनाम् ।
मन्त्ररूपेण सत्त्वानां बोधिसम्भारकारणा ॥८९४॥
G. ६४८ सर्वेषां तुष्टिपुष्ट्यर्थं पूर्वायां दिशिमाश्रितः ।
सहस्रार्धं पुनः कृत्वा आत्मनो बहुधा पुनः ॥८९५॥
भ्रमते वसुमतीं कृत्स्नां चत्वारोदधिपर्यन्ताम् ।
पूर्वेण ततः सिद्धिः *वाराणस्यां* परेण वा ॥८९६॥
स क्षेत्रस्तस्य देव्या तु पूर्वदेशः प्रकीर्तितः ।
सिद्ध्यते यक्षराट् तत्र जम्भलस्तु महाद्युतिः ॥८९७॥
भोगकामैः तदा सत्त्वैः तस्मि काले युगाधमे ।
यक्षराट् तारादेव्या तु साध्येतौ पुष्टिकामतः ॥८९८॥
क्रोधनास्तु तथा मन्त्राः साध्यतां *दक्षिणापथे* ।
म्लेच्छतस्करद्वीपेषु अम्भोधेर्मध्य एव वा ॥८९९॥
सिध्यते च तदा तारा यक्षराट् चैव महाबलः ।
हरिकेल कर्मरंगे च *कामरूपे कलशाह्वये* ॥९००॥
विविधा दूतिगणाः सर्वे यक्षिण्यश्च महर्द्धिकाः ।
T. 470 b. मञ्जुघोषेण ये गीता मन्त्रा भोगहेतवः ॥९०१॥
तत्र देशे यथा सिद्धिः नान्यस्थानेषु तथा भवेत् ।
पूर्वे दिशि विदिक्षुश्च मन्त्रा विविधहेतवः ॥९०२॥

§ 51. Madhyadeśa—Provincial

कथितास्तु तदा काले साधनीयास्तु देहिभिः ।
मध्यदेशे तथा मन्त्रो भूपाला विविधास्तथा ॥९०३॥
विस्तरां सत्त्वदौर्बल्यां अल्पबुद्धिं निबोधताम् ।
संक्षेपो नृपतिमुख्यानां सङ्कथा तेषां निगद्यते ॥९०४॥

---

८९१. ह्म्याख्येति । दशभूमिस्थिर्ति प्राप्ता । ८९५. सहस्रविधं । ८९६. चतुरुदधि-पर्यन्ताम् । ९००. तथा ।

मकाराद्यो नकाराद्यः पकाराद्यश्च कीर्त्यते ।
दकाराद्यश्च इकाराद्यः सकाराद्यश्च अकाराद्य ॥९०५॥
महात्म्यश्च कीर्त्याख्यः हकाराद्यश्च घुष्यते ।
शकाराद्यश्च भवेत् तदा ॥९०६॥
जकाराद्यो बकाराद्यो लकाराद्यः सोमचिह्नितः ।
हकाराद्यश्चैव प्रख्यातः अकाराद्य पुनस्तथा ॥९०७॥
G. ६४९ सकारो लकाराद्यश्च स्त्र्याख्या लोकविद्विषः ।
सकाराद्यो मकाराख्यः लोकानां प्रभविष्णवः ॥९०८॥
क्रमतः कृमिनः चिह्नः ब्राह्मणाश्च वैश्यवृत्तयः ।
अधर्मकर्मा भूयिष्ठाः विद्विष्टाः स्त्रीषु लोलुपाः ॥९०९॥
प्रभूतपरिवारा महीपालास्तस्मिं काले युगाधमे ।
भविष्यन्ति न सन्देहः मध्यदेशे नराधिपाः ॥९१०॥
विंशद् वर्षाणि शतं चैव आयुरेषा युगाधमे ।
मनुष्याणां तदा काले दीर्घमायुरिति कीर्त्यते ॥९११॥
तेषां मध्योत्कृष्टानां अन्तरा उच्चनीचता ।
अल्पायुषो नृपतयः सर्वे कथिता तु तदा युगे ॥९१२॥

§ 52. Miscellaneous Tracts

T. 471 a. नदीगंगा तथा तीरे हिमाद्रेश्च नितम्बयोः ।
कामरूपे तथा देशे भविष्यन्ति तथा नृपाः ॥९१३॥
आद्ये मध्ये तथान्ते च अंगदेशेषु कथ्यते ।
आद्यं वृत्सुधानश्च कर्मराजा स कीर्त्तितः ॥९१४॥
अन्तेऽङ्गपतिः तदङ्गं च सुभूतिर्भूतिरेव च ।
सवहो भवद(त्त)श्च कामरूपे अजातयः ॥९१५॥
सुभूमृगकुमारान्ता वैशाल्यां वकारयोः ।
तत्रासौ मुनिर्जातः कपिलाह्वे पुरोत्तमे ॥९१६॥
शुद्धान्ता शाक्यजाः प्रोक्ता नृपा आदित्येक्ष्वसम्भवा ।
शुद्धोदनान्तविख्याता शाक्यं शाक्यवर्द्धनान् ॥९१७॥

---

९०५. शकाराद्यो । प्रकाराद्यश्च । वकाराद्यश्च । ९०६. धकाराद्यश्च । ९०७. धकाराद्यः ९०८. अकाराद्यो । ९१४. कुलदेवी । आद्योमहाप्रधानश्च (दक्-पोडि-गृपो-बो-छेन्-पो-नि) कर्णराजः प्रकीर्त्तितः । ९१५. तत्र । सुदानो । अजायन्त । ९१६. सुभूकुमारान्ता । व-येस्युभयाक्षरम् । वैशाल्यां संभूतः । यत्रासौ । ९१७. अन्त्याः । आदित्येक्षुसम्भवाः ।

अल्पवीर्यास्तु मन्त्रा वै कथिता लोकपुङ्गवैः ।
जिनप्रोक्तास्तु ये मन्त्राः सर्वचेटगणास्तथा ॥९१८॥
तथा विविधा दूतिगणाः सर्वे वज्राब्जकुलयोरपि ।
साध्यमानस्तु सिध्यन्ते मन्त्रतंत्रार्थकोविदैः ॥९१९॥
सर्वे ते लौकिका मन्त्राः सिध्यन्तेऽत्र मध्यतः ।
विशेषतो मध्यदेशस्थाः साधनीया जिनभाषिता ॥९२०॥
G. ६५० विविधाकारचिह्नैस्तु विविधाकारकारणैः ।
विविधप्रयोगप्रयुक्तास्तु विविधा सिद्धि देहिनाम् ॥९२१॥
मध्यशेदे तथा मन्त्राः साध्या वै भोगवर्धनाः ।
T. 471 b. रक्षाहेतुपरित्राणं वश्याकर्षणदेहिनाम् ॥९२२॥
अतीतानागता प्रोक्ताः मध्यदेशे नराधिपाः ।
विविधाकारचिह्नैस्तु विविधायुष्यगोत्रतः ॥९२३॥
सर्वे नरपतयः प्रोक्ताः उत्तमाधममध्यमाः ।
त्रिप्रकारा तथा सिद्धिः त्रिधा कालेषु योजयेत् ॥९२४॥
त्रिविधास्तु तथा मन्त्राः कथिता मुनिवरैस्तथा ।

§ 53. The Scheme of Royal History

अनन्ता नृपतयः प्रोक्ता मध्यदेशेऽथ पश्चिमे ॥९२५॥
उत्तरापरपूर्वैस्तु विदिक्षुः सर्वतस्तथा ।
द्वीपेषु बहिः सर्वेषु चतुर्धा परिचिह्नितैः ॥९२६॥
अनन्ता महीपतयः प्रोक्ता अनन्ता मन्त्रसाधनाः ।
अनन्ता दिशनाश्रित्य अनन्ता मन्त्रसिद्धयः ॥९२७॥
निग्रहानुग्रहार्थाय शासनेऽन्तर्हिते मुनौ ।
मन्त्रा नृपतिषु काले वै मंजुघोषेण भाषिता ॥९२८॥
क्रीडारक्षविकुर्वार्थं कालचर्या तु कथ्यते ।
मन्त्रमाहात्म्यसत्त्वानां गतियोनिनृपाह्वये ॥९२९॥
देशकालसमाख्यातः मन्त्रसाधनलिप्सुनाम् ।
प्रसक्ता नृपतयः कथिताः शासनान्तर्धिते पथे ॥९३०॥
मन्त्राणां गुणमाहात्म्यं फलमन्ते च बोधितः ।
कथिता ह्ये परे याने नृपा पूर्वनिबोधिताः ॥९३१॥

---

९१८. सत्त्ववीर्यास्तु । ९२२. मध्यदेशे । ९२७. देशमाश्रित्य । ९२९. क्रीडा रक्षि विकुर्वार्थं ।

नानादेशद्विजातीनां पूजका ते परि द्विजाः ।
नानातीर्थाश्च गोत्राश्च विविधाचारगोचराः ॥९८०॥
समन्ताद् यतयः प्रोक्ता मानवाश्च बहुश्रुताः ।
धर्मराजा स्वयं बुद्धः सर्वसत्त्वार्थसाधकः ॥९८१॥
सर्वेषां चैव भूतानां नृदेवानां च कीर्तिताः ।
चत्वारोऽपि महाराजाः सर्वलोकेषु कीर्तिताः ॥९८२॥
विरूढो विरूपाक्षश्च धृतराष्ट्रोऽथ यक्षराट् ।
शक्रश्च अथ देवानां नियतायुः प्रकीर्तितः ॥९८३॥
सुजामा देवपुत्रश्च सुनिर्मितो वशवर्तिनः ।
राजा सन्तुषितः प्रोक्तः कामधात्वीश्वरोऽपरः ॥९८४॥
T. 474 b. शक्राद्य एकनाम्नास्तु कामधात्वीश्वरास्तथा ।
एकाश्रया सदा तेऽपि एकजापा महर्द्धिका ॥९८५॥
G. ६५५ अनन्ताः कथितास्तेऽपि नानारूपधरा सुराः ।
अतः ऊर्ध्वं समा सर्वे तेऽपि महर्द्धिकाः ॥९८६॥
एवं संज्ञा सुरश्रेष्ठाः आ संज्ञाताः प्रकीर्तिताः ।
न तेषां प्रभविष्णु स्यात् तुल्यवृत्तिसमाश्रया ॥९८७॥
अतः अवीचिपर्यन्तं न राजा तत्र विद्यते ।
नरकाष्टौ षोडशोत्सिद्धौ सपर्यन्ता तेऽपि कीर्तिता ॥९८८॥
अनृपाः कर्मराजानः यमराजा प्रेतनां विभु ।
सुवर्णः पक्षिणां राजा गरुत्मा स महर्द्धिकः ॥९८९॥
किन्नराणां द्रुमो ख्यातः भूतानां रुद्र उच्यते ।
विद्याधराणां नृपो विद्या चित्रकेतुर्महर्द्धिकः ॥९९०॥
असुराणां तथा हेतौ वेमचित्रिर्योत्तमः ।
ऋषीणां व्यास इत्युक्तः सिद्धानां च महारथः ॥९९१॥
नक्षत्राणां सोम निर्दिष्टः ग्रहाणां भास्करस्तथा ।
मातराणां तथा राजा ईशानमभिकीर्तितः ॥९९२॥
द्विपदानां प्रतिम प्रोक्तः राशीनां कन्य उच्यते ।
सरितां सागरः प्रोक्तः मेघानां तु सुपुष्करः ॥९९३॥

---

९८०. नानाद्विग् । परे । ९८१. माणवाश्च । ९८२. सत्त्वानां त्रिदिवि । ९८४. सुयामा । ९८५. एकरूपा । ९८७. असंज्ञिनः । ९८८. अधः ।

ऐरावतो हस्तीनामश्वानां हरिवरस्तथा ।
तिर्यंराजाथ सर्वत्र प्रह्लादः परिकीर्तितः ॥९९४॥
अनन्ता गतयः प्रोक्ता राजानश्च अनन्तका ।
समन्तात् सर्वतस्तेषु बुद्धो लोके नरोत्तमः ॥९९५॥
उत्तमां कुरुमाद्यः प्रभविष्णुस्तेषु न विद्यते ।
द्वीपेष्वेव परेतेषु पूर्वापरयतस्तथा ॥९९६॥
जम्बुद्वीपनिवासिस्या पूर्वाया स नराधिपाः ।
अनन्ता च क्रिया प्रोक्ता चतुर्द्वीपा समराधिपा ॥९९७॥
संक्षेपा कथिता ह्येते कल्प्यमानातिविस्तरा ।
प्रभूता भूतपतयो मुख्यां त्रिदेवासुरजम्मिनाम् ॥९९८॥
G. ६५६ अनन्तलोकधातुस्था अनन्ता गुणविस्तरा ।
अनन्ता कथिता ह्यत्र कल्पेऽस्मिन भूनिवासिनः ॥९९९॥
कथिता मन्त्रसिद्ध्यर्थे देशकालसमास्ययात् ।
सिद्ध्यन्ते मन्त्रराजानो विविधा कृतगणास्तथा ॥१०००॥
एष धर्मः समासेन कथिता मुनिपुङ्गवैः ।
G. ६६२ अधुना कथितं ह्येतत् शुद्धावासोपरिस्थिते ॥१००१॥
मञ्जुश्रियो महावीरः पप्रच्छ लोकनायकम् ।
य एष कथितो कर्म कथं चैनं धारयाम्यहम् ॥१००२॥

पेयालं विस्तरेण कर्तव्यं सर्वेषां नृपतीनां कर्म स्वकं जातकं महापरिनिर्वाणसूत्रं मञ्जुश्रियस्य कुमारस्य मुनिश्रेष्ठ ।

अभाषत बोधिसत्त्वार्थमन्त्राणां च सविस्तराम् ।
बोधिमार्गार्थबोध्यर्थं धर्मसूत्र इति स्मृतः ॥१००३॥
विसरं कल्पमन्त्राणां कर्म आयूषि भूनृणाम् ।
नृपतीनां तथा कालमायुषे परिकीर्तनम् ॥१००४॥
धर्मसंग्रहणं नाम पिटकं बोधिपरायणम् ।
मन्त्रतन्त्राभियोगेन कथितं बोधिनिम्नगम् ॥१००५॥
धारयस्त्वं सदा प्राज्ञः मन्त्रतन्त्रार्थपूरकम् ॥ इति ॥

आर्यमञ्जुश्रियमूलकल्पाद् बोधिसत्त्वपिटकावतंसकान्म-
हायानवैपुल्यसूत्रात् पटलविसरात् *एकपञ्चाश-
राजव्याकरणपरिवर्तः
परिसमाप्त इति ।

---

९८८. भयः ।

* षट्त्रिंश ।